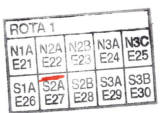

J.I. CASE

Agricultural & Construction Equipment
1956-1994

Tom Stonehouse
and
Eldon Brumbaugh

Published by the
American Society of Agricultural Engineers
2950 Niles Road, St. Joseph, Michigan

About ASAE – the Society for engineering in agricultural, food, and biological systems

ASAE is a technical and professional organization of members committed to improving agriculture through engineering. Many of our 8,000 members in the United Stated, Canada, and more than 100 other countries are engineering professionals actively involved in designing the farm equipment that continues to help the world's farmers feed the growing population. We're proud of the triumphs of the agriculture and equipment industry. ASAE is dedicated to preserving the record of this progress for others. This book joins many other popular ASAE titles in recording the exciting developments in agricultural equipment history.

J.I. Case Agricultural and Construction Equipment 1956-1994, Vol. 2

Editor and Book Designer: Melissa Carpenter Miller

Library of Congress Catalog Card Number (LCCN) 96-85682
International Standard Book Number (ISBN) 0-929355-76-8

Printed in the U.S.A.

Acknowledgments

Several people helped in the development of *J. I. Case Agricultural and Construction Equipment 1956-1994, Vol. 2* during the last two and a half years. We are grateful to the following who provided special assistance in making this project viable:

Glen Miller of Case for his interview and all his help with the Construction Equipment "theme."

Jerry Waite, retired "Father" of the Case Government Sales Department, for his interview, review, and great pictures on the military products.

Ralph Lanphere, head of the Case Design Department, for his pictures, renderings, and great literature file.

Steve Vallone, retired from Case Technical Publications, for researching technical information from Case manuals.

Judy Swetti of the Case Records Department for allowing us to access the old pictures and literature.

Lee Clark, retired Case engineer, for the many computer hours transcribing notes from disk to printer.

David Rodgers, Manager of Photography and Communication Services at Case Corporation, for all his great help in locating photos.

Lee Ann Morrelli of Case Corporation for her dedicated help in locating photos.

Jon Stonehouse and his wife, Deb, for donating their personal computer with software so the composition of this book could be manageable.

Patricia Stonehouse, for her support, encouragement, and ideas. For her patience with several research trips to Racine when she should rather have been "up North."

Introduction

This is the continuation of the story of the J. I. Case Company which began in *Volume One — Full Steam Ahead, J. I. Case Tractors and Equipment*. The story unfolds in *J. I. Case Agricultural and Construction Equipment 1956-1994, Volume Two*, with the changes in technology; the inherent culture of farming; the economics of farming; the environmental and the safety aspects of farming; and the impact all of these issues had on the design concepts of the farm machinery industry.

In the years since World War II, there have been more changes in the way food and fiber are produced than during the first one hundred years the Case Company was in existence. In the period immediately following World War II, farmers could sell everything they produced. With a shortage of farm machinery, manufacturers were able to sell all they could produce. However, times were changing. Many dramatic changes have occurred in agriculture throughout the 1950s, '60s, '70s, and '80s.

As the decade of the 1950s rolled around, agricultural productivity had been at full capacity for almost a decade and farmers were facing surpluses. Agricultural markets were expanded by extending the Food For Peace Law and the Soil Bank Act was passed to relieve the surplus.

In the 1960s the Feed Grain Program and the Food Stamp Program further helped reduce the surplus.

By the time the 1970s arrived, the surpluses had disappeared because the increased commercial demands and a booming export market. The '70s also brought a rapid rise in farm prices. The early '70s brought the Oil Embargo and increased fuel costs. As fuel prices continued to rise, farmers began looking for ways to make fewer trips across the field to prepare it for a crop. Optimum Tillage systems, Min-Till systems, as well as herbicides and pesticides were developed to fill this need. The Occupations Safety and Health Act was also passed in 1970 and helped encourage the interest and development of more sophisticated ROPS protected cabs. Environmental awareness also increased in this era which meant operator's were looking for increased protection from the environment and more comfort while operating their machines. During this decade we saw the small family farm fade and the land being gradually absorbed into larger farms. The larger farms with fewer farmers demanded larger, more sophisticated and more efficient equipment.

The most dramatic changes in farming as a business happened in the 1980s. The bottom dropped out of land values, reducing equity and causing farm loans to be recalled. Export markets dried up because most of the world had recovered from World War II and the weather disasters of the 1970s. Global competition was tough. Farm income suffered, but it has led to a very high level of sophistication in the way farm business is now conducted. Computers are everywhere, in tractors, on combines and planters, in the office, and in the shop. Satellited-based computer technology is even helping to determine the optimum time to plant and harvest. Every phase of the operation that effects cost, productivity, and the bottom line is computerized.

When the Case Company was starting in business, 90 percent of Americans lived on farms or farmland. Now that figure has dropped to less than 2 percent. Improved farm machinery and technology were the primary cause of this drop. Volume Two of this continuing story starts in the mid-1950s and progresses through the decades of the '60s, '70s, '80s, and into the 1990s. We will discuss how the needs of each of these eras influenced the design and manufacture of Case equipment that helped agriculture become the most efficient industry in the world today. Finally, we will also look at what happened as agriculture down-sized and how it influenced the diversification that resulted in the increased emphasis on the design and manufacture of construction equipment at J. I. Case in the '70s . . . and how it came full circle, to again become one of the leading full-line agricultural manufacturers in the 1990s.

The story of J. I. Case does not end here, but that story will be for other generations to tell.

This book is dedicated to all the men and women who have worked in the agriculture and construction industry, starting in the decade of the 1950s and into the '90s. Especially the farmers and their endless ability to "adapt," the machinery dealers who sold and service products, the mechanics and parts people who kept them running, and the people in the manufacturing who helped build the products. All are truly dedicated people. It was an unforgettable experience.

Table of Contents

Table of Contents

Table of Contents

J.I. CASE

Agricultural & Construction Equipment
1956-1994

Tom Stonehouse
and
Eldon Brumbaugh

The 1950s – The Search for Power

After World War II the American farmer faced a major challenge — feeding most of the world. One of the obstacles confronting the farmer was the shortage of help due to the younger generation either leaving the farm to attend college under the GI bill or getting a higher paying job in industry. This challenge led to a search for more efficient farming methods, especially in soil preparation. The first approach was to use higher horsepower tractors to pull "gangs" of small implements that were originally used with lower horsepower tractors. With this approach farmers were soon clamoring for larger implements and later for more efficient power trains. They started by making their own conversions, by taking the gasoline engine out of the Case LA, for example, and replacing it with a larger Caterpillar or GM diesel engine. The tractor companies were in the process of researching ways to meet the farmer's needs.

The Lanova System

The farmer's requests for more power caused Case to seriously investigate diesel engines. They eventually decided to design their own engine utilizing a modified closed chamber design called the Lanova System. Because Case was a late entry (1953) into the diesel market, they decided that this new engine would have the features that were lacking in many of the diesel engines of that era, such as: easy starting on diesel fuel (most of the engines in the field at that time started with gasoline or distillate auxiliary engines which cranked up the diesel), excellent fuel economy, clean burning (no black smoke), minimum maintenance, smooth running and durable (with a main bearing between each rod journal), and a rugged block that would also serve as a frame member.

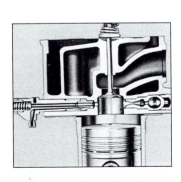

The Powrcel combustion system consisted of a fuel injector on one side (above on the left), and the combustion chamber and an energy cell Powrcel on th other side (above on the right).

This 4-cylinder engine block had five main bearings. The heavy ribbing at the bottom of the block was used to strengthen the engine block because it was an integral part of the tractor frame.

This 6-cylinder engine block had seven main bearings, one located between each rod journal.

In 1948 the J.I. Case Company hired Hans Fisher, a German consultant engineer, to provide the expertise needed to develop a diesel engine for Case. Fisher previously headed the Lanova Corporation who were responsible for the Lanova System in the Mack, Buda,

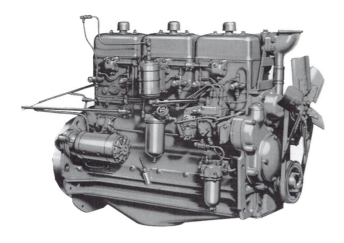

Multiple cylinder heads (one for every two cylinders) provided interchangeability between the 4- and 6-cylinder engines.

Continental, and Minneapolis-Moline engines. At Case the Lanova design was a modified auxiliary chamber-type engine which became known as Powrcel combustion. The Powrcel combustion system consisted of a fuel injector located on one side of the combustion chamber and an energy cell Powrcel on the other side. The injector sprayed atomized fuel across the top of the combustion chamber and piston into the cell. Combustion began in the fine envelope of the spray as it passed across the combustion chamber and followed into the cell, forcing the mixture back out on to the top of the piston for the power stroke.

The new Case diesel engine had a 4-inch bore and a 5-inch stroke. The engine was designed as a 4 cylinder and a 6 cylinder of the same family. The 6-cylinder crankshaft was supported by seven main bearings, one located between each rod journal. The 4-cylinder crankshaft was supported by five main bearings. The block was heavily ribbed and supported in the lower (skirt) area to accommodate the rugged Case tractor design philosophy. This design did not use a separate

frame to tie the front end and the engine to the rest of the tractor, but the frame was an integral part of the block. The same block was used for both gas and diesel engines. The head bolt pattern in the block was designed to allow for the spark plug opening used in low cost fuel (distillate), LP gas, and gasoline engines.

The multiple cylinder head design was also unique for engines of this era. A separate cylinder head existed for every two cylinders: a 6-cylinder engine used three cylinder heads and a 4-cylinder engine used two cylinder heads. This design provided complete interchangeability. Multiple heads also made quality and reliability much easier because maintaining flatness on a 6-cylinder head would be difficult.

In 1953 the new engine was first used in the Model 500 diesel tractor as a 377-cubic-inch, 6-cylinder engine rated at 63.81 PTO horsepower. The cubic inch displacement of the 6-cylinder diesel engine was subsequently increased to 401, then to 451, and finally to 504 through the years. The 4-cylinder engine was first used in 1955 in the 400 tractor as a 251-cubic-inch engine rated at 49.40 PTO horsepower. The cubic inch displacement of the 4-cylinder engine was increased to 267, then to 284, then to 301, and eventually to 336 over the years.

The Case Powrcel diesel engines started without cold-starting aids at most low temperatures. For extreme low temperatures an ether capsule injection system was provided. The Powrcel engines were more fuel efficient, quieter, and had easier to control exhaust emissions than most diesels on the market at

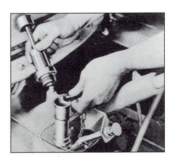

The ether injection system used a gelatin ether capsule that was inserted into a tube and punctured with the handle on the tube cover.

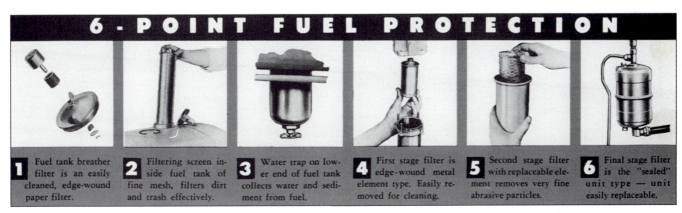

6 - POINT FUEL PROTECTION

1 Fuel tank breather filter is an easily cleaned, edge-wound paper filter.

2 Filtering screen inside fuel tank of fine mesh, filters dirt and trash effectively.

3 Water trap on lower end of fuel tank collects water and sediment from fuel.

4 First stage filter is edge-wound metal element type. Easily removed for cleaning.

5 Second stage filter with replaceable element removes very fine abrasive particles.

6 Final stage filter is the "sealed" unit type — unit easily replaceable.

The 6-point fuel filtering system made sure only clean fuel reached the precision close tolerance parts in the injection pump and fuel injectors.

The Model 500 diesel tractor closely resembled the Model LA in appearance. The yellow stripes on the side of the hood or the diesel fuel injection equipment on the right side of the engine helped distinguish between the two.

that time. The engines used in the 400 and 500 series tractors had a 6-point fuel filtering system that started with an edge wound paper filter element in the fuel tank cap, a brass filter in the neck of the tank, a water trap at the outlet of the tank, an edge wound paper first stage filter, a cotton replaceable element second stage filter, and a sealed third stage filter.

Another unique feature of the Lanova System was the decompressor. The engine was designed with a safety device that would hold the exhaust valves open when the lever was raised. This feature allowed the operator to stop the engine in an emergency, should the fuel shut-off not stop the engine. The decompressor was also used in cold weather as it allowed the engine to be cranked over breaking the cold oil seal. The decompressor was also used when preforming service procedures such as setting the tappet clearance or timing the injection pump to the engine because it allowed the service man to turn the engine by hand without fighting the 15 to 1 compression ratio. The Lanova System was maintained until 1969 when an open chamber combustion system was designed because of its ability to be turbocharged.

The 400 series tractor was the first new Case tractor in 28 years.

The Beginning of the Flambeau Desert Sunset Era

The 400 Series Tractors (1955-1957)

In the late 1940s and early '50s, Case directed a number of customer questionnaires asking for satisfaction rates (opinions) of their Case tractors. The questionnaires targeted at DC owners brought back a message that was loud and clear:

1. Get rid of the "Chicken Roost" steering system.
2. More power and more travel speeds were needed.
3. The appearance needed improvement.
4. The adjustable axle stuck out too far.
5. More operator comfort was necessary.
6. The exhaust valves and cylinder sleeve seal needed improvement.

The decompressor allowed the operator to stop the engine in an emergency (by holding the exhaust valves open) if the fuel-stop shut off did not stop the engine.

This prototype Model 400 diesel tractor was painted all flambeau red with yellow decals like the 500 (before the decision was made to go two-tone).

This top view of the transmission for the 400 tractor shows the range compartment on the left with the range fork. Notice how the rail for the fork extends through the wall into the four-speed compartment (on the right) and connects to the shifter mechanism located at the top of the picture.

7. Provide a diesel engine in a row-crop tractor. After reviewing the survey results, the Racine Tractor Works engineers started designing a replacement for the DC tractor, their mission was well defined.

The First New Tractor in 28 Years

Case took their commitment to develop a new tractor very seriously, especially since this was their first new tractor in 28 years. The engine for the 400 was designed at the same time as the 500 diesel. The 4-cylinder version was chosen since over 60% of the farmers surveyed preferred a 4-cylinder engine in this size row-crop tractor. The gas engine had exhaust valve rotators and stellate exhaust valves. A new block and sleeve design was also present in this new tractor. The 400 tractor provided four different fuel options: gasoline, LP gas, distillate, and diesel. The distillate soon began losing popularity and eventually was dropped. The LP gas was popular for a time, but that also dropped off as other uses for LP gas drove the prices up. The 30 series were the last Case tractors to offer LP gas and were discontinued in 1969.

The First 8-Speed Transmission on a Farm Tractor

Many firsts were occurring for Case as they designed a new transmission for the 400 with 8 speeds forward and 2 reverse. The transmission had a ring-and-pinion final drive rather than the previous Case roller-chain final drive. The transmission had a 2-speed range compartment and a 4-speed compartment with gears that were a sliding spur type. The shifter mechanism was very unusual in the transmission. A single shift lever controlled both the range gears and the 4-speed gears. The shifter assembly sat in the 4-speed compartment and had three shifter forks. The range fork was located in the range compartment on a shifter rail that

projected into the 4-speed compartment. The shifter mechanism had a detented swinging gate that moved from side to side, allowing the shift lever to index with the desired fork. The shift lever could then move the fork fore and aft, sliding the gear or collar in and out of mesh. Needless to say, this design was a challenge to manufacture and service. The operators also had to get used to the "feel,"

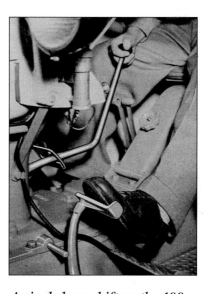

A single lever shift on the 400 tractor controlled both high and low ranges, as well as the reverse gears.

but once they got the "feel" it was quite simple to operate. This shifter design remained through the 400 and 700/800 series. The design was eventually changed

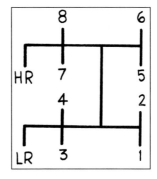

This was the shift pattern for the 400. The tricky part of the pattern was getting used to finding the path between high and low range with the single lever.

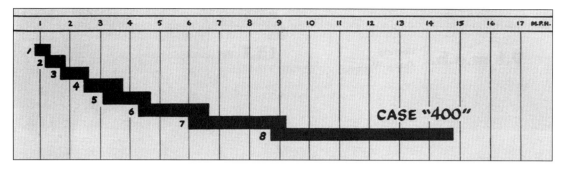

The Case 8-speed transmission was a leader in the concept of overlapping speeds in each gear (as shown in this chart) to keep the engine at full power.

on the 730/830 series (1959) to two shift levers; one for range and one for 4 speed and reverse. The two levers were affectionately dubbed the "double hand shaker" by the field service people. This 8-speed transmission was also one of the leaders in the concept of overlapping speeds in each gear to keep the engine at full power. Most tractors at that time had gaps in the working speeds, so to maintain a given ground speed the operator had to shift up and throttle back, not utilizing the rated speed of the engine.

Improvements with the 400

The End of the "Chicken Roost." The steering system on the 400 tractor was a complete new Case design. It used a vane hydraulic motor for the power steering system, along with a mechanical system. For many years Case had lived with the "Chicken Roost," a name given by Case competitors to the long steering

arm on the left side of the row-crop VA, S, and D series tractors. The arm extended from the fuel tank area, around the front of the grille, and connected the steering drop arm to the front axle. Most competitors routed this arm inside their sheet metal but the Case arm stood out about 8 to 10 inches from the side of the tractor and was very crude looking. Case management not only received many complaints from customers, but also from the Case implement plants which had to design the implements around that arm. The 400 series, by contrast, utilized a steering system that allowed the shaft to go to the front of the tractor and it stayed within the hood limitations so it would not interfere with the implements or any other obstacle (the previous tractors had been accused of interfering). This steering system allowed for a single front wheel, a dual front wheel, or an adjustable front axle (which was tucked under the front-end casting). All of these configurations utilized the same steering unit. The power steering unit was operated with a separate pump and reservoir which was driven from the front drive on the engine.

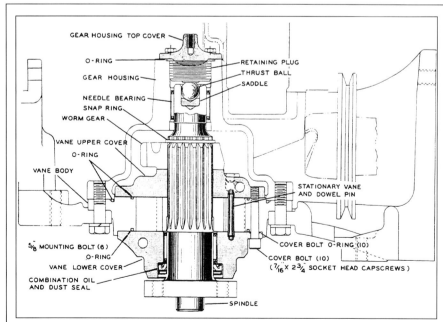

The power steering vane motor design for the 400 was unique because it allowed a common power steering system to accommodate single, dual wheel, and adjustable front axles.

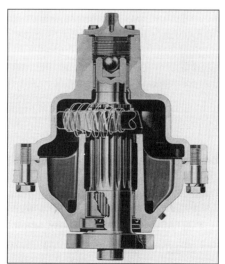

The mechanical steering unit for the 400 was designed to be completely interchangeable with the power steering unit.

The long steering arm on the DC was called the "Chicken Roost" by competitors.

The suspended seat on the 400 had an adjustable nob that let the operator reach down and soften or firm his ride on the move.

In contrast to the DC, the steering arm on the 400 remained within the hood limitations.

PARTS THAT ARE TURNING WHENEVER THE ENGINE IS RUNNING

Dual Range Drive Transmission

HYDRAULIC PUMP

PTO-HYDRAULIC PUMP DRIVE SHAFT

DRIVE GEAR

DRIVEN GEAR

PTO DRUM

FLYWHEEL

PTO STUB SHAFT AND CLUTCH

■ PARTS TURNING AT ENGINE SPEED

The power take-off and the hydraulic pump were "live" because a shaft connected to the flywheel went through the center of the clutch shaft to the rear of the tractor to drive the hydraulic pump and PTO. The PTO had a separate clutch and was totally independent of the transmission.

The dual valve pump consisted of a gear pump with two remote valves all in one package and located on the PTO housing at the rear of the tractor.

The 400 series tractors were introduced to the Case branch and dealer personnel at San Antonio, Texas, in 1955. Upon returning home, the branch and dealer personnel would hold introductions for the public, like this Lansing branch introduction held at East Lansing, Michigan.

Hydraulic System. The hydraulic system on the 400 consisted of a gear pump with two remote valves all in one package. It provided check valves so that leak down would not be a problem for the farmer operating the implements. The three-point hitch was of the eagle hitch design with the claws which allowed the operator to back up to the implement, raise the hitch arms, and the claws would snap on to the hitch pins, making the hookup easier from the seat of the tractor.

"Live PTO." The transmission was designed with a live PTO where a shaft connected to the flywheel and went through the center of the clutch shaft to the rear of the tractor and drove the hydraulic pump and the PTO output shaft. The PTO had a separate clutch and was totally independent of the transmission.

Suspended Seat. Operator comfort was given consideration by providing a suspended seat with a torsional-rubber system that was adjustable to the various operator's weights.

The End of All Flambeau Red

Because this was an all-new tractor from the engine to the three-point hitch, including the sheet metal, Case decided it should have an all-new color. Ed Smith, the paint foreman at the South Works, painted many DC tractors for a management decision. They liked the flambeau red chassis and the cream/yellow sheet metal. W. G. Thompson, the plant manager, commented that it looked like a desert sunset and the name stuck. A new

sunburst medallion as a background for the eagle was also designed for the hood of the tractor and was a result of the new color. The color change was so successful that the 300 tractor, which was developed at the Rock Island plant, adopted this same color scheme. When the 600 tractor was introduced it also used the desert sunset colors. Case used this color scheme for all agricultural and utility products until 1974.

The industrial version of the 400, like this 420 diesel, could be equipped with allied equipment such as this Ottawa loader and backhoe.

World Record Holder. The 400 diesel tractor was introduced in 1955 at 49.40 PTO horsepower. In 1957 the bore was increased from 4 to 4 1/8 inches and it was called the 400 Super Diesel at 54 PTO horsepower. In 1955 the Model 411 gasoline tractor set the world's record for fuel economy at Nebraska.

The Industrial Tractor. An industrial version of the 400, the 420 (diesel) and the 425 (gasoline), was also available. These tractors were designed for the industrial loader market. They had a heavy-duty forged front axle with 6-ply front tires and a tapered rear axle.

The Start of the Identity Confusion

In the Flambeau Era, the alphabetical nomenclature was simple: "O" stood for orchard, "C" for cultivator, "I" for industrial, and "E" for engine unit. Therefore, it was apparent right away that an SC was a cultivator tractor or that an SI was an industrial tractor. Even the start of the numerical identity with the "500" was simple because there was only one configuration. The "400" being a row-crop model presented a whole new "ball game." For example there was:

The identity of 400 series agricultural tractors was quite simple when given names, such as in this advertisement. When it came to ordering a tractor, each front end type, each fuel, and each fender type had a separate numerical model designation and the identity confusion began.

- The 400 Diesel — a solid front axle, fan fender, non-adjustable rear axle model.
- The 401 Diesel — a single front wheel, or dual front, or an adjustable front axle. The rear axle was adjustable and it had fan fenders
- The 402 Diesel Orchard Vineyard — had an 82-inch wheel base and a 56.5-inch height over the hood. The overall length was 128 inches.
- The 403 Diesel High Clearance — a 33.5-inch under-axle clearance-differential fertilizer drive, as well as a full-mesh protective-radiator screen.
- The 405 Diesel Orchard — instead of just a full swinging drawbar like the 402, the 405 had an eagle hitch.
- The 409 Diesel — an engine power unit.
- The 400 Western Special Diesel — this model had full fenders and a low platform like the 500. It did

not have a hitch but did have a full swinging drawbar and non-adjustable rear wheels. This unit was designed for the Western Plains, thus the low platform to protect the operator from the elements as much as possible.

- The 410 — the same as the 400 except it had a spark-ignition engine with either gasoline, LPG, or distillate.
- The 411 — the same as the 401 except it had a spark-ignition engine.
- The 412 — the spark-ignition version of the 402.
- The 413 — the spark-ignition version of the 403.
- The 414 — a grove-orchard LPG with a 76-inch wheelbase, an overall length of 118.5 inches, and a height over radiator of 54.5 inches.
- The 415 — the spark-ignition version of the 405.

This Model 412 orchard tractor is equipped with a sprayer. The 412 had full flowing sheet metal from the grille to the rear fender, including the LP gas tank so tree branches did not get caught and broken off as the tractor passed.

- The 419 — the spark-ignition version of the 409 power unit available in either LPG, natural gas, or gasoline versions.

Oranges, Apples, Peaches, or Grapes?

Back in the days of the "C" and "D" series, Case had enjoyed a good market share in orchard or grove specialty tractors, so when they designed the "400" this specialty was part of the program. One of the first prototypes was sent to one of the larger dealers in this market, the Pounds Tractor Company in Florida, for their evaluation. Pounds said it was too long, too high, that there was no market for a diesel, and that they didn't need a hitch. Their reasoning for the tractor being too high, too long, and without a hitch was the

row spacing and type of trees which they farmed. Pounds made their own specialty implements so they didn't need a hitch. They had no market for diesel because they were LPG dealers. The other markets, however, did not share these problems. As a result Case ended up with grove orchard LPG tractors for Florida that had only a swinging drawbar and a 6-inch shorter wheelbase. It was 2 inches lower than the orchard/vineyard tractors used in the other markets that required all fuels and a hitch and didn't need to be that short or that low. The first literature and price lists were very confusing because they were all designated 402 or 412. Later Case changed the model numbers to 414 for the Florida LPG and to 405 and 415 for the California groves and vineyard tractors. The 405 and 415 were unique since they had a higher platform and eagle hitch.

This Model 412 was pulling a disk harrow. Notice that even the disk has a shield to protect the tree branches from the disk blades and axles.

The Model 415 came equipped with a hitch rather than a swinging drawbar like the 412.

The Model 415 only had fender skirts and hood sides rather than full sheet metal like the 412.

The styling of the 300 created the most dramatic change in appearance of any Case machine in 30 years.

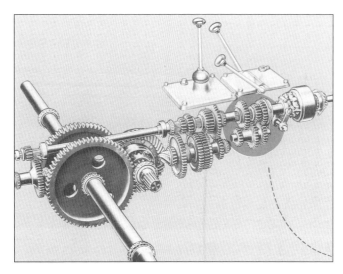

The 300 offered a 12-speed transmission by adding a 3-speed range section to the existing VA transmission (shown in the highlight above) and a multiple disc traction clutch on the main drive shaft.

The Beginning of the Desert Sunset Era

The 300 Series Tractors (1956-1959)

Case management felt for several years that they had not taken full advantage of the power possibilities of the SC. They also felt that the SC and the VAC appeared too close together in horsepower to properly cover the market in their respective fields. The 300 series tractors were a replacement for the SC and an upgrade of the VA series. Its design was influenced by the customer response to the surveys and questionnaires distributed on the SC and VA series. More power, a larger selection of speeds, operator controls, operator comfort, and appearance were paramount.

Engines. The spark-ignition engine displacement was increased from 124 cubic inches on the VA series to 148 cubic inches on the 300 series. This was a Case designed and built engine. The 300 series also saw the addition of a Continental diesel engine.

Transmissions. The transmission gear speeds were increased from 4 to 12 speeds by adding a 3-speed range section to the existing VA 4-speed design. The Triple Range Transmission, as it was called, had two clutches. A single disc clutch located at the flywheel was controlled by a foot pedal and started and stopped the traction, belt pulley, and PTO, all at once. A multiple disc clutch located on the main driveshaft to the transmission was controlled by a hand clutch and could only start

and stop the traction. This design allowed the PTO to operate continuously even when the tractor was stopped. The Triple Range Transmission was offered as an option and the original 4-speed transmission was standard.

Styling. The styling of the 300 created the most dramatic change in appearance of any Case machine in almost 30 years. This advanced sheet metal design, together with the Desert Sunset\Flambeau Red paint, gave the 300 excellent showroom appeal. The operator area also drastically changed with all the gauges (including speedometer and tachometer) located in a self-contained cluster. The hand throttle was moved up to the dash. The 300 was the first Case tractor to have a key start and a cigarette lighter.

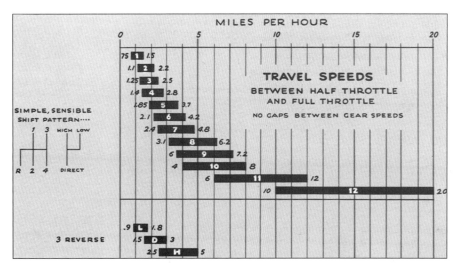

The travel speeds for the 300 overlapped similar to the concept of the 400. There were two shift levers, one for range and one for the 4-speed which simplified the shift pattern.

The spark ignition engine displacement was increased from 124 cubic inches in the VA to 148 cubic inches in the 300.

The 300 also introduced a diesel engine which was designed and built by Continental Motors of Muskegon, Michigan.

Hitch. The major shortcoming of the 300 was the hitch system. This tractor was positioned to compete with the Ford-Ferguson which had a draft-sensing hitch. The 300 had the eagle hitch which was similar to the 400. These tractors used this hitch system because it was L. R. Clausen's (Case's Chairman of the Board) opinion that a draft control system allowed the plow to be automatically raised when it hit a hard spot. He believed that plowing should be done at a constant depth rather than at varying depths, and that after hitting a hard spot the farmer did not want the implement to raise. He felt that the farmer really needed to plow deep in the hard spot and loosen up the ground. The rest of the industry, however, did not share his opinion and were successfully utilizing some sort of draft sensing to operate their 3-point hitches.

1956-57

The 300 series tractor was introduced in 1956 with the diesel at 30.8 PTO horsepower and the gasoline version at 33 PTO horsepower. It was part of the Case tractor line until 1959 when it was replaced by the 30 series in 1960. In 1957 another spark-ignition model, the 350, was introduced in gasoline and LPG versions. The 350 had a 164-cubic-inch engine and was rated at 42 PTO horsepower.

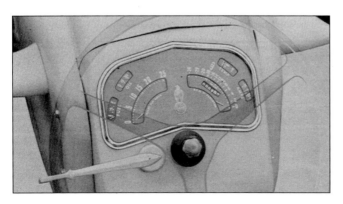

The 300 was the first tractor to have all of the gauges in a self-contained cluster.

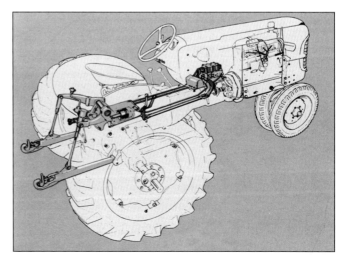

The 300 offered the 3-point Eagle Hitch system when most of the competition was offering draft-sensing hitches.

The Utility Tractor

The introduction of the utility tractor is one of the major contributions of the 300 series. The 300 utility could be equipped with a foot throttle, a choice of a 4-speed transmission or an 8-speed shuttle transmission, or a 12-speed triple range transmission. A high-speed road gear (20 mph) was also available. The 300 utility was a low-profile tractor with a heavy-duty forged front axle and offered engineered allied equipment such as: a loader, backhoe, fork lift, dozer, crane, auger, and post driver. This tractor became the foundation for the loader backhoe market.

The 300 utility tractor offered numerous attachments such as a loader and a backhoe.

One of the major contributions the 300 will be remembered for in the industry was the introduction of the utility tractor.

The Identity Crisis Continues

The 300 presented as much of an identity problem as the 400 with the new numerical identity system.

For example, there was:

- The 300 Diesel Utility — with a heavy-duty non-adjustable forged front axle with a fixed tread of 47.5 inches and adjustable rear tread of 48 to 68 inches, with a swinging drawbar and no hitch.
- The 301 Diesel General Purpose — with a single front wheel, or a dual front, or an adjustable front axle.

The 350 was introduced in 1957 at 42 horsepower with a 164-cubic inch engine.

The 311 gasoline general purpose tractor was available with a single front wheel, a dual front, or as shown here, with an adjustable front axle.

In late 1956 the 500 transmission was modified to increase the forward travel speeds from four to six and was introduced on the 600 tractor. The additional 2-speed housing is visible in this photo immediately under the front brace for the rear fender on the side of the transmission case.

The End of the Postwar Boom

Customers were well satisfied with the 300, 400, and 500 series tractors as replacements for their VA's, S's, D's, and LA's. As a result of their satisfaction, sales were very brisk. In the postwar era larger tractors were needed to satisfy the trend toward fewer but larger farms. The Model 500 diesel, introduced in 1953, rapidly became a strong favorite of large-scale farmers, not only because it was one of the larger tractors on the

The 600 tractor was the second generation of the Model 500 and adopted the sunburst medallion on front of the radiator top tank and had the desert sunset/flambeau paint similar to the 300 and 400.

The 900 was the second generation of the 600 tractor and had the eyebrows on the front grille cap with the cast aluminum Case eagle. The rear fenders were also rounded off at the corners.

market, but also because it started without cold starting aids or an auxiliary engine, was economical, and had plenty of torque for an engine of its size. The 500 was also the first agricultural tractor to offer power steering. Since the new features of the 500 met those market trends, the 500 was a very popular tractor. It also helped cause the retirement of the "Poppin' Johnny." The huge demands of the postwar era had generated new companies and intensified the competition, saturating the tractor market. The market for 400,000 units per year was over.

The Desert Sunset/Flambeau Era

The 600 and 900 Tractors (1957-1958)

As the competition intensified in the shrinking marketplace, transmission design became an important issue. Case engineers had developed the triple-range transmission for the smaller tractors, but now it was time to upgrade the 500 transmission.

In late 1956 the Model 600 was ready for production. The 600 was a modification of the Model 500, with increased travel speeds to 6 forward and 1 reverse. The 500 only had 4 forward speeds and competition was offering 5 and 6 speeds in the same size tractor. Six speeds were provided by adding an additional housing to the left side of the existing transmission case, thereby allowing two more change gears to be added to the cross-shaft transmission. This modification brought the cross-shaft transmission design with the 2-inch pitch chain final drive to the limit as far as horsepower was concerned. As a result, future development was dropped. The chain-drive configuration was originally adopted on the Model L in 1929.

The 500 and 600 were a strong favorites with large scale farmers and many could be seen in the western irrigated areas pulling land leveling scrapers getting the fields ready for the next crop.

The 600 adopted the sunburst medallion and desert sunset/flambeau paint similar to the 300 and 400, but the rest of the appearance was like the 500. The 600 transmission was reliable and worked well. The 600 was only built for one year and was then reidentified as the 900 in 1957 when all the model numbers were changed.

Case Enters the Small Tractor Market

The 200 Tractor (1958-1960)

The 200 gasoline tractor was announced in 1958 as Case's new entry into the small tractor market. The engine was rated at 1,900 engine rpm. As a comparison, the highest engine speed ever announced by Case up to this point was the LA at 1,150 rpm and the 500 at 1,350 rpm. The 200 was built as a 210 utility tractor and also as a 211 general purpose tractor. The 200 was powered by a 126.5-cubic-inch engine at 30.84 horse-

The 200 utility tractor with a loader was very popular with farmers for material handling. As a chore tractor it was used for practically everything imaginable.

A 300 series 188 diesel type I power unit. The customer provided the cooling system (usually right off the well) and the fuel tank.

A 300 series 148 type II natural gas power unit with a radiator but no fuel tank. The customer usually ran the engine directly off a gas pipeline or gas from the oil well it was pumping.

A 400 series 4-cylinder natural gas type II power unit with radiator, grille, and hood.

A 6-cylinder diesel type III power unit, complete with radiator, grille, hood, and fuel tank, as well as flywheel and clutch.

This type II 6-cylinder power unit was pumping water from an irrigation well into an irrigation ditch.

power which was approximately 3 horsepower less than the 300 gas which was powered by a 148-cubic-inch engine. Originally, the standard 4-speed and the triple-range transmissions were provided as options. Later, an 8-speed transmission with a synchronized mechanical shuttle was added with 8 speeds forward and 8 speeds in reverse. Two hitches were offered, either the eagle hitch or a 3-point hitch with swinging draft arms. The swinging draft arms were a first for Case.

Power Units (200, 300, 400, and 500)

During the Flambeau Era, Case had always enjoyed a market of 600 to 1,000 engine power unit sales per year. This trend continued with the 200, 300, 400, and 500 series engines. These engines were used as power plants for sawmills, irrigation pumps, oil well pumps, generator sets, etc. The power units were sold in three configurations:

- Type I — Water pump to flywheel with an SAE flywheel housing (No. 1 on larger engines and No. 4 on smaller engines). The customer provided the heat exchanger and output drive on these engines.
- Type II — This unit came with standard equipment, radiator, fan, generator, ammeter, and SAE flywheel housing (no fuel tank).

- Type III — This full unit came with standard equipment, radiator, grille, hood, fan, generator, ammeter, fuel tank, and SAE flywheel housing

Fuels. The 200 and 300 were offered in gasoline, LPG, or natural gas. The 400 was offered in diesel, gasoline, LPG, and natural gas. The 500 was offered in diesel, LPG, and natural gas. The natural gas and LPG units generally ran off the gas generated from the oil well they were pumping.

Selling these units required some on-site engineering by Case dealers to determine the horsepower torque and fuel consumption required by the engine to match the requirements of the application. Eventually the competition from the automotive engines (especially in the irrigation engines) made the engineering aspects unprofitable for dealers. Farmers would pick up an automotive engine for a few hundred dollars and when it quit, they would push it aside and install another one and still not have made the investment of a power unit. The power unit business was most profitable for Case through the 1950s and '60s.

This type II 6-cylinder power unit was pumping water from a reservoir to an irrigation sprinkling system.

17

The 1960s – The Desert Sunset/Flambeau Era

This experimental Case-O-Matic tractor was disguised in 400 tractor sheet metal (note the transmission case for the torque converter).

As the decade of the 1950s drew to a close, the farm machinery industry's search for the "complete" transmission started to appear in the marketplace. For example, there were transmissions that could match changing loads "on the go" like hydrostatics; variable speed drives were available; and there was the Case offering – the torque converter. Needless to say, these first attempts were not the ultimate answer but they were a good start.

In November of 1956 the Case Board of Directors approved the acquisition of the American Tractor Corporation (ATC). Marc B. Rojtman, the president of ATC, came to Case and later became a vice president after the acquisition was completed in 1957. Rojtman was a very flamboyant individual and pushed for many changes. Prior to the acquisition of ATC, Case engineers had been experimenting with a torque converter made by the Twin Disc Company of Racine, Wisconsin, that was used in place of the traction

clutch. The torque converter was in operation in the field and was being used in many different applications, but it was not at a stage where it could be put into production. When Rojtman heard about the torque converter he wanted to adopt it for the Case agricultural tractors. The South Works tractor engineers were concerned about it because this was a crash program and they knew compromises would have to be made, but decided in working with the Twin Disc Company it could be a viable project if they accomplished one goal — they needed to provide a torque converter lock out. Essentially, when the torque converter was not needed it could be operated in the lock out position without losing substantial efficiency of operation.

A meeting was held with the management of the Twin Disc Company and a very aggressive program was laid out to adopt the torque converter to the agricultural tractor. A 13-inch converter was decided upon rather than the 15 inch that Case had been using. An 11-inch converter was designed for the 400, the 500, and the 600. The Twin Disc design included a single disc clutch that could lock the turbine against the torus (converter housing). The converter was mounted to the engine flywheel with a multiple disc clutch at the transmission end, to engage and disengage the transmission. This was a very ambitious program with a deadline of less than a year to build and test the vehicles. Case did not have tractor endurance testing at that time, so the test tractors pulled load machines around the perimeter of the South Works Plant 24 hours a day. The lights circling the plant all night stirred the curiosity of the neighbors, suppliers, and dealers. Everyone was asking, "What's going on?" While curiosity was building over the Racine testing, the field testing was quietly going on primarily in the southwestern United States where they farm almost year round and tractor hours accumulate very quickly.

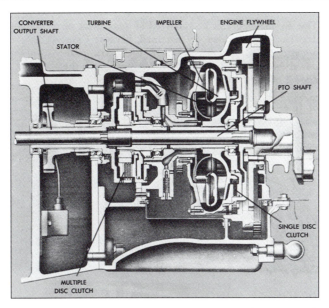

A 13-inch torque converter was used in the 700 and 800 series Case-O-Matic tractors. The direct drive clutch locked the stator to the turbine when the converter was not needed. The multiple disc clutch engaged or disengaged the transmission.

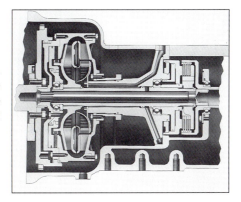

An 11-inch converter was used in the 400, 500, and 600 tractors.

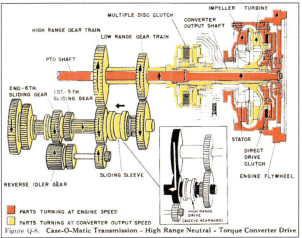

This drawing shows the power path from the flywheel through the converter which is driving the transmission at converter speed. The PTO is being driven at engine speed.

The participants at the 1957 World Premier had a chance to get "hands on" experience in the numerous corrals that were set up for demonstrations.

1957 World Premiere

It Changed the Thinking of an Entire Industry

The testing was completed and the torque converter daubed Case-O-Matic drive was put into production in time for the Phoenix, Arizona World Premiere in December 1957. The World Premiere was a totally new concept for introducing a new product line. Previously, Case and the rest of the industry had staged regional shows to introduce new products. The World Premiere was an awesome experience for more than 3,000 Case dealers, wives, bankers, and others.

This first Premiere lasted six weeks as the dealers were flown in for their three-day stay. Case even invited 700 competitive dealers. The highlight of the show was the Case-O-Matic "Tug-O-War." In the center of the large circus tent a Case-O-Matic tractor was hooked up to a competitor's tractor with the same horsepower and size, drawbar to drawbar. The drivers started their engines and the competitor's tractor immediately began pulling the Case-O-Matic tractor backward. A hush came over the crowd, then the driver of the Case tractor started gradually opening the throttle on his tractor. As the torque converter multiplied the engine torque, the Case tractor started pulling the competitor backward. The driver of the competitor's tractor would stand on the brakes to try and stop from being pulled backwards, this would finally cause his engine to kill and the crowd would roar! Did this bit of showmanship work? It certainly did — 30,000 tractors were ordered from that show. The World Premiere show changed forever how the industry introduced a new product line. Competitors rushed to follow suit. When John Deere

The World Premier held in Phoenix, Arizona, in 1957 changed the industry's thinking in the way they introduced new products.

introduced the New Generation tractors at its Dallas show in 1960, it imitated the Case concept. With this show in 1957, Rojtman and Case taught the industry that tractors could be sold automotive-style.

Sometimes It's Hard to Teach an Old Dog New Tricks

Because the Case-O-Matic drive was an accelerated program, certain compromises were made in the design. Engineering decided that the clutch control for the torque converter would be an on/off control to prevent slippage and the generation of heat. They thought the operator should start the tractor and engage the main clutch with the engine at idle and the foot on the brake,

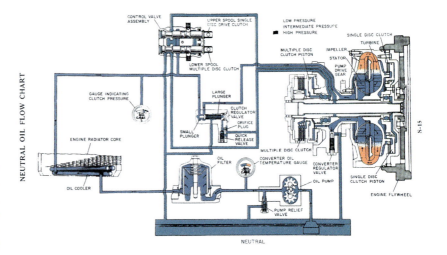

This drawing shows the components in the Case-O-Matic drive system from the converter oil cooler in the radiator bottom tank through the converter, oil pump, filter, temperature and pressure gauges, as well as the regulator and control valves.

similar to starting an automatic transmission in a car. This method was first demonstrated in the "Tug-O-War." The concept of this particular design compromise never really became popular since most farmers had been accustomed to just pulling the throttle wide open and letting the clutch out slowly to pick

In the Tug-O-War demonstration the crowd roared when the Case-O-Matic pulled the competitive tractor backwards.

up the load. This technique caused the torque converter in the early Case-O-Matic tractors to jerk. As a result, Case engineers designed the "F" circuit converter that had a modulated clutch where oil was fed to the clutch to allow for slippage and smooth engagement at high speed.

Case-O-Matic – Ahead of Its Time

The introduction of the "F" converter offered the farmer the ability to start out loads at full throttle. The "F" converter worked especially well for PTO work where it was occasionally needed to unplug a baler or a pull-type combine with the engine at full throttle. The converter pulled the plow or other tillage equipment through tough spots without shifting, the converter

CASE 200   CASE 300   Case-o-matic DRIVE 400

CASE 500   Case-o-matic DRIVE 600   CASE 900

CASE 310 CRAWLER   CASE 610 CRAWLER   CASE 810 CRAWLER

CASE 1010 CRAWLER   CASE 210 WITH FRONT LOADER   CASE 310 WITH LOADER-BACKHOE

All of the wheel and crawler tractors had the same "look" by 1957, except the 310 which changed in 1959.

The development of Case-O-Matic also provided an opportunity for a military product like an Air Force towing tractor in the 530 size. Case was the only manufacturer that built a torque converter tractor for this application from 1960 into the 1980s. The smooth start of the converter tractor made it ideal for towing ground support equipment for aircraft. Case had this business to themselves for many years until the government combined several orders, making it worthwhile for Ford to install a torque converter in their tractor. Ford later got the contract from Case.

Placing the torque converter in the 530 also provided a good chassis for the loader backhoe and gave Case the advantage over everyone else in the industry for loader backhoe operation. The torque converter in the 530 for the loader backhoe did not have a lock up clutch. Case gained leadership in this size of loader backhoe, which they have never lost.

lock-out feature allowed the tractor to operate efficiently in direct drive at lighter loads. The lock-out feature was ahead of its time, for the same device is used on present-day automobiles to achieve over-drive on automatic transmissions.

Case-O-Matic never realized its full potential in the agricultural tractors because the "F" converter was not introduced early enough to make a difference. Many of the old configurations in the field caused resistance to the acceptance of the Case-O-Matic drive. This old or original configuration also had a problem with the ball bearing at the rear of the torque converter. The original bearing supplied by the Twin Disc Co. completed all the Case tests without a failure, however, when production started the bearing supplier was changed and the substituted bearing had a shorter life. The bearing was supposedly interchangeable but it did not provide the required life in this instance. Many of the converters in the field prior to the "F" style had to be recalled. Many Case-O-Matic agricultural tractors are still working in the field. In these instances, the owner couldn't replace it with a unit with similar features and didn't want to give it up.

Styling Changes for Case-O-Matic

For the Phoenix World Premier introduction in 1957 the front grille cap was changed from the round bullet nose styling with the sunburst medallion that originated on the 400 in 1955 to the recessed head lights or "eye brows" as they were tabbed. The entire tractor

The development of Case-O-Matic provided an opportunity for a military product like the U.S. Air Force towing tractor. Case was the only manufacturer of these products from 1960 until the 1980s.

21

The 210 was developed for the agricultural/utility markets and was painted flambeau red and desert sunset. Case agricultural dealers sold this tractor.

The 420 loader backhoe was the first loader backhoe made by a single manufacturer. The torque converter drive was an off-shoot of the Case-O-Matic drive and made Case the leader in loader backhoes. The 420 was the forerunner of the 530/580 loader backhoes.

The 320 was designed for the small contractor and had a solid bar front axle, heavy-duty power steering, grille guard, and was available with a loader and a host of attachments.

In 1960 the long black stripe on each side of the hood was added and became a Case styling hallmark that carried into the mid-1990s.

line, including the newly acquired line of crawler tractors, had this same "look" which lasted on the construction and utility equipment until 1967 and on agricultural tractors until 1969.

The Savage 1960s

During the 1960s both the United States and Case faced one of the most trying decades in their histories. The United States faced the assassination of a president and civil unrest. Case encountered bankruptcy and the possible liquidation of an icon of American agriculture. The Rojtman era had brought an encumbering debt on Case, and caused his resignation from the company. William Grede (a member of the board of directors) was elected as president of Case on February 1, 1960. At that time Case owed $178 million to 92 banks. Grede tried to move quickly and decisively to lower the debt. One of his cost-cutting moves was to slash the engineering budgets and lay off one hundred engineers. Needless to say, things were pretty austere for product development for the next few years.

During 1961 assistant controller, James Ketelsen, worked with other executives and was able to develop an innovative strategy for repayment of the debt to the banks, while letting Case eventually return to profitably. The bank agreement, which came in December of 1961, was to run for 10 years. It called for a reorganization of the company and in March of 1962, Merrit D. Hill, former president and general manager of Ford Tractor and Implement Division, was named president of Case. Hill started refocusing the company by taking responsibility for the operations, engineering, product development, and the public relations department. Case was on the road to recovery by the mid- to late-1960s. Only a strong company, with a backbone of extremely loyal and dedicated employees and a loyal dealer organization, could have survived such an ordeal. It was impressive that they were able to establish new product concepts, such as the utility tractor, improved operator comfort and safety with the Comfort King, the Draft-O-Matic, the four-wheel-steer Traction King, and hydrostatic drive garden tractors. All of these advancements were done with the most meager of facilities and financial investment.

The 30 Series Tractors (1960-1970)

The 430, 530, 630, 730, 830, 930, and 1030

In 1960 Case introduced the 30 series tractors. The 430, 530, and 630 were built at Rock Island and replaced the 200, 300, 400, 500, and 600 tractors. The 730, 830, and 930 were built at Racine and replaced the 700, 800, and 900 models. In 1960 the 1,000 rpm take off was introduced on the 930 which still had the chain drive transmission. The 1030 was not introduced until 1966.

Refinements, Options, and Improved Performance of the 30 Series

The Case Hallmark. In 1960 the styling was again changed by the addition of a long wide black stripe on each side of the hood. This hallmark of Case styling remained into the 1990s with only minor changes to fit the changing hood lines.

Comfort Kings. The Comfort King series began in 1962 with the 930 tractor when a foot clutch was introduced, the hand clutch remained an option until 1967. Also in 1962, the platform was raised on the 930 and the fuel tank was mounted behind the operator. The

In 1962 the platform was raised and a new seat suspension was added to the 930. On the 930 Comfort King the operator sat ahead of the rear axle and up out of the dust. A 50-gallon rear-mounted diesel fuel tank was also added.

The 930 Comfort King LP gas tractor had a rear-mounted fuel tank with a 48-gallon capacity. These large rear-mounted fuel tanks were the first in the industry.

Comfort King series was later expanded to the 730 and 830 series in 1964.

The term Comfort King was coined because the operator sat up on the elevated platform with visibility in every direction. The Comfort King seat was also a breakthrough in operator comfort. It had contoured rubber seat cushions mounted on a torsional rubber mounting that could be adjusted to suit the operator's weight and moved easily forward or back to suit legroom needs. The seat also flipped out of the way when the operator wanted to stand.

The rear-mounted fuel tank design answered the ever-increasing request from larger farms for a large tank "that only had to be filled once a day." The 930 was the first two-wheel-drive tractor in the industry with a large rear-mounted fuel tank. The diesel tank held 50 gallons which was advertised to work 15 hours under average conditions without a refill. The LP gas tank held 48 gallons. An interesting note, in touting the 930's diesel fuel economy, the advertising literature of the day stated many Case owners reporting plowing for 14-cents an acre. The 730 and 830 tractors did not have rear-mounted tanks until the 70 series was introduced in 1969. The 730 and 830 Comfort Kings fuel tank capacity was increased from 22 to 31 gallons as part of the raised platform design. The Comfort King design was well accepted and was in production until 1969.

Draft-O-Matic. The engineering group at the Rock Island Plant started the Draft-O-Matic hitch design around 1960 for the 430/530 series size tractors, but the design was completed and expanded for use on all tractors by the Clausen Works engineering group. The design for the small tractors was an upper-link sensing system. This system sensed the load through the third point (turn-buckle) by compressing or relaxing a coil spring at the end of the third point. In 1961, when the tractor production and engineering were consolidated into the Racine Clausen Works, the design of the Draft-O-Matic valve was expanded so it would work on both the small tractors with upper-link sensing and the larger tractors with lower-link sensing. Draft-O-Matic (DOM) was introduced on the small tractors on a limited scale in Tifton, Georgia, in 1962, and full production began in 1963. Large tractor production with Draft-O-Matic began in 1964. DOM allowed the operator to select the sensitivity to fit the job by simply positioning the lever for either load or depth. In the load position for tillage

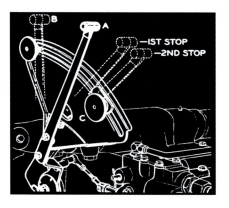

The 430 and 530 tractors were the first Case tractors with draft sensing hitches. A single lever allowed the operator to choose either draft control or position control.

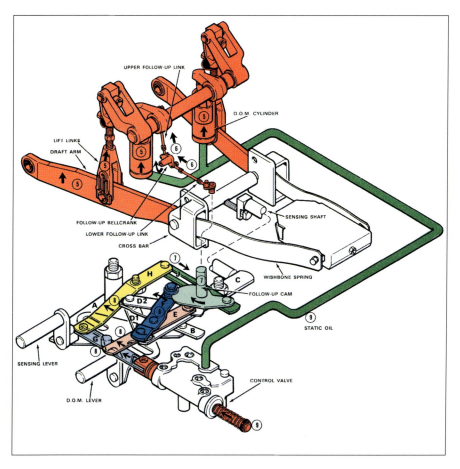

Labels on diagram: UPPER FOLLOW-UP LINK, D.O.M CYLINDER, LIFT LINKS, DRAFT ARM, FOLLOW-UP BELLCRANK, LOWER FOLLOW-UP LINK, CROSS BAR, SENSING SHAFT, WISHBONE SPRING, FOLLOW-UP CAM, STATIC OIL, SENSING LEVER, D.O.M. LEVER, CONTROL VALVE

Draft-O-Matic lower link sensing on the larger tractors was comprised of a series of sensing levers connected to the DOM valves. This series of levers made the system very sensitive and allowed it to make only small depth corrections as needed.

Model 930 General Purpose Tractor

In 1964 the 6-cylinder engine was married to what was essentially the 730/830 chassis which became the 930 General Purpose tractor. This gave Case a row-crop tractor in the 85+ horsepower category and satisfied customer demands for larger row-crop tractors such as the Deere 4010 and 4020. The 830, the largest Case row-crop tractor prior to the 930, was at 64.26 PTO horsepower. The 930 GP, as it was called, was designed with the rear-mounted fuel tank, a Comfort King platform, and a new contour seat with arm rests and extended back rest. The 8-speed dual range transmission was modified to accept the increased horsepower.

operation the valve was very sensitive — it sensed — it started to lift — it canceled out — the valve did not move the implement any more than necessary. In the depth mode, the valve would maintain a constant depth regardless of the terrain, this feature was especially popular for tool bar planters. The DOM valve was extremely successful and is still used in the 1990s with some variations. Valves were even sold to Versatile for use on some of their tractor models.

Draft-O-Matic was standard and three choices of fuel were offered: gasoline, LP gas, and diesel. The 930 GP remained in production until 1969. The 930 with the 6-speed transmission (930 Comfort King four-wheel standard as it became known after the 930 GP introduction) remained in production until 1967.

1030 Comfort King

During the 1960s there was constant market pressure for larger and larger row-crop tractors, but there was little research and development taking place due to the financial constraints of the bank agreement. As a result, Case engineers couldn't "go to the cupboard" so to speak and pick up a transmission — the engine was on the shelf but the transmission wasn't. R.J. Miller, then Vice President of Engineering, decided to gamble against the better judgment of his design engineers and

The 930 General Purpose tractor was a marriage of the 730/830 transmission and the 6-cylinder engine.

The 1030 was a case of the 930 General Purpose transmission being stretched too far for the heavy use in some areas of the country, such as the Mississippi Delta, where it was not successful.

stretch the 930 transmission. It didn't work. The 1030 was produced but had reliability problems in certain areas of the United States, such as the Mississippi Delta. The 1030 was introduced in 1966 at 101.79 PTO horsepower and was only available with a 451-cubic-inch diesel engine. The 1030 did have a first — it was the first Case tractor with a dry-type air cleaner.

The Rest of the 30 Series

In the 1960s Case started marketing a new concept of tractors, "The Utility Tractors." These tractors, the 430 and 530, were equipped with new heavy-duty drop-forged front axles, heavy-duty double-acting

The 730 Diesel Comfort King had a raised platform and the deluxe seat suspension, but the fuel tank remained in front of the operator.

steering cylinders, a power shuttle transmission, and larger diameter induction-hardened rear axles. They were then combined with Case-designed-and-built loaders and backhoes. Box scrapers, lawn mowers, brush mowers, cutter-bar mowers, crane booms, log forks, and a dozer blade were made by outside suppliers. An all-terrain forklift was built around the 430 chassis. Case was now ready for both the light construction and agricultural markets. With the newly acquired construction equipment dealer organization through the American Tractor Company acquisition and the existing agricultural dealerships, Case hit the ground running in this market — a lead they have never relinquished.

Specialty Tractors

Case offered an expanded line of orchard-grove tractors in the specialty tractors. The 630 and 730 were offered with full grove sheet metal in either Case-O-

The 1030 was the first tractor to use a dry-type air cleaner for longer life and ease of service. Prior to this only oil bath cleaners were used.

The fuel capacity on front-mounted fuel tanks for the 730/830 Comfort King tractors was increased about 9 gallons.

The specialty tractor for orchard grove work came in all sizes and configurations. This 530 with a tree hoe is a low center of gravity (LCG) tractor with turf tires. It was usually sold to golf courses and park commissions for mowing grass.

This 430 tractor with a sprayer is equipped with orchard rear fenders.

In the 30 series Case still made the 730 with full orchard sheet metal.

This 730 with the tree trimmer does not have the raised platform but it does have the orchard fenders without the skirts and a brush guard in front of the radiator. Case offered more specialty tractors in the 1960s than at any other time.

Matic or dry clutch versions. Only drawbar models were available. The 430 and 530 models were also offered with orchard rear fenders, Case-O-Matic or dry clutch, and Draft-O-Matic hitch or drawbar only.

Garden Tractors

After acquiring the Colt Manufacturing Company of Winneconne, Wisconsin, in 1964, Case was into the 10- and 12-horsepower garden tractor business. By 1966 Case was offering the first commercial production hydrostatic drive garden tractor. See page 146 for more details on the garden tractors.

The End of the 1960s

The 1200 Traction King

In the early 1960s, as Case was searching for the answer to the marketplace demand for 100- and over horsepower tractor, they studied their competition. International Harvester had the 4300 at 214.23 drawbar horsepower, four-wheel drive four-wheel steer (independent front and rear and crab); Deere & Company had the 5010 at 121.12 PTO horsepower, a two-wheel drive; and Minneapolis Moline had the G 706 at 101 PTO horsepower, a two-wheel drive with a power front-wheel drive. Case realized the horsepower limits of two-wheel drive since two-wheel drive over 100 horsepower could only deliver limited traction under most field conditions. The only solution to avoid wheel slippage was to add weight to the rear

In 1964 Case entered the garden tractor business by acquiring Colt Manufacturing Company and started out with a 10-horsepower model and the 12-horsepower model shown here.

Another specialty tractor was the conversion of 310s to forklifts. The platform modification and mast was made by the Harlo Corporation. The forklifts were sold mostly with pallet forks but some attachments like this dozer blade were also offered.

wheels, but this was self-defeating because the extra weight caused more soil compaction. Case began investigating mechanical front-wheel drives like the Elwood axles and a few others. They even sold some but the problem was cost. Considering the base price of a 930 GP was under $7,400 it didn't make sense to add between $2,000 and $3,000 for mechanical front-wheel drive. In the case of the IH 4300, the concept seemed to make more sense because the four-wheel drive divided up the power delivered to the front and rear of the tractor and reduced the slippage and compaction problems. The four-wheel steer also had a shorter turning radius than the Deere 8010, 215-horsepower four-wheeler which was articulated. But in those days there weren't many implements available for a 214-horsepower and 215-horsepower tractor, so Case opted for a lower horsepower, higher volume machine.

With only limited resources available, Case decided to use off-the-shelf components and pick up proven axles and a transmission from outside suppliers. They also intended to use the Case engine to develop a 120-horsepower four-wheel-drive tractor. The original plan was to use a 451-cubic-inch, 105-PTO-horsepower diesel similar to the one used in the W12 loader, but the Marketing Group complained it wouldn't sell against the Deere 5010 at 121 PTO horsepower.

Design Requirements

In 1963 the design responsibility for the 1200 Traction King was assigned to the Industrial Loader Design Group at the Racine Clausen Works (formerly the South Works) since the concept wasn't much different than their previous design work — a fabricated chassis with an engine, transmission, drive axles, and a hydraulic system. In June 1963 the following design requirements were presented for approval:

- four-wheel drive
- four-wheel steer
- 120 PTO horsepower
- drawbar pull to handle eight bottoms in most field conditions
- maximum comfort
- distinctive styling
- 451 Case diesel engine
- modified Clark R500, 6-speed transmission
- Eaton, Wisconsin Axle Division axles similar to those used in W 10 loader
- Open deck-type operator's platform that would use the Comfort King seat
- rear-mounted fuel tank
- 1,500 PSI, 24-gpm hydraulic system
- hydrovac vacuum brakes
- 1,000 rpm PTO, 3-point hitch
- rear wheel steering hydraulically independent of front steering

The transmission and axles on the 1200 were purchased from Clark Equipment. The transmission was a vertical design and had to be lowered out of the chassis for most service work, but it was a very reliable unit and required very little service.

The Four-Wheel-Steering System. One of the most unique design features of the 1200 Traction King was the four-wheel-steering system. The front wheels were controlled by a hydrostatic steering pump attached to the steering wheel and was completely independent of the rear steering. The rear steering was controlled by either a hand lever on the dash next to the steering wheel or by a rocker-type foot pedal that was handy when the operator's hands were busy with the steering wheel and hydraulic levers. The lever and pedal operated a rear steering valve thru mechanical linkage. Rear steering could either be coordinated with the front steering or could be independent from the front.

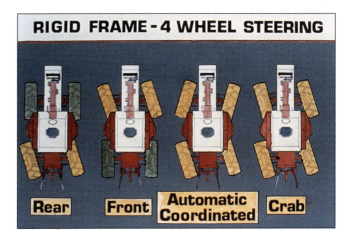

The 1200 was the first four-wheel-steer tractor in the industry to offer automatic coordinated steering.

Mechanical cables were used to control the hydraulic rear steering system, starting with the 1200 in 1964 until it was replaced with an electronic system in 1983.

Front-Wheel Steering Only. Front-wheel steering only was used for better control in row-crop work. Front-wheel mode was also designed for safer control in road travel. Most people have seen the old rear-steer front-end loaders going down the road backwards. The reason was that at higher speeds with rear steering and traveling frontward the operator tended to oversteer and drove down the road like a waddling duck. The Case design of independent front steering eliminated this problem because the rear steering could be locked in the straight ahead position, thereby giving the tractor conventional front-wheel steering.

Rear Steering Only. The rear-steering mode was widely used for attaching to implements, especially since the implements used behind the 1200 were large and heavy. It wasn't easy to move those implements

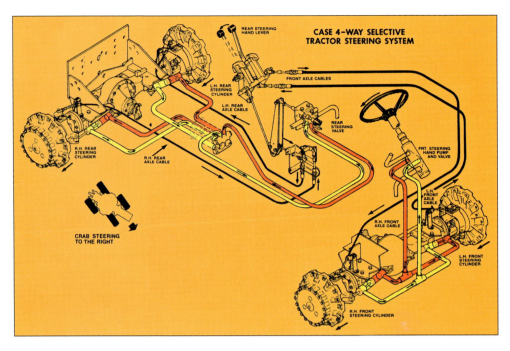

and rear steering made backing and hooking up to them easier. The back end of the tractor was steered right into the implement.

Coordinated and Crab Steer. The Case 1200 was the first large four-wheel-drive tractor in the industry to offer coordinated steering. When the rear steering lever was put in the coordinated mode, the steering of the rear wheels was controlled by the steering wheel. Coordinated steering was used on short turns at the end of the row because the front and rear wheels turned in the opposite direction (for example: front wheels to the left, rear wheels to the right made a very tight left turn). One of the major uses of crab steer was when working on hillsides. Gravity tended to pull the heavy implement downhill and on an articulated tractor it pulled the rear of the tractor downhill also,

The open platform design of the 1200 allowed the operator to enter or leave the operator compartment from either side. The rear steering lever is under the steering wheel on the left. The steering foot pedal is not visible in this picture.

The ability to crab steer on the hillsides developed in the 1200 made the Case four-wheel steer one of the top selling four-wheel-drive tractors in to the early 1990s.

The vertical transmission allowed the engine flywheel to mount straight into the clutch housing and the transmission output shafts were in line with the axles without the need for a separate drop housing. The auxiliary pump and PTO drives were also located at the top of the transmission and were driven directly off the engine.

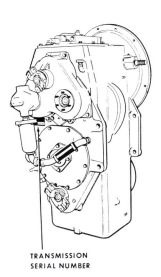

TRANSMISSION
SERIAL NUMBER

and in some extreme cases caused an upset. In this situation the operator could put the 1200 tractor in crab steer with all four wheels turned in the same direction slightly uphill and the tractor and implement would track straight ahead. Crab steer also worked well in compensating for side draft in tillage operations.

Transmission. The 1200's transmission was a vertical design and was mounted in the chassis so the engine flywheel was mounted straight into the clutch and transmission input shaft. The transmission output shafts were in line with the axle differentials. The vertical installation was not remembered for its serviceability, but luckily it was a very reliable transmission. The transmission was controlled by three levers located on the right counsel: a range lever, a forward/reverse lever, and a Hi-Lo lever that was pulled up for "Hi" and pushed down for "Lo." There were six speeds forward and four reverse.

Axles. The original plan was to use the same axles on the 1200 as were used on the W10 front-end loader. It was later decided, however, that the Rzeppa joint, a type of large ball joint designed for intermittent loading and the tight turning of the industrial loader application, would not work in the constant heavy-duty straight loading of the agricultural tractor. As a result, the universal joint steering knuckle (constant velocity joint) was finally decided upon and Clark Equipment Company of Kalamazoo, Michigan, became the supplier.

Engine. The engine became the biggest design challenge. Originally the plan was to use the 451-cubic-inch naturally aspirated engine at 105 PTO horsepower, but the most they could get out of it was 115 horsepower as a naturally aspirated engine. Marketing would have no part of it, because it didn't meet the 120-horsepower competition in this class and price of tractor. Case had no other engine, so the only answer was to turbocharge it.

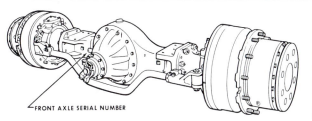

FRONT AXLE SERIAL NUMBER

The original axle design called for a Rzeppa type joint design like the front-end loaders, but field testing soon determined that this type of joint did not stand up under the constant heavy loading of an agricultural application. The design was changed to a constant velocity joint before production. The 1200 had individual drum brakes on each wheel, this was changed on the 1470 which used a caliper disc brake on the driveline.

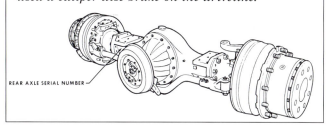

REAR AXLE SERIAL NUMBER

The Lanova system did not lend itself to substantial turbocharging because of the injector/Powrcel relationship where the injector has to inject fuel across the combustion chamber into the Powrcel. Turbocharging made the air in the combustion chamber more dense and the penetration from the injector became more difficult. The solution was to move the Powrcel closer to the injector. This change required reducing the diameter of the exhaust valve, which restricted the breathing of the engine and limited the horsepower of a given displacement engine. The Powrcel location was another problem. The fuel from the Powrcel could be concen-

The turbocharged Lanova 451-cubic inch engine was only used in the 1200 tractor and was discontinued in 1969 when the 504-cubic-inch open chamber engine was introduced in the 1470 Traction King which replaced the 1200.

trated in a spot on the cylinder head, resulting in a hot spot. If operated under heavy loads for a long period of time, combustion temperatures could reach unacceptable levels. When diesel exhaust temperatures rise above the 1,200 to 1,300 degree mark, metallurgical damage can occur in the piston dome and top ring area which is the hottest part of the combustion chamber. Piston scoring between the top ring area or piston skirt and the cylinder sleeve often resulted in too much high temperature operation. To overcome this problem, a pyrometer (an instrument for measuring very high temperatures) was mounted in front of the operator in the cockpit with a large decal warning the operator not to exceed 925 degrees Fahrenheit on the pyrometer. It also warned to cool the engine down to 400 degrees before shutdown. Overfueling became more critical in the Lanova engine than the open chamber engine, so the operator's manual for the 1200 warned that over-fueling could potentially cause excessive combustion chamber temperatures and result in internal engine damage.

With limited resources in the early 1960s the usual clay models were not made for styling approval, instead a full size wood and art board mock-up was made to get the effect of the size of this large tractor. The engine in this picture was an enlarged photograph mounted in the mock-up.

Styling. Because of the urgency of this program a few styling renderings were made. The Case styling department crew made a full-size wooden and art board mock-up for effect and it received overwhelming and quick approval.

Production Begins – 1964

In January 1964 the 1200 was released for production pending the test results of four prototypes. One unit was tested on the new test-center test track

in Racine. The second unit was sent to the stress lab, then to the hydraulic lab, and finally to the Arizona proving grounds. The third unit was sent to Texas for three weeks for advertising photos and returned to Racine to the Technical Publications Department for the Operator Manual and Dealer Service Manual work.

The wooden and art board mock-up achieved its purpose. Someone could climb up and sit in the seat and get the feel of what a big tractor was like. Notice the plywood wheel discs and wooden hitch arms in this photo.

Case built a special prototype tractor that was used to make the Dealer Service Manual. This manual was available when the tractor was introduced to the dealers and when they needed it most — on a new product.

Many of the special tools Case dealers would need to service the product, such as the splitting stands shown here, were developed in the Case Technical Publications photo studio/shop while the Service Manual was being completed.

The writers and mechanics in the publications department developed the procedures and techniques needed to service a tractor. These procedures were then photographed step by step and printed in their Service Manual so the dealer service personnel could quickly grasp the techniques. As a result, language was not left to the mercy of translation.

A Case designed and manufactured cab was not available on the 1200 and very few tractors had after-market cabs installed. This is a very rare picture of a 1200 with a cab.

The technical publications crew completely disassembled and worked on the unit in the same modes a dealer/serviceman would, for example; clutch overhaul, axle seal replacement, valve refacing, hydraulic system testing, etc. through the whole tractor. Case was the only company in the industry that built a special prototype tractor just for technical manual work. They felt very strongly about having an Operators Manual, a Parts Catalog, and a Dealer Service Manual available when the tractor was introduced so dealers had the necessary information when they most needed it — on a new product. A pilot run of 22 units were produced in March of 1964 to resolve any production problems. Full production began on March 23, 1964. The loader assembly line in Racine produced 304 tractors. Racine built 18 more in 1965 before the loader and Traction King production were moved to the Case facility in Rockford, Illinois. A total of 1,549 1200 Traction Kings were built until it was replaced by the 1470 TK in 1969.

Considering all the concerns about turbocharging a Lanova engine, the 1200 did quite well — two engine problems occurred in the first one-third of the units built. One problem was the failure of the camshaft drive gears, the original gears were made of cast alloy but was later changed to harden steel. The second problem occurred with the fire ring on the head gasket. It allowed coolant to enter the combustion chamber. A one-piece gasket was designed and solved the problem. Also a vacuum build-up in the turbine housing of the turbocharger caused oil to be drawn through the bearing and seal into the intake manifold causing excessive oil consumption. A vent tube between the engine-valve cover and the turbine housing fixed this problem. All units were recalled and each problem repaired.

The 1200 established Case in the four-wheel-drive tractor business. Case was number three in market share in 1975, number one in 1976, number six in 1977, number two in 1980, number four in 1981, and number five in 1982. Very interesting, considering they were the only four-wheel-steer tractor in the marketplace and all the rest were articulated.

The 1470, which replaced the 1200, offered a Case factory installed cab.

The Case plant in Vierzon, France, started out producing small tractors for the European market in 1958. The tractors were less than successful. It wasn't until the 1960s when they began producing U.S.-designed hay balers and loader backhoes that the plant became profitable.

de Gaulle's Revenge

Until 1958 Case had never manufactured a locally-made product overseas. At that time, the French Case distributor was having difficulty with competition from Massey Ferguson and IH who were selling locally-made products. Also, Case did not have a small 2- or 3-cylinder diesel engine. In 1958 Case bought The Societe Francaise which was founded in 1848 from a

Mr. Arbel. It had profited from the postwar boom but was now in financial trouble because its engineering was outdated, but it was working on a two-cylinder tractor. The plant was located in Vierzon, France. Case sent several people from manufacturing, finance, and engineering to evaluate it. The report was: "it could be salvaged" and would provide a local-made European product and a small diesel engine. Never have so many people been so wrong! The current tractors, the 303 and the 403, had major engine problems and were not considered acceptable by the dealers. The CF 250 and CF 350, the new models, were, after a tremendous amount of testing and suggested redesign by the Racine Test Center, well accepted and had no field problems. The only major problem was the high manufacturing cost. The Vierzon plant was never profitable until the late 1960s when it started producing the European version of the 530 CK loader backhoe and its successors. The Vierzon plant losses were one of the financial anchors around Case's neck during the 1960s.

Light at the End of the Tunnel

By the end of the 1960s, things were definitely improving for Case. In 1967, Tenneco Inc. of Houston, Texas, acquired Kern County Land Company with its controlling interest in Case. In 1969 Tenneco increased its interest in Case to 91% through a stock purchase and in 1970 Case became a wholly-owned subsidiary of Tenneco. Net sales increased 20% to $430.8 million. Tenneco's backing and the business upturn were the financial boost Case needed to enter the 1970s, when farm exports grew 150% and agricultural productivity skyrocketed.

This side-shift backhoe was produced at the Case Vierzon plant. The loader backhoe became so successful in Europe that Vierzon had to stop producing hay balers and shift that capacity to loader backhoes.

The 1970s – End Desert Sunset, Begin Power Red

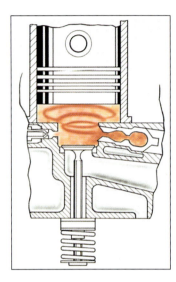

The Lanova combustion system was difficult to turbocharge because the fuel was injected across the combustion chamber. Turbocharging caused the air to become more dense and in turn made it very difficult for the fuel to penetrate the combustion chamber and enter the cell.

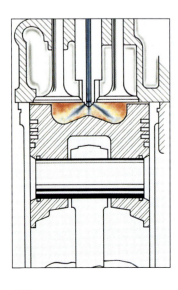

Case designed the open chamber combustion system to replace the Lanova design because the open chamber was easier to turbocharge.

The groundwork for the tractors of the 1970s actually began in June of 1965 when the open chamber engine design was approved. This design utilized the same basic cylinder block as the Lanova design and ran over the existing machine tools. The open chamber engine required new machine tools for the cylinder head. The cylinder bore size was increased from 451 to 504 cubic inch displacement on the largest 6-cylinder engine and from 301 to 336 cubic inch displacement on the largest 4-cylinder engine. Because the open chamber design was quite easily turbocharged, Case eventually developed 254 horsepower out of this design with turbocharging and aftercooling. This open chamber engine design became the cornerstone for the tractors of the 1970s and 1980s, until it was replaced by the Family 1 and 2 Case-Cummins engines in the late 1980s.

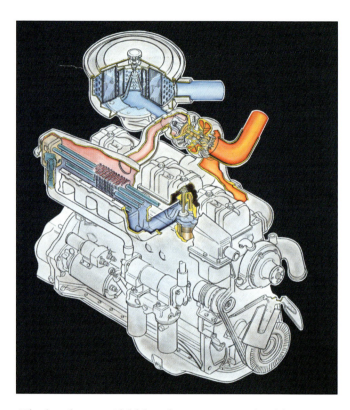

The intake manifold has been cut away in this picture. Note the aftercooler in the intake manifold which cooled the air from the exhaust before it entered the combustion chamber.

One Giant Step For Case – Intro 70

In 1969, while the rest of the country was concerned with going to the moon, Case was preparing for a major launch of its own — the 70 series tractors at Intro 70. Case dealers, sales people, marketing personnel, bankers, the press, manufacturing, and engineering all gathered at an an abandoned air base in southeastern Wisconsin in August 1969 for Intro 70. The Bong Air Base, just southwest of Racine in Kenosha County, Wisconsin, had recently been declared obsolete (before it was even finished) so Case leased the facility for its largest product introduction. It was virtually a city in the middle of the Wisconsin prairie.

Old Abe Retires

The first major change launched at Intro 70 was the replacement of Old Abe, the Case eagle trademark of 100 years. (Old Abe made his first appearance on the Eclipse thresher in 1869.) In 1969 Morris Reid, Executive Vice President, engaged Lippincott & Margulies Inc., a New York firm specializing in corporate images, to design a new logo that better reflected the company's diversification objectives. The two major reasons for Old Abe's retirement were: (1) the memories of the Civil War and what Old Abe symbolized had long ago faded and (2) Case was swiftly moving into a new field — construction equipment —where the eagle trademark was not as well recognized. Needless to say, many agricultural dealers and longtime agricultural employees found this a bitter pill to swallow at first, but over time found that the "chips" (as they called Case's name stamped in metal treads of black) were easier to recognize as a corporate symbol. But on a machine it was harder to read from a distance, such

as identifying a Case product in the field or on a construction site from the highway because only 60% of the logo was letters. So in 1978, the products were changed to the logo with the helvetica bold Case name. This new logo had vision. When Case acquired International Harvester the two logos fit together like hand and glove. The eagle logo, on the other hand, would have been a difficult fit.

Case may have retired Old Abe from prominence on the products and dealer signs in 1969, but the eagle has remained on many product castings to this day. Old Abe has also made some cameo appearances through the years, such as appearing on the steering wheel hub on the 1896 and 2096 tractors and it was the symbol for the Case 150th anniversary celebration in 1992.

A New Era of Operator Consciousness

Intro 70 ushered in a totally new era of operator consciousness. During the 1950s and mid-1960s the farm equipment industry concentrated on larger horsepower tractors that were more efficient and could run longer hours on a tank of fuel. But what about the operator sitting out in the elements hour after hour? The noise, dust, heat, and cold could all lead to fatigue. First, umbrellas were installed to shade the operator from the sun, then around 1966, roll over protection with special guards and frames became available. Canopies appeared over these frames but they were never well excepted. They were very noisy since these frames were attached to the axle housing or transmission case and telegraphed the noise right past the operator's ear. The acceptance of these roll-over protective structures was so poor that Deere and Company gave them away as a promotion. As the 1960s drew to a close more and more farmers started buying "will fit" cabs for their tractor with heaters and air conditioning. Some of these cabs were noisier than a tractor without a cab because the noise stayed within the cab.

The 70 series tractors and the other new Case products made their debut at Intro 70 in August of 1969. Case virtually built a city in the middle of the Wisconsin prairie.

Author Tom Stonehouse (at Intro 70) explains how the RPS 34 transmission works to Tenneco management, as Case Chairman of the Board, Meritt Hill, looks on. The full-size working transmission cut away was powered by an electric motor and the clutches were actuated by air pressure.

The Isolated Platform on 70 Series Tractors

During the development of the larger 70 series tractors (770 - 1070), Case engineers decided by isolating the operator's platform from the rest of the tractor with iso mounts (rubber biscuits) they could lower the noise level below the competition. These rubber mounts especially isolated the operator from the noise, heat, and vibration common to most of the transmission and hydraulic systems of that era. Designing the correct durometer (stiffness) and choosing the right material was quite a challenge when considering the environment these mounts had to survive, such as:

The development of the isolated platform by Case was the first attempt by a major manufacturer to address the vibration, noise, and heat of the operator's environment.

This tractor illustrates Case's attempt during the 1950s to satisfy the market demand for a cab. The cab was a step above the umbrella, and the designs of the 1960s showed a vast improvement in operator comfort.

The vendor cab on this 930 tractor was just one example of a fast-growing industry of the mid-1960s — the after-market cab. The major tractor manufacturers were not responding to the demand for operator comfort in a cab. These vendor cabs were not the answer — they were noisy and had very little or no ROPS protection

heat, dirt, mud, grease, and to top it off — survive a roll over. Needless to say, a lot of specialized testing had to be done before it was successful. With the platform isolated, it was time to encase it with an enclosure that was dust free (as much as possible) and climate controlled. The result was the comfort cab.

A New World of Comfort and Quiet

The comfort cab design began at the operator's feet with a platform that floated on air and rubber. The four rubber biscuits (one at each corner) reduced vibration and the insulating cushion of moving air under the platform reduced the noise and heat from the transmission and hydraulics. The cab was mounted on the isolated platform with doors, windows, a floor, and a control console sealed against noise, dust, dirt, heat, and cold. A cellular foam padding with vinyl covering was also used to insulate against noise as well as heat and cold. Two pressurizing fans that gave six air changes a minute through a filter kept out additional dust and pollen.

In the search for the best location for the filter, the first priority was operator convenience. The engineers decided the best location would be accessible from the operator's seat. It was a poor decision because when the operator removed the filter all the dirt fell in his lap. As a result, the location was changed to the outside and to the rear. Even though the rear of the tractor got dust, it was away from exhaust noise and soot. The intake air filter was placed at the rear of the cab for several reasons. The first reason was to reduce noise. Another reason was to prolong the life of the filter. After slamming the cab door shut the air going back through the filter would tend to clean some of the dirt from the filter, thereby providing a longer filter life for the cab.

The cab had other improvements for the operator. For their personal convenience, optional heat and air conditioning were available. In addition, a tilt and telescoping steering wheel was offered, together with an

Whenever the cab door was slammed shut, the air going back through the filter would clean some of the dirt and provide a longer filter life.

The cab air filter was moved to the rear of the cab to get away from the exhaust noise, soot, and also to prevent the dirt from falling into the operator's lap when the filter was changed.

The Case comfort cab was designed with maximum visibility. The engine exhaust stack and intake prescreener were moved to the left, out of the line of visibility, the hood was sloped and tapered, and wide deep windows allowed the operator to easily see the row and the ground.

operator control console, a radio, and a choice of three seats.

The first unofficial University of Nebraska sound tests were made on a 970 manual transmission diesel tractor (Test No. 1034). This experience eventually became part of the sound test that began at Nebraska in 1971 when an 870 cab tractor tested out at 88.5 dB(A). The first Case-designed comfort cabs were manufactured by an outside supplier, but because of delivery problems, Case decided to manufacture its own cab — a first in the industry.

The tilt and telescoping steering wheel took into consideration the fact that during long days in the field, the operator would like to occasionally change positions. This was the first attempt at that since the tilt back seat to let the operator stand back in the 1940s.

Visibility – All Around

The comfort cab was designed with maximum visibility. First, the engine exhaust stack and intake prescreener were mounted in line to the operator's left side. The hood sloped and tapered in front and wide deep windows were in the front, allowing the operator to easily see the rows and the ground. The fuel tank was also contoured so the operator could easily see the drawbar and hitch.

Roll Over Protection Structure and the Comfort Cab

From the very beginning of this new operator environment concept, Case decided that the cab would be provided with a roll-over protective structure (ROPS). They would not offer a cab without ROPS. Case decided very early in the development to have a supplier design and build the cab. The supplier delivered the first cab for testing and Case engineers mounted it on the tractor platform. The engineers took it out to the 7 Mile Proving Ground north of Racine for roll-over testing — the cab totally collapsed! Case decided that if they were to control their own destiny with the ROPS cab concept, they would have to design their own cab. Case engineers designed the cab with maximum visibility, low noise level, and ROPS protection. They recognized that if by offering two cab options, one with and one without ROPS, the buyer would choose the cab at the lowest price. This proved to be a very good decision because these cabs were very successful and served Case from the 70 series in 1969 to the Magnum in 1987.

ROPS Testing. Initially the ROPS testing started by rolling tractors over and the concerns were simple: Maintain an envelope for the operator through the complete roll; Make sure the glass explodes out of the cab rather than implodes into the cab; Insure that the operator has a means (the seat belt) to stay supported and confined to the seat to prevent injury from flying around the cab during an upset. The concerns were simple but the collection of test data was very complicated. Before the tractors were rolled they were strained gauged to determine the forces on the roll-over

At the start of the 70 series design program the plan was to have an outside supplier design and build the cab. When the first prototype cabs were delivered, one of them was designated for a roll-over test. These frames depict the results of this test — the cab completely failed. It was at this time that Case decided that if they were to control their own destiny, they would have to design and build their own cab.

If the tractor was still drivable after the side roll, all photos and measurements were taken and it was immediately driven up this ramp and rolled over backwards.

The object of the roll-over test was that if the cab did crush, that an adequate envelope was always maintained for the operator.

All of the roll-over testing was done on a test site on the banks of Lake Michigan, just north of Racine, Wisconsin. The test course was run from west to east so the early morning light was good for motion picture and television recording of the test. The problem was, the end of the course was only about 300 yards from a 50-foot drop off a bluff and down to the lake. To prevent a remote controlled tractor (that had a mind of its own) from diving off the bluff, a safety pit was located at the end of the course.

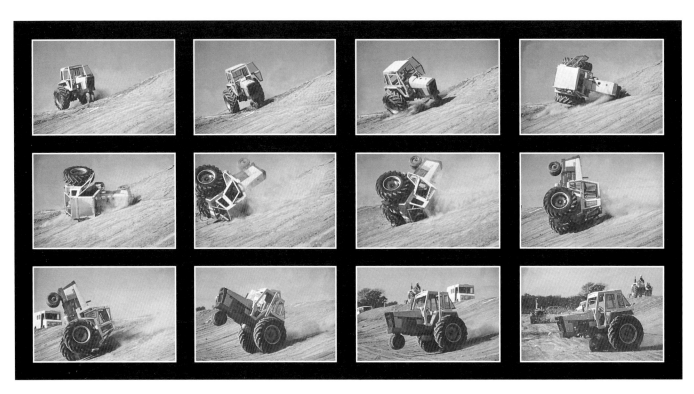

As the roll-over testing matured, all tests were only conducted when the ambient temperature was zero degrees Fahrenheit or below, and the tractor had been put in this environment overnight. Most tests were conducted at the first light of day. The cold was one of the reasons the tractor bounced around so much as shown in these frames — the slope was a frozen clay surface. The cold also made the metal brittle, so it was a good testing environment.

Just so the reader does not get the impression that tractors were easily rolled over, we have included these frames of what happened quite frequently — the tractor just went down the hill and never tipped over. Also notice on all these tests the doors and windows were open, the reason for this was so they didn't add any support to the ROPS structure.

This roll-over dummy had a lot of exciting rides and survived them all because he was using his seat belt.

protective structure. These forces could be duplicated in the lab without having to roll the cab and tractor. The roll overs were recorded on 16-mm color motion picture film, 35-mm color still film, and black-and-white television tape so the exact type and severity of the roll could be analyzed — somewhat like analyzing the game films in football. This type of analysis, using pictures and strain gauge data in a computer model, was very successful and eventually became so predictable it was unnecessary to roll the cab.

The actual roll overs were very exciting, especially in the beginning when everyone was learning. The roll-over tractor was controlled from a stationary drone tractor. Hundreds of feet of hydraulic hose for steering and electrical wire for stopping and starting and recording were carefully laid out on the edge of a steep cliff. The operator of the drone tractor then started the roll-over tractor moving along the cliff — trying to tip it over the cliff. Due to the length of the steering hose, there was a response delay in the steering and needless

to say, there were some exciting moments not knowing at just what point the roll-over tractor was going to respond. If it could be restarted after the side roll, the tractor was immediately put through a rear roll. A mechanical dummy was used in all the rollovers to test the seat belts.

After watching the tapes and films it didn't take long to become a disciple of the use of seat belts and roll-over protection on farm tractors. The structure of the same cab for ROPS protection was available without the glass or other internal features of the cab for those who wanted ROPS but did not want to purchase a cab.

Another Industry First for Case — The Nonmetallic Fuel Tank

In 1962 Case was the first tractor manufacturer with the rear-mounted fuel tank on the 930 Comfort King. In 1969 they were again first with a rear-mounted seamless nylon fuel tank. Case engineers went to the nylon tank to utilize space, they wanted to have a large tank. Initially the tank started out at 50 gallons and later increased to 80 gallons. Almost everyone can visualize a 50 gallon drum, so where do you hide it on a tractor? A nylon or nonmetallic tank utilized all of the available space. The first tanks were made out of nylon because high-density polyethylenes were not developed in the late 1960s. Some other materials such as fiberglass would wick, so liquid nylon was poured into a Rotocast and rotated.

Many pluses came with using the nonmetallic tank. The old metallic tank constantly had problems when turnplate material was used. The problem occurred at the point where the seam welding was done because

Case was the first in the industry to use a nonmetallic fuel tank. This tank not only solved large capacity tank space problems, it was also very durable and safe. One tank survived eight roll-over tests and never ruptured.

One of the problems with rear-mounted tanks was that they obscured the operator's view of the drawbar when backing up to hook up an implement. The ability to sculpture the nonmetallic tank solved this problem.

the welding would cause rust to form at the seam inside the tank and get into the fuel – clogging the fuel filter. The nonmetallic tank eliminated this problem. Safety was another big plus, especially in roll-over testing. One nonmetallic tank on a tractor was rolled eight times and never ruptured, whereas the metal tank would have ruptured every time.

The Range Power Shift Transmission. Intro 70 introduced the first power shift transmission on a Case tractor. The range power shift transmission (RPS) was developed using the "backdoor" design concept. When the Ford contingent assumed Case management in 1962 the new Vice President of Engineering, Raymond J. Miller, pushed for an 11-speed power shift to be designed to compete with the Ford 10 speed. The prototype was designed and after all the numbers were

presented, it was decided the cost effectiveness or investment return was just not there (especially considering that the Ford power shift had not excelled due to early reliability problems and cost). Case also tested an Allison full power shift transmission and again felt the cost was too high. Rather than just designing to meet competition, the tractor plant product engineers designed around the most frequently used power shift applications in the farming operation. The first range was for very low-speed PTO work, such as hay and forage, or for crop production such as planters. A second range was available for heavy tillage. A third range was used for higher field and transport speeds.

Case again went back to the shelf to dust off a design they had been working on using the 4-speed gear box from the 30 series coupled to a 2-speed range power shift. To meet their "most frequently used" criteria, Case engineers upgraded the original design to a

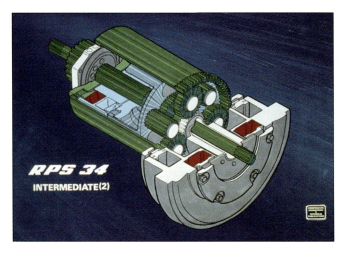

The engagement of clutches 1 and 4 (indicated in red) determined the power path through the planetary for the intermediate range.

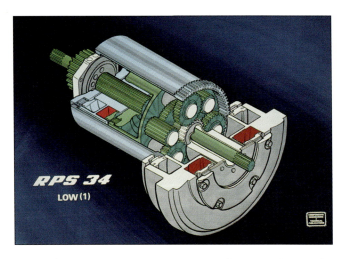

When RPS clutch number 1 and 3 (indicated in red) were engaged, they determined the power path through the planetary for the low range.

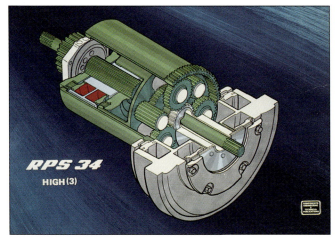

Clutches 3 and 4 (indicated in red) were engaged for the high range path through the planetary.

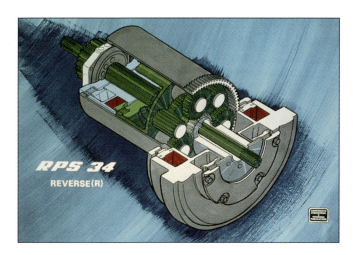

Clutches 2 and 3 were engaged for reverse. Clutch 2 held the planetary gear to reverse the direction of rotation of the planetary gear set.

3-speed range power shift, giving 12 speeds forward and 4 reverse. The 3-speed range power shift consisted of four hydraulic multiple disc clutches connected to a compound planetary gear set. The multiple disc hydraulic clutches determined the power path through the planetary resulting in a high, low, intermediate, or reverse range to drive the 4-speed transmission. The RPS 34 transmission was very well designed, but it had its idiosyncrasy — the adjustment of the retard valves.

Normally the RPS operated with two clutches engaged. For example, clutches number 1 and number 2 were engaged for Low; clutches number 1 and number 3 for Intermediate; and number 2 and number 3 clutches for High. When the operator power shifted, all three clutches were engaged for a moment to give a smooth shift, this was called clutch overlap. The clutch overlap adjustment was made at a set screw on the valve with the help of a "blinky box" or a clutch monitor tool which had a red, yellow, and green light. The green light was the correct overlap. Customers sometimes measured the mechanics skills by how well he could set the clutch overlap because it determined the smoothness of the power shift. The RPS design was used in tractors from the 770-up, including the four-wheel drives starting with the 2470. It was later expanded to 6-power shift speeds in four ranges. The RPS served Case well and remained in the two-wheel-drive tractor line until the Magnum in 1987 and the four-wheel drives until the 9100 series.

Standard 8-Speed Transmission. The standard 8-speed transmission developed in 1954 continued to be offered as an option on the 770 through the 1070.

Dual Hydraulic Pump (770 through 1070 Tractors). Case was one of the first companies to offer a dual hydraulic pump in which the rear section of the pump supplied 8-gpm oil to the steering and power brake systems. The front section supplied 16-gpm oil to the hitch and hydraulic systems. This design assured plenty of power for steering at the end of the field even when it was lifting a heavy implement.

Reversible PTO. For the first time the 770-1070 tractors offered Case customers an option of a dual-speed PTO with both 1,000 and 540 rpm. A single shaft with 540-rpm straight-sided splines on one end and the other end with 1,000 rpm involute

C-2 RETARD VALVE - LOW TO INTERMEDIATE

CLUTCH MONITOR A42743

RESET SWITCH

WHITE
AMBER
BLUE
GREEN
RED

BLACK GROUND CLIP

RED PLUS (+) CLIP

WIRE PLUGS

170 PSI SWITCH

50 PSI SWITCH

C2 RETARD

C3 RETARD

The smoothness of the power shift was regulated by the retard valve adjusters with the aid of the clutch monitor ("blinky box") and two pressure switches.

The dual hydraulic pump on the 70 series tractor was unique because the rear section supplied 8 gallons per minute to the steering and power brake system . The front section supplied 16 gallons per minute to the hitch, PTO, and remote hydraulic systems. This dual system assured plenty of power to the steering system at the end of the field, even when lifting a heavy implement.

HYDRAULIC SYSTEM-POWER SHIFT

DUAL
REMOTE
VALVE

STEERING
CONTROL
VALVE

DRAFT-O-MATIC
CONTROL VALVE

DUAL
HYDRAULIC
PUMP

POWER SHIFT
CONTROL VALVE

POWER BRAKE
VALVE

HYDRAULIC P.T.O. CLUTCH

10 MICRON
FILTER

CLOSED
SHUT-OFF VALVE

CASE FLOW DIVIDER
AND P.T.O. CONTROL VALVE

25 MICRON
FILTER

STEERING SYSTEM
RELIEF VALVE USED
WHEN NOT EQUIPPED
WITH POWER BRAKES

HYDRA-SLEUTH

TO SUMP

770-870-970-1070 TRACTORS

splines, could simply be reversed by removing a snap ring with a pliers and turning the shaft end-to-end and then replacing the snap ring. Competitors at the time offered two separate shafts that had to be carried in the tool box, but they lost oil when the shaft was changed. The Case design had a unique spring-loaded sleeve and shifter collar that indexed with the 1,000-rpm drive gear when the short end of the shaft was inserted and the 540-rpm drive gear when the long end was inserted.

Power Brakes. The 70 series tractors were the first Case tractors to have power and self-adjusting brakes. The brake valve was designed and manufactured by Case at the Rock Island plant. The pressure regulating spool made it unique. When actuated by the power brake piston, the pressure regulating spool restricted the flow from the pump to the steering system to ensure

The dual speed PTO on the large 70 series tractors could be quickly changed from 540 rpm to 1,000 rpm by removing a snap ring and the PTO shaft — then simply reversing the end of the shaft — and installing it back in the tractor and securing it with the snap ring.

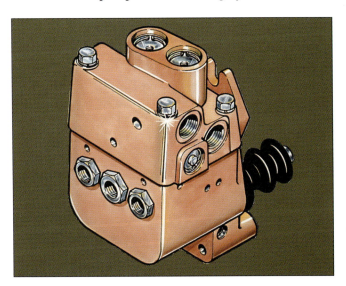

The power brake valve used on the 70 series tractors had a unique pressure regulating valve that could restrict the flow of oil from the pump to the steering system to ensure there was adequate pressure for breaking.

there was adequate pressure for braking. Hydraulic self-adjusting brakes were also available as an option.

New Engines For The 70's. Intro 70 ushered in all new engines from the 770 to the 1470. The 770 gasoline had a 251-cubic-inch 4-cylinder engine rated at 53.53 PTO horsepower and was the last gasoline tractor tested at Nebraska by Case. The other engines sizes were:
- The 770 diesel – 267-cubic-inch at 56.36 horsepower
- The 870 diesel - 336-cubic-inch at 70.53 horsepower
- The 970 diesel – 401-cubic-inch at 85.31 horsepower
- The 1070 diesel – 451-cubic-inch at 107.36 horsepower
- The 1470 diesel – 504-cubic-inch at 144.89 horsepower (The first Case turbocharged open chamber engine)

All the tractors introduced at Intro 70 were naturally aspirated and one of the first turbocharged two-wheel-drive models was the 1170 in 1970. The Intro 70 tractors were also the first complete line of Case tractors to use dry-type air cleaners.

Styling and Paint. The 770-1070 tractors were introduced with a new sloping hood and a squared off styling. The 1470 did not have the forward-sloping hood but rather a rear-sloping square front grille. The 1470 also did not have a Case comfort cab. There was little change in the 470 and 570 other than the decals and power red paint — all the models had the power red paint scheme. The difference between flambeau red and power red paint was obvious to the eye when the two tractors were side-by-side. The flambeau had an orange glow whereas the power red had more of a red glow, but looking at them individually it was hard to tell the difference. Customers had complained that the flambeau red faded too fast, therefore the paint was changed to power red.

An early full-scale clay model of the 70 series before the isolated platform design was complete and also before "Old Abe" was retired.

A later version full-scale model with isolated platform, fully painted, and the new Case logo.

The 1470 was restyled from the 1200, including a new 100-gallon fuel tank, but it was still metal and the hood and grille were different than the large 70 series row-crop tractors. The transmission speeds were increased from six on the 1200, to eight on the 1470 and the brakes were moved from the wheel ends to the drive shaft.

The 1470 was the first model to use the new 504-cubic inch turbocharged open chamber engine at 144.9 PTO horsepower.

The 1470 Traction King Replaces the 1200 Traction King

In addition to the new turbocharged 504 engine, the 1470's brakes were redesigned from the wheel ends on the 1200 to the driveshaft on the 1470. The new brake was a disc type which gave a smoother stopping action. The forward speeds in the transmission were increased from 6 to 8 speeds and the fuel tank was increased from 50 gallons on the 1200 to 100 gallons on the 1470. The cab, not of Case design, was an option and purchased from an outside supplier. The 1470 had a quiet introduction in January 1968 and was reintroduced with the rest of the 70 series in August 1969. The 1470 was produced at the Rockford, Illinois plant from 1968 until 1970 when the Rockford plant closed and then it was moved back to Racine, Wisconsin. The Traction King designation remained with Case four-wheel-drive models through the 2870 until 1978. Both the Traction King and Agri King designation were dropped from product identification with the introduction of the 90 series in 1978.

The 1470 did not have the isolated platform and Case cab, instead it had a vendor-designed cab.

In 1970 Case began specializing in large tractors, the 1090 was the first attempt at this market approach with heavier differential, a hefty drawbar, as well as a "beefed-up" hitch and front axle.

The 1090 and 1170 Two-Wheel-Drive Tractors

Case began specializing in large tractors in 1970. The 1090 had the same 100 PTO horsepower as the 1070, but was designed to take the punishment of the rice levees in the Memphis, Tennessee area. Working against the grain of the levees was punishment to both man and machine. The suspended platform helped the man some, but a heavier differential, a hefty drawbar, a beefed-up hitch, and front axle were also needed. Power-assisted caliper disc brakes were necessary to survive in the mud and water of the levees. A dual-element dry air cleaner was needed for the engine to handle the dust. Case engineers designed all of these features into the 1090. After the tractors were working in the field and were debugged the word came back: "They were working just fine — but — how about 20 more horsepower?"

Following this repeated request, the 1170 was created. The additional 20+ horsepower was achieved by turbocharging (which was the easy part). Calculations showed that the final drive would be unable to absorb the increased horsepower without the addition of a planetary gear set to reduce the load on the differential and final drive. Outboard planetaries were added at the outer ends of the rear axles which created a fixed wheel tread design. The planetaries were

purchased from outside suppliers. These features, together with all the heavy-duty features of the 1090, made up the 1170 at 121.93 PTO horsepower.

Demonstrators and Black Knights

One of the marketing plans for the 70 series tractors was for dealers to have special tractors equipped with the horsepower common to their territory for demonstrating. The dealers were to actively demonstrate these tractors to their potential customers, especially to owner's of competitive makes. The object was to have the tractor properly serviced, weighted, and fitted with the correct tire equipment. In other words, the tractor needed to be sufficiently broken in and not just a new tractor. The idea was to leave the demonstrated tractor and implement with the potential customer for a few days (if the customer so desired). At the end of the season this demonstrator model could be sold to a local farmer.

To give the program visibility, Case offered specially painted and decaled tractors for the demonstrator program. The first demonstrator tractors had the hood painted black with a large gold decal covering the hood and side panels. A black decal with the gold lettering:

A 1070 Black Knight Demonstrator. The original idea was to have dealers actively demonstrate with tractors that were properly serviced, weighted, and fitted with the correct tire equipment. The black decaling gave a distinct appearance and made them highly visible. Today, these models are especially sought after by collectors — even the Black Knight toys carry a premium with collectors.

The demonstrator program was so successful that the black paint and decaling was expanded to all the areas normally painted with desert sunset colors like this 1470.

"Demonstrator" was above the side windows. The program became so popular and successful that after the first session the black paint was extended to replace all of the normally desert sunset area of paint. This paint made the tractor stand out even more.

A myth arose among the farming communities that these tractors were "souped up" and they became (and still are) collector's items bringing a premium price even in the toy tractor market. The truth is that a precise job of weighting, breaking in, and tire selection for the application made these tractors preform so well.

Intro 70's New Manufacturing and Test Facilities

The New Test Center

On June 26, 1964, one of the most modern research and test centers in the industry was dedicated in Racine. Located on the northeast corner of the Clausen plant property, this facility centralized many testing labs. Included were: the engine testing that was located in a tin shed facility and was constantly fighting a shutdown by the EPA; the stress lab was temporarily occupying a 1940 building located at the Main Works; the hydraulic lab was located in a similar building; the chemistry lab; the design center (styling department) which was homeless; and the electrical lab and cold room which was built with the new facility. Unfortunately the transmission testing had to move into the tin shed which had been redone.

The dirt test track, which had been built during the later years of Case-O-Matic testing, was paved with

August of 1966 saw Case begin construction of a 336,000-square-foot facility to manufacture transmissions in Mount Pleasant, Wisconsin. In May of 1968, Factory Magazine named the transmission plant to their "Top Ten Manufacturing Plant" list.

The new facility included a transmission test stand area that completely tested all phases of function, as well as noise, before shipment to the tractor plant in Racine.

concrete. Without this modern facility the development of the open chamber engine, the suspended platform, ROPS cab, and RPS transmission could not have been accomplished in the tight time frame demanded for Intro 70. All were paramount to the success of the 70 series.

The New Transmission Plant

In August 1966 Case began construction of 336,000-square-foot facility to manufacture transmissions, together with 50,000 square feet of office space. Starting in February 1967, 370 machine tools moved from the Clausen Works to the new transmission plant just west of Racine in the town of Mount Pleasant, Wisconsin. In May 1968, *Factory Magazine* named the transmission plant to their "Top Ten Manufacturing Plant" list. Initially they were producing 30 series transmissions.

New Assembly Line

In January 1968 one of the world's largest moulding complexes, the Taccone Unit, was put into operation in the foundry located at the Clausen Works. During early 1969 a complete modernization of the tractor assembly line began at the Clausen Works. It was simply a case of too much too soon. The tractors for the Intro 70 Show were produced just before the summer shut down and change over period. They were only partially built on

In June of 1964 Case opened a new test and research center and concrete test track facility on the shores of Lake Michigan, just northeast of the Clausen plant.

the assembly with a lot of help from the Engineering Experimental Department. When the dealers saw the tractors at the Intro they were awed and wanted immediate delivery. Morris Reid, Executive Vice President, promised the dealers they could have tractors for the annual buying frenzy at the end of the year (November and December). This was the time when farmers were faced with decisions of capital investment

Author Eldon Brumbaugh and his engineering management team were responsible for the 70 series tractor design and celebrated the first tractor off the assembly line.

In January of 1968 one of the world's largest moulding complexes, the Taccone Unit, was put into operation at the foundry in Racine. The Case management had a lot more gray hairs before this unit was running smoothly.

versus tax on profits, based on the type of year they had. At that point Murphy's Law took over. The Taccone Unit in the foundry started to get temperamental and couldn't produce enough good castings for the machine shop to keep the line running; the cab supplier couldn't produce cabs fast enough; and the Rock Island plant that was now producing hydraulic components, couldn't produce enough good brake valves to keep the line going. So in typical Case fashion, everybody rolled up their sleeves and "went to work to make it work." Tractors built with shortages were marshalled into holding areas where personnel from engineering, experimental build area, field service representatives, and test center personnel were called in to complete the tractors with shortages. The hydraulic lab at the Test Center tested and re-built brake valves, while others in the offices expedited parts. By November 1, 1969, everything was on schedule coming off the assembly line.

1970 — What a Year

The decade of the 1970s began with quite a bang. Construction equipment became 65% of Case production and agricultural products, which had been two-thirds of its production, dropped to 45%. Ketelsen and Tenneco announced that "Case would concentrate on large agricultural tractors." There were about 900 farm equipment producers. Seven companies, including Case, were full-line producers accounting for about two-thirds of the industry's total volume. Three of the seven manufacturers had larger volumes than Case.

The Rockford plant was closed in 1970 and Uni-Loader production was moved to Burlington, Iowa, and a few remaining implements were moved to the Bettendorf, Iowa plant. Bettendorf started to manufacture Case cabs.

1972 — "The Big Tractor Specialist"

In 1972 Case announced they were getting out of the combine business. The previous year nine companies sold only 28,000 units and the Case market share was less than 7%. The Case design was over 10 years old and new development could run into millions of dollars. With such a limited sales potential it would take years to recover the investment. Tractors, on the other hand, were a different story. Seven manufactures shared a wheel tractor market of 131,523 units, so Case announced they were going to concentrate on large agricultural tractors — "The Big Tractor Specialist" — which they were for the next 12 years.

Construction Equipment Production Climbs To 70%

With the rapid growth in the construction equipment business, Case could sell more loader backhoes than they could make. In order to gain capacity for loader backhoes Case acquired David Brown Tractors of Meltham, England, and discontinued production of the 470 and 570 tractors in August 1972. This acquisition allowed the Clausen Works to ship 2,000 more loader backhoe chassis to the Burlington and Vierzon plants because of the discontinuance of the 470/570 agricul-

Before the 1972 acquisition of David Brown tractors of Meltham, England, Case was essentially a domestic producer. The David Brown worldwide distribution system introduced Case into the world markets.

The David Brown assembly line in Meltham, West Yorkshire, England. The emblem on the front of the tractor was a white rose and a red rose, commemorating the War of the Roses between Yorkshire and Lancashire.

tural tractors. At the same time the 2,000-plus market for the small tractors was not lost since the gap was filled by the four basic David Brown models. This acquisition eventually provided a David Brown built loader backhoe transaxle and engine for Vierzon production and the European market. It also furnished engines for the Leeds, England crawler plant.

The David Brown acquisition left Case with the worldwide distribution system it needed. Up to this point Case was essentially a domestic producer, with some sales in South America and Australia. David Brown provided Case access to the fastest growing markets which were outside the United States, outlets especially needing the larger tractors.

David Brown Tractors

The David Brown Company was originally part of an old, respected English manufacturing company that had not previously worked with tractors until becoming involved with Harry Ferguson. David Brown built the first Ferguson-designed system. After several years of manufacturing the Ferguson system, David Brown eventually became a major tractor company manufacturing the David Brown tractor that Ferguson had designed. The David

The basic David Brown tractor line at the time of the acquisition included the 885 series, the 990 series, and the Model 1210.

Brown tractor was introduced in 1936. The tractor was mechanically successful but gained acceptance slowly. Ferguson lost interest in David Brown before sales improved and he went to work with Ford and later with Massey Harris in the 1940s and '50s. David Brown was acquired by Case through their parent company, Tenneco, in 1972.

Brown's (as they were called in Meltham) produced four sizes of tractors that fit quite well into Case's plans, for example:

Four basic models
- 885 with a 164.4-cubic-inch diesel engine at 43 PTO horsepower. Also, the 885 with a 146-cubic-inch gasoline engine at 41 PTO horsepower
- 990 with a 195-cubic-inch diesel engine at 53 PTO horsepower
- 995 with a 219-cubic-inch diesel engine at 58 PTO horsepower
- 1210 Synchromesh with a 219-cubic-inch diesel rated at 65 PTO horsepower and the 1212 Power shift was the same as the 1210

Two special models:
- 885 narrow orchard vineyard tractor
- 885 Special LCG (low center of gravity) utility tractor

The engine had opposed manifolds for efficiency like the large Case engines and had a Mexican hat combustion chamber like the 470/570. These engines got excellent fuel economy, with dual fuel filters and air filters like Case tractors. It also came with a lifetime porcelain muffler.

The hydraulics had a draft control single lever like Case. They called it Selectamatic.

The transmission had 12 speeds with synchromesh between ranges, a slow range for crop production and forage, a second range for heavy tillage, a third range for lighter tillage and hay and forage, and a fourth range for transport. They had a differential lock and power shift on the 1212, offering three ranges with four on-the-go power shifts. They also offered mechanical front wheel drive (MFD).

All of the models had hydrostatic power steering.

The David Brown 995 working in South Africa. This was one of the markets opened to Case after the acquisition.

In Pursuit of Large Tractors

Case introduced four new tractors over 120 horsepower (the 1175, 1270, 1370, and the 2470) in 1972.

The 1175

The 1175 was a like a beefed up 1170. The horsepower for the 1175 remained at 121.9 and it offered the same heavy-duty side rails, front axle, and outboard planetary as the 1170, but the hitch was increased to a category II with solid arms. The 1175 was in production from 1972 until 1978.

The 1270

The 1270 was truly a new tractor and required all new tooling for the transmission. The success of the cab since Intro 70 was phenomenal, around 75% of the tractors were ordered with cabs. With this in mind, Case engineers designed the transmission case with a closed top so there would be no need to remove the cab and platform for service, as there was full access from the sides and bottom of the case. Much of the hydraulic

tubing was eliminated because passages were cored into the transmission case eliminating heat and vibration. Serviceability was the key word in this design.

PFC Hydraulic System. The hydraulic system was a pressure-flow compensated system (PFC). The heart of the PFC system was the variable volume axial piston pump which could change the amount of flow as it operated. The system was constantly monitoring its own pressure, flow, and load — and adjusting its performance accordingly for maximum efficiency. The result was a faster response, a longer pump life, more efficient usage of horsepower, and greater fuel economy. The system was designed as the common sump and the transmission case was the common reservoir for the hydraulic system, transmission, brakes, power steering, PTO, and differential lock.

Case was a pioneer in the common sump concept in 1957 with the 700/800 tractors. The advantages included a single fluid for all systems and the elimination of leakage between housings. The disadvantage was that the gears tended to generate contamination and the piston pumps didn't tolerate it very well. If the filter was placed on the suction side of the pump it could cause cavitation. To solve the problem Case engineers installed a large low-pressure pump that digested some of this contamination in the system. This low-pressure pump took oil from the sump, pressurized it, and pushed it through a large filter to the piston pump. The result was clean oil to the piston pump, as well as to the various systems. Case was the first to use the "dirty oil pump" concept.

The 1175 replaced the 1170 in 1972. In addition to all the heavy-duty components offered on the 1170, the 1175 also had a category II hitch with solid lift arms.

The transmission case for the 1270 was designed with all of the component access openings on either the sides or the bottom of the case, so there was no need to remove the cab for service. Much of the heat-generating hydraulic tubing was eliminated by using cored passages in the transmission case.

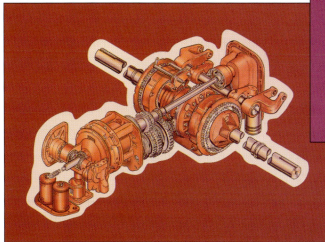

The 1270 was the first Case tractor that had inboard planetaries and allowed for adjustable rear wheel axles. This transmission also had an internal wet brake design.

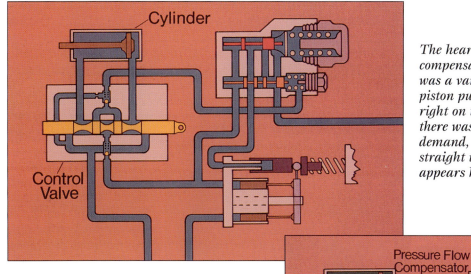

The heart of the pressure flow compensated hydraulic system was a variably volume axial piston pump (shown at the lower right on this drawing). When there was no hydraulic system demand, the pump plate was straight up and down as it appears here.

When there was hydraulic system demand, the pump plate would swash just enough to allow the pistons to pump only what the system needed. The result was faster response, longer pump life, and more efficient use of horsepower.

This Model 1270 tractor had the full western-style fenders but without cab or ROPS. The 1270 was introduced at 126.7 PTO horsepower.

The 1270, at 126.70 PTO horsepower, was the largest two-wheel-drive tractor Case had ever built. The transmission was designed with inboard planetaries to allow for adjustable rear wheels — a change from the fixed rear wheel tread like the 1170 and 1175 with the outboard planetaries. The new inboard planetary design also included a new wet brake design to overcome the problems of the 70 series which were dust and water sensitive. The new brakes were totally enclosed and designed as a continuous disc with a totally annular piston. This system was much smoother and didn't grab as much as the John Deere three-button system. A differential lock was also provided in this design.

The 1370

The 1370 had the same features as the 1270 except for the power. It used the Case 6-cylinder turbocharged 504-cubic-inch diesel engine at 142.51 PTO horsepower. The 1270 and 1370 were in production until the 1370 was increased to 150 horsepower in 1973 and the 1270 was increased to 135.39 in 1974. Both were replaced by the by the 90 series in 1978.

The 2470

The 2470 was the first four-wheel-drive tractor with all Case major components. For the first time Case was able to build a four-wheel-drive tractor from components on its own shelf. The transmission was essentially the 12-speed RPS transmission used in the 1270 and 1370. The 2470 was rated at 174.20 PTO horsepower at 2,200 rpm, 100 rpm faster than the 1370. The planetaries in the axles were from the 1270 and 1370 with new housings, the differentials were purchased from Eaton (Wisconsin Axle Div., Oshkosh, Wisconsin). The hydraulic system was the PFC system from the 1270 and 1370. A category II hitch and four remotes were also offered. Draft control was not available. The first couple of years the Factory Price List included two-wheel steering as standard and four-wheel drive as an $850 option. Lack of two-wheel-drive orders soon changed four-wheel steering to standard. The 2470 was the last full-size Case tractor introduced with the Desert Sunset paint scheme and was in production until it was replaced by the 4490 in 1979.

The major new feature of the 2470 was the POD cab which incorporated the cab and platform as an integral unit. Even the instrument panel, fire wall, operator console, steering wheel, seat, and operating levers were part of the POD cab. This type of construction made sealing out noise and dirt a lot more successful because the sealing and testing could all

About 75% of the 1270's were sold with a Case cab. The horsepower was increased to 135.39 in 1974.

The 1370 was introduced with a 504-cubic-inch Case turbocharged engine at 142.51 PTO horsepower. In 1973 the horsepower was increased to 150.

be done before the cab was set on the tractor. The official sound level tests reflected this theory with 82-85 dB(A) results — one of the quietest cabs in the industry at that time.

Case had another first with the 2470 — a self-cleaning air induction system. This air cleaner was under the hood to eliminate the stacks from obscuring the operator's view. The air was taken in at the front of the tractor and passed through an aspirated strata tube (a series of tubes and fins that broke up the dirt particles as the air passed through it). The larger particles were aspirated off by the exhaust stack and blown away, the fine particles were trapped in the two-stage air cleaner filter. Daily, the operator could raise the hood and squeeze a little rubber boot on the air cleaner can and fine particles dropped out on the ground. The air cleaner didn't need service unless the warning light came on. This design was conceived from test results that showed that

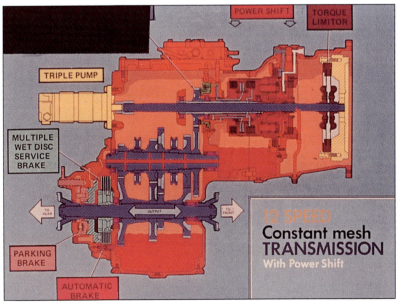

The 2470 was the first Case four-wheel-drive tractor with a Case designed-and-built transmission. The components were similar to those of the 1270 and 1370, a 12-speed RPS, PFC hydraulics, 1270/1370 planetary gears in new outboard housings with purchased differentials.

This Case model maker put the finishing touches on a scale model of the 2470. The 2470 was the last model introduced with the desert sunset/flambeau red paint scheme.

The self-cleaning air induction system was located under the hood and air was taken in at the front of the tractor. The air then passed through the aspirated strata tubes that broke up the dirt particles. The larger particles were aspirated off by the exhaust system and blown away. The smaller particles were trapped by the two-stage air cleaner.

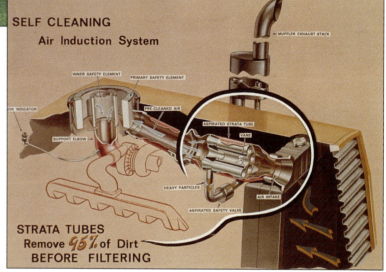

Th Model 2470 was the first four-wheel-drive tractor to have the new POD cab design which incorporated the cab and platform as an integral unit. Instrument panel, fire wall, operator console, steering wheel, seat, and operating levers were all part of the POD.

This 2470 was pulling a field cultivator in the Western Great Plains. Case introduced the Assured Availability Program in 1972 that assured the customer a free loaner should his tractor have a mechanical failure during his peak productive period.

more damage was done to air filters due to over-cleaning, than to those cleaned only when necessary.

A Busy Year

In addition to the new models introduced in 1972, Case also introduced a new warranty with assured availability and started selling tractors in the United Kingdom after a 20-year absence.

- The Assured Availability Program assured the customer a free loaner tractor should his tractor have a mechanical failure during his peak productive period — and if the Case dealer could not repair the owner's tractor in 24 hours, during the warranty period. The warranty was a no-fault one-year warranty.
- The 970 tractor was introduced in England. Case machinery had not been sold in the United Kingdom for about 20 years.

The Power White\Power Red Era

The 70 Series (1974-1978)

Case agricultural equipment sales increased 46% in 1973, with earnings almost tripling those of 1972. In the spring of 1974, farmers were facing an acute machinery shortage. The tractor plant in Racine was working at capacity. The production of the 870 was discontinued in 1974, as had the 770 in 1973, to allow for capacity increases in the larger, faster-growing models. The agricultural outlook was good since farm income more than doubled between 1970 and 1973. U.S. agricultural exports skyrocketed as the Soviet Union started buying grain in the world market. The worldwide demand for food imports in developing nations continued with population growth and the desire for more protein. Case had been stepping up its activity in worldwide markets since 1972.

To keep the momentum going in the worldwide markets, Case decided a common "look" or identity was needed. They decided to marry the Case and David Brown color schemes keeping the Case power red and the David Brown white — creating the Power White/Power Red era. It was important in this era of rapid growth to have a product in the marketplace that had a common look. David Brown also adopted the hallmark black hood stripe. On tractors produced for the North American market only, the Case logo appeared. For the worldwide markets, however, the David Brown logo appeared at the front of the stripe and the Case logo at the rear of the stripe. In 1974 Case and David Brown sold three times as many tractors as Case alone sold in 1967.

The 2670 Introduction (1974)

When Case first introduced the four-wheel-drive tractor in 1964, the concept was not an immediate success. In fact, the idea of four wheelers didn't catch on until 1972 when it became the fastest growing segment of the North American market. The 2670 had all of the features of the 2470. In addition, the 2670 had a complete new hydrostatic steering system.

This new steering system was hydrostatic on both the rear and the front. It was in contrast to the hydraulic assist rear steering used on the 1200, 1470, and 2470. Hydrostatic rear steer was equipped with a control valve and the operator could use the steering mode selector switch on the console to select any of the four different modes. Once the mode was selected, the operator could move a rocker switch right or left to turn the rear wheels, the wheel would stop turning once the

In 1974 Case decided to marry the David Brown white and the Case red to create a common "look" in the marketplace. The hallmark black Case stripe was also added to the Browns.

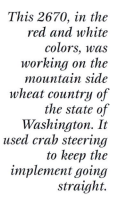

This 2670, in the red and white colors, was working on the mountain side wheat country of the state of Washington. It used crab steering to keep the implement going straight.

rocker switch was released. An electronic rear wheel position indicator was mounted on the dash indicating the position of the rear wheels. Later model 2670's were available with electronic draft sensing and variable flow control to the remotes for operating hydraulic motors. The 2470 and 2670 both had adjustable wheel spacing.

The power for the 2670 was the Case 6-cylinder 504-cubic-inch turbocharged and intercooled engine rated at 219.44 PTO horsepower. The 2670 was the first Case tractor to have both a turbocharger and an intercooler. The intercooler cooled the intake air. Cooler air, which is more dense, can use more fuel to increase power because there is enough air for combustion. Case ended 1974 with sales surpassing the $1 billion mark for the first time.

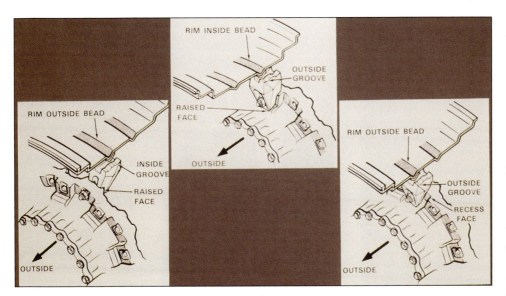

MEET THE FUEL MISER...
economy performance champ / 80 pto hp

1410 Synchromesh (STD.)
1410 Range Power Shift (OPT.)

The 1410 and the 1412 were designed to fill the niche left by the discontinuance of the 770 and 870.

1410 and 1412 Announced (1975)

The 1410 synchromesh and the 1412 hydra-shift were upgraded to 70 horsepower from the 65 horsepower 1210 and 1212. These models were designed to fill the niche left by the discontinuance of the 770 and 870. International sales had increased over 500% in the last five years and now accounted for 29% of Case's total business.

The 1570 and Spirit of '76 (1976)

As the United States was celebrating the bicentennial year, Case was introducing the 1570 and the Spirit of '76. The 1570 had all the same features as the 1370, plus a larger turbocharged power plant of 180 PTO horsepower. The rear axle diameter was increased to 3 7/8 inches versus 3 1/2 inches on the 1370. For 1976 only, the 1570 was offered with Stars and Stripes decals — as the Spirit of '76.

The wheel tread spacing adjustment on four-wheel-drive tractors was accomplished by moving the wheel lugs and rim in and out on the wheel.

The 1570 was introduced in 1976 at 180 PTO horsepower. The Spirit of '76 model with the stars and stripes could be ordered from the factory for a limited time to celebrate the bicentennial year.

The 2870

The 2870, the grandaddy of the 70 series, was rated at 300 horsepower and was powered by a 674-cubic-inch Scania 6-cylinder engine. The 2870 took three years to develop. Even though the transmission and axles were similar to the 2670, they had to be redesigned for the greater capacity required to meet the increased horsepower of the 2870. The larger capacity differentials were provided by Eaton's Wisconsin Axle Division. The pod cab structure also had to be modified to meet the ROPS standards for that size tractor. The engine design also had to be changed to meet Case standards, for example, keystone piston rings and valve rotators were not available on Scania engines but Case required these changes for their application.

The 90 Series (1978-1983)

By 1978 the 70 series had run over nine years and had built an enviable record, but it was time for a change. In 1976 the industry tractor market was down 5%. Case's market wasn't down, but it was flat and the time was right for some consolidation and stimulation — the 90 series. In the two-wheel-drive tractors four new models replaced the six previous models.

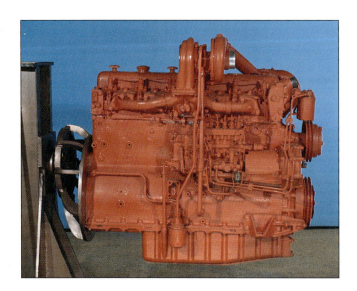

A Scania 674-cubic-inch engine was used in the 2870. The engine was purchased from Waukesha Motors who was the agent for Scania.

The 2870 was rated at 300 horsepower and the 2670 axles and transmission were redesigned to handle the increased horsepower, larger capacity differentials were also used.

This Model 2090 tractor was chopping cotton stalks in Litchfield Park, Arizona. The 2090 replaced the 1070 and was rated at 108 PTO horsepower.

128 pto HP.   **est.**

The 2290 replaced the 1175 at 129 PTO horsepower. Both the 2090 and 2290 had a redesigned transmission with inboard planetaries and adjustable rear axles.

The 2090 and 2290 tractors essentially replaced the 1070 and the 1175. The 2090 was powered by the 6-cylinder 504-cubic-inch naturally aspirated engine and rated at 108 PTO horsepower. The 2290 was powered by the 504-cubic-inch turbocharged 6-cylinder engine and rated at 129 PTO horsepower. The rest of the features were the same for both models

Transmission. The transmission was new in the 90 series, it had inboard planetaries and the power-shift valve was located on the side of the case similar to the 1270. The transmission could be serviced from the sides except for the hydraulic pump drive which was serviced from the top and required the cab to be removed. A differential lock and park lock were standard. Every once in a while a new model seems to have its millstone. The park lock was the millstone for the 2090 and 2290, as it had to go through several rework programs and was eventually redesigned. The powershift was the same one used in the 1070. The 8-speed transmission was also the same as the 1070, except for the transmission case and the hydraulic system. The brakes were located in the planetary area of the transmission, similar to the 1270, and therefore overcame the problems of dust and water that plagued the 1170.

Hydraulic System. A closed-center pressure-flow compensated hydraulic system was used with flow control to the remotes for operating hydraulic motors. The design of the hydraulic pumps was unique since

The PFC hydraulic system dirty oil pump and the piston pump were a unique design because they were piggyback, rather than individual components like the 1270.

The 90 series, with a new grille and hood, had a distinct new look from the 70 series.

the dirty oil gear pump was piggyback to the piston pump. Limited space, rather than the individual design of the 1270, dictated the piggyback.

Mechanical front wheel drive (MFD) was offered for those that wanted a four-wheel-drive option. The MFD axle and drop box were manufactured by Carraro in Padua, Italy.

"Ease of Maintenance" Enhancements

The Silent Guardian Cab

The silent guardian cab, as it was called, had a major revision. The air conditioning evaporator and air handling fans for the cab were moved to the rear of the cab and the fans were put in the same enclosure as the air filter. The purpose of this design change was twofold; first, the original mounting of the fans at the front of the cab required the removal of the cab roof to service the fans and evaporator. This task was time consuming, especially resealing the roof. Second,

as the air passed across the plenum of the cab, dust accumulated in the plenum and the cab roof again had to be removed to clean the plenum and sealing was again a problem. The new design allowed the self-contained unit to be lifted from the rear of the cab for servicing or cleaning. When cleaning the new unit with a pressure washer there was no worry of getting the cab interior dirty. The instrument cluster was a modular design with a circuit board as first used in the 2670.

Swing-Out Batteries

The battery tray was designed to swing out from under the cab for ease of service.

The new hood was tapered to provide the operator with greater visibility to the rows and the ground ahead. The instrument cluster was a modular type that could be simply unplugged and lifted out for service.

the 1370. The horsepower of the 2590 was 180 — the same as the 1570. The 2390 and the 2590 had essentially the same features as the 1370 and 1570 except even more serviceability was added. The 1370 and 1570 had been known for their serviceability with all components accessible from the sides or rear of the tractor, but with the 90's even more was added with the silent guardian cab, swing-out batteries, tilt hood, and modular instrument cluster that could be unplugged and quickly replaced.

The styling changes on the 90 series were all geared to easier maintenance, like the tilting hood and the engine side panel just below the hood that could easily be lifted off.

New Styling and Hood

The 90 series had a distinct new look from the 70 series with a new grille and hood. The new hood tilted forward assisted by two cylinders, there were also two side panels that could be easily lifted off to give unequalled access for regular maintenance. Not only had Case been working to extend maintenance intervals, but now made maintenance easier. The goal was to keep the tractor in the field rather than tied up for maintenance.

1978

The 2390 and 2590 replaced the 1370 and 1570, respectively. The horsepower of the 2390 was 160 compared to 142 horsepower on

The 2590 tractor replaced the 1570 with the same horsepower.

The 2390 replaced the 1370 with an increase in horsepower from 142 to 160.

The 1980s and '90s – New Technology/New Company

At the start of the 1980s Case had essentially a new line of tractors in place.

During the 1970s many people believed the United States should increase agricultural production to meet the growing world demand for food and the American farmers enthusiastically expanded to meet these market demands. As American agriculture entered into the 1980s everyone expected the prosperity to last. Never have so many experts been so wrong! Inflation was increasing at 15% a year when the Carter Administration had the Federal Reserve apply the brakes which sent interest rates spiraling from 15.5 to 21.5% in six weeks. On top of that,

President Carter put a ban on grain sales to the Soviet Union. By 1982 other countries had stepped in to supply grain to the Soviets and the dollar had gotten so strong the developing countries could not afford American food purchases. U.S. exports of grain tumbled from a high of 71,000 metric tons in 1979 to 54,000 metric tons by 1983. When world demand for agricultural exports dropped, commodity prices plummeted. As surpluses grew and interest rates skyrocketed, farmers were having a hard time making ends meet, much less buying new tractors. In 1981 alone, the

The 90 series general purpose tractors were built in Meltham, England, at the former David Brown plant.

sales of over-100-horsepower two-wheel-drive tractors dropped 14%. Farm equipment dealers weren't faring too well either. Many were selling equipment practically for cost, while hundreds were going out of business. The farm equipment manufactures were also suffering: White went out of business; Deutz bought Allis-Chalmers; Massey-Ferguson and International Harvester were in financial trouble; just to name a few. The industry was in disarray with business and financial failures the likes of which had not been seen since the Great Depression.

Cautious . . . Growing . . . Innovative

At the start of the 1980s Case essentially had a new tractor line in place, so with the depressed market the first half of the decade was spent filling a few gaps in the line and adding innovative features to the rest of the line. There were five new David-Brown-built models, a new line of constant traction models, and a new large four-wheel-drive model from the Racine plant. In addition to the new models, solid state electronics and microelectronics technology added features to steering and transmissions. The remainder of the decade was spent integrating the products of International Harvester and Case (as described later in this chapter).

The 1190, 1290, 1390, 1490, and 1690 were introduced in 1983 to complete the 90 series line. The major changes were in improved serviceability with the tilt hood and snap-off side panels. A new cab was also designed that could be tailored to serve world markets. The Brown's now looked like the 90 series. The 1690 was a replacement for the 970 with increased horsepower at 90 PTO horsepower.

The Constant Traction — 3294, 3394, and 3594

Ever since Case introduced the 1200 in 1964 some markets had been asking for a smaller four-wheel-drive tractor. Lowering the cost of the smaller four-wheel-drive tractor wasn't feasible since a majority of the cost was in the driveline. In this instance smaller was not necessarily cheaper. Mechanical front-wheel drives (MFD) for general purpose tractors were not a very popular alternative in the early days, until farmers began to realize what a four wheeler could do. As a result, mechanical front-wheel drive was introduced as an option on the 2090 and 2290 and it became very popular. As the economy went into a nose dive, many farmers felt they couldn't afford a large four wheeler, but still had the need for four-wheel drive. The 3294, 3394, and 3594 were designed with full-time constant traction MFD (there was no shifting the MFD out) to further reduce the cost and because the farmer felt the constant traction four-wheel drive fit his needs. The 3294, 3394 and 3594 nicely filled the four-wheel-drive gap without a large tooling investment on Case's part because the axles were purchased either from Carro (an Italian Manufacturer) or ZF (a West German Manufacturer).

The 4994 — The Big Tractor That Didn't!

The 4994 was introduced in 1984 with a Scania turbocharged V8 engine rated at 400-gross-engine horsepower. It also had a 12-speed-forward, 3-speed-reverse Twin Disc power shift transmission, along with ZF four-wheel-steer planetary axles. This tractor was a proverbial locomotive. The author had a chance to observe the 4994 in Phoenix, Arizona, while videotaping an introductory program. The 4994 in the video was pulling a tool bar chisel with 48-inch chisels. At the

The constant traction Model 3294 was designed with full-time mechanical front-wheel drive (there was no shifting the MFD out) to fill the demand for a smaller four-wheel-drive tractor.

The constant traction 3294 was the smallest four-wheel-drive Case tractor produced in the mid-1980s.

The 4994 was the largest four-wheel drive produced in the mid-1980s. It was powered by a Scania turbocharged V-8 engine at 400 gross engine horsepower.

The 4994 had a 12-speed full power shift twin-disc transmission and ZF four-wheel steering planetary axles.

The 4994 was introduced in 1984 and slightly over 200 tractors were produced.

The 94 series family of black and white tractors were produced from 1983 until 1985. These were the last tractors produced under only the Case name.

end of the scene the operator, just out of curiosity, gradually buried the tool bar to the ground —the resulting black smoke looked like a locomotive pulling 200 freight cars up a mountainside but the 4994 never quit. But as some models do, it had its millstones — namely the transmission and the axles. The transmission did not have a skip-shift feature which meant the operator always had to start out in low gear after pushing in the inching pedal (the pedal always downshifted to neutral) and power shift one gear at a time to the desired operating gear. This method seemed to take forever when shifting into transport gear. The axles also had problems when they were operated continuously under maximum load conditions. Case ended up reworking all of the 4994 axles. By the time the axle problem was identified and corrected, Case had acquired Steiger Tractor and had replaced some of the Case four-wheelers with the Steiger models, so only slightly over 200 tractors were built.

The Black and White Era — A Short One! 1983-1985

In 1983 government regulations went into effect that stated specifically how paint containing lead chromate must be handled in a manufacturing environment. Case had to make a decision about their paint color since all bright red and bright yellow paint contained lead chromate. Keeping those colors required a major capital investment in plant remodeling and new painting equipment, such as robots. Already three years into a disastrous market and with no end in sight, Case opted to change the power red paint to black rather than invest money in a project that would have a very long payback — if ever. So in 1983 all the models were painted black and white with new red and black decals. This color scheme lasted until 1985 when the new colors changed to Harvester red and Case black chassis and decals with silver accents. These tractors were rei-

dentified as the 94 series. At the same time the 1690 was dropped and brought back as the 1594 at 5 horsepower less (85 horsepower). Also, a Case designed-and-built 24-speed power shift transmission was added to the Racine-built tractors.

New Technology

During the 1980s Case used solid state electronics and microelectronics to add features, solve problems, and improve serviceability for their products because they were easily serviced, reliable, and user-friendly. Inaccurate centering of the rear wheels sometimes occurred with the four-wheel mechanical steering control which was soon replaced with improved electronic technology. The follow-up or feedback mechanism between the rear steering control valve and the rear axle had been a mechanical link or cable on the four-wheel drives since the 1200. When the operator returned the rear steering control to straight ahead, the cable would cancel out when the rear wheels were centered. The problem occurred when the centering was

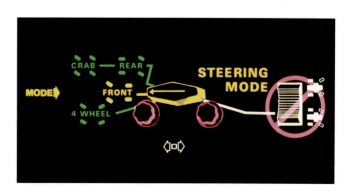

In 1983 the rear steering mode selector on the four-wheel-steer tractors was changed from a mechanical lever to an electronic selector switch and a microprocessor.

The 94 series four-wheel-drive tractors offered the latest in electronic technology with electronic steering and transmission controls, the Intelligence Center, and a true ground speed radar sensor.

wheels. This sensor also made possible the design of the electronic rear steering with the selector switch as used on the 94 series four-wheel drives — it gave the rear steering a more responsive feel, it was easier to operate, and it was more accurate.

Electronic Transmission Controls

In 1983 the 94 series tractors were introduced. The power shift control for the RPS 34 transmission was changed from mechanical links to a solenoid control. The shift lever operated a speed selector switch which indirectly determined which clutches would be engaged or disengaged through the solenoid. Each clutch on the power shift was engaged or disengaged by an individual solenoid. The inching pedal operated a clutch cut off microswitch. The clutch retards were now also controlled by microswitches, no longer needing a mechanic to adjust them. The electronics also simplified the design of the 24-speed controls, because fewer links were required. Electronics also simplified service and diagnosis, but more significantly it made the controls work faster and easier for the operator.

off a degree or two because of the hysteresis or lag in the cable. As technology improved an electronic sensor was mounted on the steering knuckle cap on the rear axles. This device sensed the exact position of the rear wheels and therefore could accurately center the rear

The electronic steering sensor was mounted on the steering knuckle cap on the rear axle and sensed the exact position of the rear wheels.

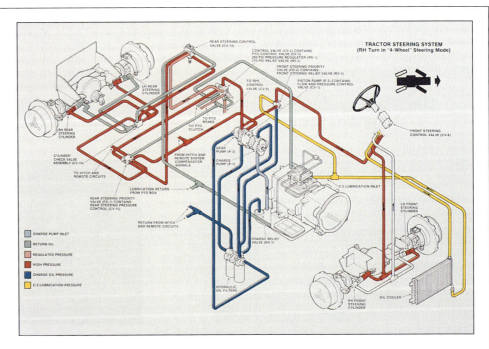

With the introduction of the electronic sensing steering system on the 94 series four-wheel drives, there were no more mechanical cables which eliminated any hysteresis problems caused by mechanical parts.

The electronic steering mode selector controlled the steering modes illustrated below.

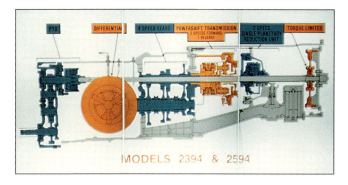

Cut-away drawing of the 24-speed dual-range power shift transmission introduced on the large Racine-built 94 series general purpose tractors.

The 24-Speed Power Shift Transmission

A 24-speed power shift transmission option was announced for the 2094 through the 4894 tractors during their 1983 and 1984 introductions. The 24 speeds were achieved by adding a second planetary gear set with two additional clutches in front of the existing planetary gear set and four clutches. This combination of two planetary gear sets and six clutches provided 24-speeds forward and 3-reverse speeds. Despite the difficult farm economies, these 94 series tractors sold very well.

Solid State Electronics and the Intelligence Center

The digital instrument cluster or "Intelligence Center" was first introduced on the 94 series tractors. It was very unique and unlike any cluster on the market at the time. Take these service monitors, for example:

- Air cleaner restriction allowed the operator time to clean the air cleaner the next morning without suddenly loosing power in the field.
  - The water level was monitored with a probe in the radiator top tank which indicated when the water level started to drop.

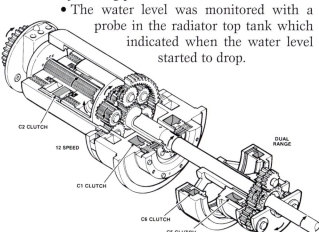

The power shift portion of the 24-speed transmission showing the original 12-speed RPS (on the left) and the second planetary with two (C5 and 6) clutches that were added (on the right) to increase the power shift to 24 speeds.

The four-wheel-steering modes: front wheel (upper left), rear wheel (upper right), crab (lower left), and four-wheel coordinated (lower right).

The digital instrument cluster (Intelligence Center) was first introduced on the 94 series tractors and was unlike any cluster on the market at that time.

- A normal light let the operator know that things were all right at a glance.
- A transmission oil monitor checked both temperature and pressure in the transmission.
- A transmission filter monitor had a light that let the operator know when it was time to change the filter and transmission fluid before starting the next days operation.
- An exhaust temperature bar graph helped the operator regulate load and speed.
- A fuel level bar graph was another monitor on the Intelligence Center (some makes of tractors didn't even have a fuel gauge at that time).

In addition to the service monitor, the Intelligence Center had a minicomputer allowing the operator to communicate with the tractor. For example, the Intelligence Center reported how many acres were covered in an hour, a day, or a week. The operator could monitor wheel slip, PTO speed, and ground speed. Five program buttons were available to the operator. By programming in the tire size and the implement width, the operator could monitor the amount of acreage that was covered. The Intelligence Center would constantly compute the area being covered and any time the operator pushed the "Area Covered" button, the amount would be displayed on the screen.

Wheel slip could also be monitored through the Intelligence Center. During the late 1970s an Oklahoma State University study revealed that farming under continuous drawbar load at speeds above 5 miles per hour would produce a transmission life of approximately 10,000 hours, while farming with heavier loads that required operating at only 4 miles per hour would produce a life of just 6,500 hours. The study also recommended that a wheel slip of 10 to 15% be maintained. The Intelligence Center calculated wheel slip by measuring the actual ground covered with a true ground speed sensor (a radar-type device) and comparing it against a

The True Ground Speed Sensor (a radar-type device) was mounted to the tractor frame and pointed to the ground comparing tractor movement against a magnetic sensor which was measuring transmission gear speed.

magnetic sensor which was measuring transmission gear speed. When the operator pushed the wheel slip button on the cluster, the wheel slip would read out on the screen. The operator could also constantly monitor the true ground speed.

The Rapid Farming Concept

Case called farming at 5 miles per hour "Rapid Farming" and widely promoted this concept because their tests concurred with the university study. From 1961 to 1978, average tractor horsepower had increased from 70 to 180 horsepower but the weight of the tractor had dropped in half. As a result, farmers were pulling larger implements at slow speeds and tying the rear wheels to the ground with added weight. If they didn't over weight the tractor they were encountering 20 to 30% wheel slip and were going nowhere. Case promoted pulling a smaller implement and farming at 5 miles per hour and maintaining 10 to 15% wheel slip because Rapid Farming would promote longer transmission life, better tire wear, less fuel consumption, less soil compaction, and more productivity (several acres per day with a narrower implement). The Intelligence Center gave farmers a means to monitor this performance.

Case promoted the Rapid Farming System for longer transmission life, better tire wear, less fuel consumption, less soil compaction, and more productivity.

Bill Simpson, a well-known Case Marketing Manger and creator of the Rapid Farming concept, campaigned all over the world against over-weighting of tractors. He promoted farming at 5 miles per hour and maintaining 10 to 15% wheel slip for longer transmission life.

The Consolidated Diesel Connection

The saga of the start of the joint venture between the Cummins Engine Company and J.I. Case reads like the script for a foreign intrigue film. The partnership, which was formed in 1979, was called the Consolidated Diesel Corporation (CDC). In 1977 the machine tools that had been producing the two families of Case diesel engines since 1953 were starting to show severe wear. On top of that, these engines had been stretched to their limit. The engines had given their all and had no more to give. To get higher horsepower engines for the 2870 and 4994 tractors, the Agricultural Division had to buy Scania engines. Retooling was out of the question because Case did not have the volume of engines to make it profitable. Case also did not have the testing equipment (dynamometers) or the design and test personnel to develop a family of engines from scratch, in a short period of time. For example, in their study of other engine manufacturers Case found that Cummins, Caterpillar, and General Motors had around 80 to 85 dynamometers for development work at each of their research centers. They even talked to Hercules and Mercedes-Benz about engines, but none met the requirements for the horsepower ranges or the rpm. They also could not meet the requirements for standardization of parts between the 4- and 6-cylinder engines.

It wasn't until Tom Guendel, CEO of Case, met Henry Schacht, CEO of Cummins, at a trade show that things began to happen. They discussed engines and a possible joint venture. Now the intrigue begins — fol-

The family I CDC engines: (from left) the 6-cylinder turbocharged, the 4-cylinder turbocharged, and the 4-cylinder naturally aspirated engine.

The intercooler is the housing at the top of this CDC family I turbocharged and intercooled 6-cylinder engine. It obscures the view of valve covers and part of the turbocharger.

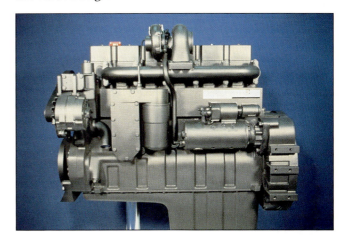

Here is the CDC family II 6-cylinder turbocharged engine. The family II engines are the largest horsepower CDC engines.

The Consolidated Diesel Corporation (a joint venture between Cummins Engine Company and J.I. Case) built this plant in Rocky Mount, North Carolina, to build the CDC engines. The first engine was built in 1983, just four years after the joint venture was announced.

lowing their initial discussion. Guendel wanted the plan done very quietly with only three or four Case people involved. The reason for the secrecy probably was to avoid "analysis paralysis," thereby slowing the entire process if the whole company had gotten involved studying the project. Case put together their needs starting with an engine of the horsepower of the 580 and future 580's (67 SAE net horsepower) and then make it a 3-cylinder engine. Next on the agenda was the need to develop a 6 cylinder, then turbocharge it, then intercool it, and then calculate the horsepower. A larger 6-cylinder engine was also required. Case met with Cummins in Indianapolis, Indiana, at an airport motel so other Cummins people wouldn't know about the project. As the project progressed, meetings were held anyplace other than Racine, Wisconsin, or Columbus, Indiana.

Cummins agreed with the family I, 3-, 4-, and 6-cylinder engines, but proposed a V8 instead of the big 6. Case responded that the V8 wasn't big enough, so Cummins did a market study on a big 6 and found it would also fit in their market. Both Case and Cummins agreed to a family II, 6-cylinder naturally aspirated, a 6-cylinder turbocharged, and a 6-cylinder turbocharged intercooled engine. So lines were started on paper and to help in the design Case furnished 188 and 207 Case engines, as well as engines from Deere, Ford, and David Brown. It took several pickup truck trips to get all the engines to Cummins because Case didn't want to risk a common carrier. One of the four insiders drove the pickup to a designated drop-off point outside Columbus, Indiana, and delivered the engines. Cummins then picked the engines up. Because this was a multipurpose engine to be sold to other users by Cummins, as well as to be used by Case, the traditional heavy-ribbed self-supporting block was ruled out. Case would have to support the engine with chassis frames which made good sense because frame steel was cheaper than block iron. They also decided that the

joint venture plant would only make cylinder heads, connecting rods, and cylinder blocks. They would buy other components — some from other Cummins plants and still others from specialty manufactures. It was agreed that the assembly line would be high tech and highly automated. As a result, engine testing was computerized and $350 million was spent on a new plant in Rocky Mount, North Carolina. The first engine was used in the 580 in 1983, just four years after the joint venture was announced.

The rest of the Case world did get involved with Cummins after 1979 and the rest is history. The CDC engine turned out to be one of the most efficient engines with the lowest emissions in the industry. A second plant was added to produce CDC engines by renovating the existing Cummins plant at Walesboro, Indiana, because these engines became so popular in the automotive industry, especially in pickup trucks like Dodge. The engines were also used in Japanese excavators. The first Case agricultural tractors to use the CDC engine were the 1896 and 2096. The Magnum and Maxxum, as well as the former Steiger models, also were produced with the CDC engine.

Case IH

In early 1985 Case, through its parent company, Tenneco, acquired selected assets of the International Harvester Company agricultural equipment operations. This acquisition made Case the second largest farm equipment manufacturer in the industry. By consolidating International Harvester operations with Case agricultural operations, Case again became a full-line agricultural equipment producer. Case did not purchase the Farmall plant in Rock Island, Illinois, or the Memphis plant from IH. This acquisition cut tractor manufacturing capacity in the United States by 35% and increased market share for Case to about 35%, second only to Deere & Company's 40%. The acquisition had

CURRENT PRODUCT LINE

ENGINE HORSEPOWER

- 300
- 250
- 200
- 150
- 100
- 50

60 SERIES — 6788, 6588, 6388

"D" FAMILY — 1255, 1455

"C" FAMILY — 1056, 956, 856, 844

"B" FAMILY — 743, 745, 833, 733, 633

"A" FAMILY — 433, 533

200 SERIES — 234, 244, 254, 284, 274

30 SERIES — 3088, 3288, 3688, 3488H

50 SERIES — 5088, 5288, 5488

WORLDWIDE — 484, 584, 684, 784, H84, 884

This diagram illustrates the IH family of tractors at the time of the acquisition. Case and IH brought together more than 50 tractor models, along with a painful decision as to which models should be cut to get down to 37 models.

its painful decisions because it brought together more than 50 tractor models which had to be cut. In the 90- to 185-horsepower models they dropped the IH 50 series and 2 + 2 for three reasons: one, because they did not buy the Farmall plant and only purchased selected tooling; two, Harvester had new ideas on the drawing board and were going to replace the IH 50 series anyway; and three, the Case 94 series was only two years old and the 50 series was four years old.

In the smaller series there was no question about keeping the IH A, B, C, and D series made in Neuss, Germany, because they were very popular tractors in

The A and B family of tractors were manufactured at the Case International plant in Neuss, Germany, and served primarily the European market.

This IH A family Model 635 had a restyled hood and grille as well as Case International decals. The 635 was the smallest A family tractor at under 50 horsepower.

This restyled IH B family 745 was the smallest B family model in the approximately 70-horse-power class.

The C and D family were also produced in Neuss for the European market.

The Model 1455 was the largest of the D family at just under 150 horsepower.

The Model 1056 was the largest of the C family at over 100 horsepower.

The IH 84 Hydro series, produced in Doncaster, England, was one of the models dropped from the product mix.

This is IH 584 before the hood and grille were changed to the Case International styling. It was reidentified as the 585. The rest of the 84 series were also changed to the 85 series. The 85 series were produced at the Case International plant in Doncaster, England, for the United Kingdom, and the rest of the world markets including North America. The IH symbol was not used very much outside of North America, the rest of the world knew them as International.

Europe. There was also no question about keeping the IH 85 series made in Doncaster, England, and exported to North America because it was mechanically a more state-of-the-art tractor than the David Brown produced tractors where the tooling dated back to the 1940s, '50s, and '60s.

In 1985 the Case IH tractor line consisted of the IH-designed tractors built in Neuss, Germany; St. Dizier, France; and Doncaster, England; and the Case-designed 94 series tractors built at the Racine plant. All of the Case IH tractors were painted Harvester red with Case black chassis and decals with silver stripes. The parts that were painted Harvester red for the Racine plant were the cab, which was made and painted at the Case IH plant in East Moline, Illinois, and the fiberglass hood which was colored by the supplier. The production of Case-designed 94 series was discontinued in 1987 just prior to the introduction of the Magnum series. No four-wheel-drive tractors were produced from 1987 until the acquisition of the Steiger Tractor Company of Fargo, North Dakota

The Case IH Magnum tractor series was the result of combining the set designs of both companies, Case and IH.

The Magnum – The Best of Both Worlds

Harvester engineers had been working on a power shift transmission based on their mechanical version and were pretty far along before the acquisition. This power shift transmission would be used on the Magnum, the newest tractor added to the line and a collaboration between Case and Harvester. Case built

and tested a new frame for the new CDC engine, so it was a matter of adapting the Case engine and frame to the Harvester transmission. The cab was a Harvester design but Case management wasn't happy with the shape — it was too square. As a result, Ralph Lanphere and the Case Styling Department designed a rounded windshield. Lanphere rounded the square corner posts of the original design. He also drafted the interior design, the fenders, the hood, grille decals, paint scheme, and also married the Case and the IH logos.

The Harvester red paint could now be used because Case shut down the Racine tractor plant for three months to completely remodel it into one of the most

First Generation Magnum Series (1988-93)					Second Generation Magnum Series (1993-94)				
Model	PTO Hp	No. Cylinders*	Displacement (cubic inch)†	Speeds	Model	PTO Hp	No. Cylinders*	Displacement (cubic inch)†	Speeds
7110	130	CDC 6	505 TC	18F/2R	7210	130	CDC 6	505 TC	18F/4R
7120	150	CDC 6	505 TC	18F/2R	7220	155	CDC 6	505 TC	18F/4R
7130	170	CDC 6	505 TC	18F/2R	7230	170	CDC 6	505 TC	18F/4R
7140	195	CDC 6	505 TCI	18F/2R	7240	195	CDC 6	505 TCI	18F/4R
					7250	215	CDC 6	505 TCI	18F/4R

* CDC = Consolidated Diesel Corporation.
† TC = turbocharged.
   TCI = turbocharged and intercooled.

* CDC = Consolidated Diesel Corporation.
† TC = turbocharged.
   TCI = turbocharged and intercooled.

The first generation of Magnum tractors (from 1988 to 1993): the 7110, 7120, 7130, 7140, and 7150.

state-of-the-art factories in the country, which included a robotic paint system. The steering mechanism was a modification of a Case design. Both Case and Harvester used the same Vickers hydraulic pump, which was easily integrated. The hitch was modified from the hitch on the 50 series. Case had been working with Bosch on a sensing hitch pin that flexed when the load changed on the hitch arms. When the pin flexed it changed the magnetic field and sent a signal to the valve. It made for very smooth sensing and was used on the new Magnum. The rear axles and wheel hub design was the Case key-way type rather than the double-notch type used on the 50 series that was difficult to adjust. The Magnum also was equipped with the Intelligence Center. The Magnum was a tribute to two great companies — truly the best of both worlds.

Magnum — The Second Generation (1993-1994)

The Magnum line of tractors set the standard for large horsepower row-crop tractors for six years (from 1987-1993). In September 1993, Case IH introduced the new 7200 series that not only kept the tradition, but with hundreds of customer-driven refinements it was again advancing the standard. The major refinements included: improved machine process on the final drive gears for increased life, the engine side panels were sculpted and additional steering stops on MFD tractors together improved the turning radius by 11%, a new "Multi Mode" MFD switch that controlled "ON," "Alternate ON," (which helped get through wet spots, but saved fuel when it wasn't necessary) and "OFF," and finally an optional rear-mounted up/down

This 7120, involved in a spring tillage operation, was equipped with a mechanical front-wheel drive (MFD).

This 7110 tractor was working on a midwestern U.S. farm with a Cyclo Air planter.

This 7130 tractor was equipped with an adjustable front axle for row-crop work.

This 7140 MFD had front fenders and rear duals as it worked in a disking operation.

This 7150 was working with a laser-controlled land plane to level a field. The 7150 was introduced in 1993 at 215 horsepower and was the first of the Magnum series with the sculpted hood and the short turning MFD axle. In 1994 it was changed to 7250 with the rest of the 7200's.

The sculpted engine side panels, together with some steering stop changes, increased the turning radius on 7200 series MFD tractors up to 11%.

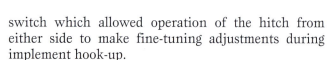

The panoramic view from the Silent Guardian II cab provides unequalled visibility to the field and implement. Optional mounting brackets were available for right front or rear posts to mount monitors or even a cellular phone. The state-of-the-art seat even let the operator swivel for easy exiting or entering the cab. The large climate controls were also easily within reach.

switch which allowed operation of the hitch from either side to make fine-tuning adjustments during implement hook-up.

A fourth reverse speed was added and the oil flow to the remotes was increased from 22 to 25 gallons per minute on all the reidentified 7200 series. There was very little reason to make any major change in the Silent Guardian II cab because it was already at the leading edge of technology. The ergonomics of the cab were already leading the industry, for example, the steps were more like stairs that led to a landing in front of the cab door. The operator could stand and open the cab door assisted by a gas-filled door opener — rather than standing on a ladder and trying to hang on with one hand and open the door with the other hand like so many competitive models. Other benefits included the

An optional up/down switch allowed convenient operation of the hitch from either side of the tractor for fine-tuning adjustments during implement hook up.

right-side control console with the color-coded control knobs at the operator's finger tips, the forward-mounted instrument panel with the Intelligence Center, the air-over-oil ride seat suspension, the seat with an adjustable lumbar support, fore/aft and lateral isolators that took the pitch and yaw out of the ride over rough ground, ride control, back cushion tilt, folding arm rests, automatic weight adjustment on the seat, a tilt and telescoping steering wheel mounted in the rubber mounted and isolated pod cab. All of these features created comfortable, as well as safe, operating conditions for the operator whether it was a petite farm wife or the "Incredible Hulk."

This Maxxum 5130 was equipped with an adjustable front axle.

The Maxxum — A World Tractor

In the early 1980s Case started designing a replacement for the transmission used in the Browns and the 580. This design was eventually used for the transmission of the Maxxum. A team of engineers from both Case and IH finalized the design. The transmission, which was built by Case in St. Dizier, France, was a sliding spur gear in 1st and 2nd and a synchromesh in 3rd and 4th. A power shift version was also available. It offered a power shuttle and the engine was a CDC. The cab was built in Croix, France. The rest of the tractor was designed and built in Neuss, Germany.

This tractor had the customer design influence aimed at customer needs and contributed by customers. After the production prototypes were built, they were sent to the engineering center in Hinsdale, Illinois. Potential customers were brought in to Hinsdale to meet with the engineers. Farmers found fault with several features and indicated that unless these changes were made, they would not buy the tractor. These faults were fixed before production began.

The tractor design allowed the customer to customize their tractor before it was built. This opportunity was very important in Europe and England because the farmers also used their trac-

This cut-away of a Maxxum tractor shows the drive line including the MFD axle. Notice the front hitch and escape hatch in the top of the cab so the operator could get out in case of an upset. Both of these features are common in Europe.

This Maxxum specialty tractor was designed for the vegetable farming market. The large front wheels on an MFD axle are for working in muddy conditions. When the crop is ready for harvesting, the vegetable farmer can't wait for a dry field to harvest — freshness to the marketplace is of the essence. These "Vege Specials," as they are called, usually are equipped with a creeper gear because the vegetable transplanters and harvesters are mostly semi-automatic and require a lot of hand labor which need very slow speeds — usually under 1 mile per hour.

tors as trucks. The European farmers have an assortment of trailers: some dump, some stake, and some covered — some large and others small. They travel to and from town in their tractors, just like a U.S. farmer in a truck. The tractors in Europe are licensed and because they travel in cities they must have special braking systems, lighting, and drawbar hitches. The worst part was that every little hamlet throughout Europe had its own rules so this tractor was designed to offer the customer what he needed in that respect. This is a problem with U.S. manufactured tractors shipped to Europe, they must go through a homologation for each country where they are sold and these specialties are added.

The Second Generation of Maxxum tractors were introduced in the fall of 1992 and the line was increased from three to four models.

This Maxxum Model 5120 at 77 horsepower was equipped with a ROPS.

This Model 5130 with a ROPS and adjustable front axle was rated at 86 horsepower.

This 94-horsepower 5140 was equipped with MFD and a cab.

First Generation Maxxum Series (1990-92)				
Model	PTO Hp	No. Cylinders*	Displacement (cubic inch)†	Speeds
5120	77	CDC 4	239 TC	16F/12R
5130	86	CDC 6	359 NA	16F/12R
5140	94	CDC 6	359 TC	16F/12R

* CDC = Consolidated Diesel Corporation.
† TC = turbocharged.
  NA = naturally aspirated.

Second Generation Maxxum Series (1992-94)				
Model	PTO Hp	No. Cylinders*	Displacement (cubic inch)†	Speeds
5220	80	CDC 4	239 TC	16F/12R
5230	90	CDC 6	359 NA	16F/12R
5240	100	CDC 6	359 TC	16F/12R
5250	112	CDC 6	359 TC	16F/12R

* CDC = Consolidated Diesel Corporation.
† TC = turbocharged.
  NA = naturally aspirated.

The 5250 Maxxum was introduced in 1993 at 112 horsepower. This Maxxum is equipped with a Case IH loader for handling round bales.

The 62-horsepower 695 tractor was manufactured in Doncaster, England, along with the 35-horsepower 395, the 42-horsepower 495, the 52-horsepower 595, the 62-horsepower 695, the 72-horsepower 895, and the 85-horsepower 995. The 395 was discontinued in 1994 and the rest were replaced with the 3200/4200 series.

In the fall of 1992 the Maxxum series was repositioned in the marketplace with increased horsepower in all models and reidentified as the 5200 series. A larger 112-horsepower model, the 5250, was added to the series. The 5250 had the sculpted engine side panel for a shorter turning radius on MFD models, also on some electrical system changes were made to make servicing easier on all 5200's.

The 3200 and 4200 Series

In 1994 the Case IH 95 series 42- to 85-horsepower range tractors (which were the original IH 84/85 series and changed to 95 series in 1990) were replaced by the 40- to 90-horsepower 3200/4200 series. These tractor series (85, 95, 3200/4200) were all built in Doncaster, England. Both the 95 series and the 3200 and 4200 series served the North American and world markets for this size of tractor.

The 3200 and 4200 used a synchromesh transmission with 8-forward and 4-reverse speeds. The brakes were single-disc hydraulically actually. The clutch

Model	PTO Hp	No. Cylinders	Displacement (cubic inch)*	Speeds
3220	42	3	179 NA	8F/4R
3230	52	4	206 NA	8F/4R
4210	62	4	239 NA	8F/4R
4230	72	4	268 NA	8F/4R
4240	85	4	268 NA	8F/4R

The 3200 and 4200 Series (1994)

* NA = naturally aspirated.

This 3220 tractor was working with a Bush Hog rotary cutter.

The hood on the 3200/4200 series was styled for greater visibility and the engine side panels were sculpted like the larger tractors. The fenders on this 4240 were intended for the European market.

material was cerametallic. The hydraulic system was open center. Two optional front axles were available either straight adjustable or mechanical front drive and the hitch was a category II with draft and position control. The PTO was independent at 540 rpm. A two-post ROPS was standard on all models and an optional ROPS iso-mounted cab was offered for all models except the 3220. The cab offered air conditioning, a tinted windshield with wipers and washer, twin outside mirrors, right transmission controls, and a roof hatch that was required by most European countries for escape in case of a rollover.

The 200 Series Compact Tractors

In 1987 Case IH introduced the 200 series, a line of compact diesel tractors designed and manufactured for Case IH by Mitsubishi. The 235 was rated at 15 PTO horsepower, the 245 at 18 PTO horsepower, the 255 at 21 PTO horsepower, the 265 at 24 PTO horsepower, and the 275 at 27 PTO horsepower. These compacts had the features just like the "big ones": tilt hood, 3-point category 1-hitch, mechanical front-wheel drive, rear-mounted and mid-mounted PTO's, adjustable

wheels, and a choice of either a mechanical or hydrostatic transmission. A line of attachments was also available for the 200 series which included: front-mount mowers, mid-mount mowers, rear-mount mowers, a dozer blade, a snow blower, and a front-end loader. In 1990 the 200 series was consolidated by dropping the 15- and 18-horsepower models and three remaining models were reidentified as the 1100 series with the 1120, 1130, and 1140.

The 9100/9200 Series — Case Bends in the Middle

In 1987 Case (again through its parent company, Tenneco) acquired the Steiger Tractor Company of Fargo, North Dakota, who were in Chapter 11 bankruptcy proceedings. After the Magnum production began Case needed a plant to build four-wheel-drive tractors. This situation was ideal for Case since Steiger had an excellent product that had fallen victim to the economic disaster in the farm equipment industry of the 1980s. Steiger purchased Cummins engines for their tractors, so the CDC engine was perfect. From 1987 until 1990 the Fargo plant built the Case IH 9100

The Case IH compact line of tractors were manufactured by Mitsubishi and filled the 21 and 27 horsepower requirements.

Early 9100 series were marketed under both Case IH and Steiger name plates.

The Case IH 9150 was rated at 250 horsepower and used the Cummins 10-liter 6-cylinder 611-cubic-inch turbocharged intercooled engine.

The 9190, the largest of the 9100 series, was rated at 505 horsepower and powered by a Cummins 18.9-liter 1,150-cubic-inch turbocharged and intercooled engine. The 9190 was discontinued in 1990 with the introduction of the 9200 series.

Two models of four-wheel-steer, four-wheel-drive tractors were produced in the 9200 series. The 9240 (shown here) replaced the Case 4494 and the 9260 replaced the 4894.

The four-wheel-steer models were built on essentially the same chassis as the articulated models except without the articulation joint. This 9240 is in the rear steer mode.

This 9240 is in the coordinated mode. The 9240 and 9260 were discontinued in 1994.

One of the reasons some areas of the world preferred four-wheel-steer over articulated steering is shown here in the crab mode which was used for working on slopes.

The 9200 family of four-wheel drives included both articulated and four-wheel-steer models and were manufactured at the Case IH plant in Fargo, North Dakota.

9100 Series Four-Wheel-Drive Tractors
The First Generation (1987-90)

Model	Steering*	PTO Hp	No. Cylinders†	Displacement (cu. inch)‡	Speeds
9110	Articul.	168	CDC 6	505 TC	12F/2R
Puma	Articul.	168	CDC 6	505 TC	12F/2R
9130	Articul.	190	CDC 6	505 TCI	12F/2R
Wildcat	Articul.	190	CDC 6	505 TCI	12F/2R
9150	Articul.	245	Cum 10 L6	611 TCI	12F/2R
Cougar	Articul.	245	Cum 10 L6	611 TCI	12F/2R
9170	Articul.	300	Cum 14 L6	855 TC	12F/2R
Panther	Articul.	300	Cum 14 L6	855 TC	12F/2R
9180	Articul.	340	Cum 14 L6	855 TC	12F/2R
Lion	Articul.	340	Cum 14 L6	855 TC	12F/2R
9190	Articul.	505	Cum 18.9 L6	1,150 TCI	24F/4R
Tiger	Articul.	505	Cum 18.9 L6	1,150 TCI	24F/4R

* Articulated.
† CDC = Consolidated Diesel Corporation.
  Cum = Cummins.
    L = liter size of Cummins engine.
‡ TC = turbocharged.
  TCI = turbocharged intercooled.

series which were painted Case IH red and black with the 9100 silver and black decaling to fit into the Case IH identification system. They were sold through the Case IH dealers.

During this same period the Fargo plant also continued to build the Steiger models: the Puma, Wildcat, Cougar, Panther, Lion, and the Tiger which were sold through Steiger dealers. A fourth model, the Bearcat, at 218 PTO horsepower and used the Cummins 6-cylinder 611-cubic-inch 10-liter engine, was offered by Steiger dealers. The 190- through 340-horsepower models came with a 12-speed power shift similar to the Case 4994. The 505-horsepower model offered a power shift transmission with 24-forward speeds and 4-reverse speeds.

The 9110, Puma, 9130, and Wildcat had singe reduction inboard planetaries with a bar axle that provided for 60-to 130-inch tread settings. These same models offered an optional front steerable bar axle that allowed the operator to independently steer the front wheels approximately 6 degrees for row-crop work. The Bearcat, 9150, and Cougar also had inboard planetaries with bar axles that accommodated the 60- to 130-inch tread settings, but did not offer the steerable front axles. The brakes were single caliper, dual piston, hydraulically actuated, and mounted on the front axle. Hydraulics were closed center, load sensing, pressure compensating with two remotes standard on the 168-

The Model 9200 row-crop special was an articulated model with a bar front axle that had 6 degrees of front-wheel steer with a 12.8-foot turning radius.

dash along with the warning lights. The steering wheel had tilt and telescope features. As an option for the Bearcat, Cougar, Panther, and Lion, Steiger offered a Caterpillar engine at the same horsepower as the Cummins. The dual Case IH/Steiger distribution system was gradually phased out by 1990 after many Steiger dealers became Case IH dealers.

1990-1994

and 190-horsepower models with three remotes standard on the rest of the models. The cabs were rubber isolated ROPS, with an aspirated cab pre-cleaner. The standard cab offered a full adjustable seat with fore and aft travel, three position height adjustment, swivel, weight adjustment, and lumbar support. In addition, the deluxe cab offered an air-over-oil seat suspension. The hour meter, volt meter, engine water temperature gauge, engine oil pressure gauge, transmission oil pressure gauge and fuel level gauge were all mounted on the front right cab post. The engine tachometer, PTO speed indicator, and speedometer were digital displays on the

In August of 1990 the Second Generation Case IH four-wheel drives, the 9200's, were announced. Several across the board changes were made for all models. One new feature was the unique "skip-shift" transmission controller that shifted from 1st to 4th to 6th to 8th gears in 3 seconds for faster highway startups and more efficient field operation. The skip-shift transmission also provided a third reverse gear at about 8 miles per hour. The upper transmission shaft was changed from spur to helical gears for a quieter and smoother operation. The transmission and hydraulic coolers were relocated to the front of the radiator for easier access and cleaning. The manufacturing process for the hood was changed to provide a smoother finish and better appearance. Two storage compartments were added in the cab — one behind the seat

The 9260 four-wheel-steer tractor at 265 horsepower powered by a Cummins 10-liter turbocharged and intercooled engine. The 9260 was discontinued in May of 1994.

The hour meter, volt meter, engine water temperature gauge, and fuel gauge were mounted on the front right cab post — just in front of the console on the 9100 and 9200 series tractors.

The deluxe cab on the 9200 series offered an air-over-oil seat suspension with fore and aft travel, three position height adjustment, swivel, weight adjustment, and lumbar support.

and the other in the left corner. The ROPS posts were padded, studs were added for mounting monitors, the Case IH air-over-oil seat suspension was adopted as standard. A sun visor, coat hook, beverage holder, and a new AM/FM radio with larger buttons were also added to the cab. The 9120 replaced the 9110 and the 9230 replaced the 9130 with a 100-engine rpm increase from 2,100 to 2,200 rpm. The 9240, a four-wheel-steer tractor, replaced the 4494 with new axles, 25% engine torque rise (which was 10% more than the 4494) and a 124-inch wheel base for a smoother ride. The 9250 replaced the 9150 with 35% more torque rise from an updated Cummins 10-liter engine that had a new turbocharger, improved cam shaft timing, injectors, pistons, piston bowl, as well as reduced fuel consumption. The 9260, another four-wheel-steer tractor, replaced the 4894 with 35% torque rise which is 5% more than the 4894 and 12% better fuel economy than the 4894. The 9270 replaced the 9170 with eight more horsepower. The 9280 replaced the 9180 and had four more horsepower.

In May of 1994 Case IH discontinued the 9240 and 9260 with no replacements, but this still left 21 different horsepower tractors ranging from 21 to 344 horsepower. Case IH was truly the best of both worlds.

9200 Series Four-Wheel-Drive Tractors
The Second Generation (1990-94)

Model	Steering*	PTO Hp	No. Cylinders†	Displacement (cu. inch)‡	Speeds
9210	Articul.	168	CDC 6	505 TC	12F/3R
9230	Articul.	190	CDC 6	505 TCI	12F/3R
9240	4Wheel	202	CDC 6	505 TCI	12F/3R
9250	Articul.	246	Cum 10 L6	611 TCI	12F/3R
9260	4Wheel	265	Cum 10 L6	611 TCI	12F/3R
9270	Articul.	308	Cum 14 L6	855 TCI	12F/3R
9280	Articul.	344	Cum 14 L6	855 TCI	12F/3R

* Articulated.
† CDC = Consolidated Diesel Corporation.
  Cum = Cummins.
      L = liter size of Cummins engine.
‡   TC = turbocharged.
    TCI = turbocharged intercooled.

New in 1994, the 9250 row-crop special offered a steerable planetary front axle design that provided 18 degrees of front axle steer. This design was to take the place of the discontinued 9260 four-wheel-steer tractors.

The 9270 replaced the 9170 and the horsepower was increased from 300 to 308.

The 9280 replaced the 9180 with increased horsepower going from 340 to 344. The 9280 was now the largest tractor in the Case IH line as the 9190 was discontinued.

In the mid-1990s Case IH did some feasibility work with a Quad Track on the 9200 series, targeting farmers that felt they needed a crawler tractor.

Tillage Equipment

Moldboard Plows

The 1950s

In the 1930s and '40s the largest population of moldboard plows were pull-type, either by horses or tractors. Some mounted plows were available, but it was truly the start of a transition era. For Case and the rest of the industry the next two decades revolutionized the moldboard plow. Case started in 1949 with the first 3-point-hitch breakaway plow that allowed the plow to unhitch if it hit an obstruction. By 1950 Case was releasing the first pivotal breakaway 3-point-hitch plow. In 1954 they introduced the Eagle Bottom, a throwaway plow share that was developed because of a decline in the number of blacksmiths who could sharpen plow shares. In 1956 Case introduced the first box section as a rear beam brace on a moldboard plow.

The standard of pull- or wheel-type plows of the 1950s and '60s was the Case A series wheel-type moldboard plow. The A series was known for its large trash capacity. It offered a constant high level lift which could either be hydraulic or oil bath clutch controlled. The rear beam and bottom could be removed for use in extra-tough soils. The A offered 3 to 6 bottoms in 14- or 16- inch sizes with 16-, 17-, and 18-inch rolling coulters, 17- and 18-inch notched coulters, or 16-inch concave coulters.

The 1960s

In the 1960s Case offered plows with spring release trip bottoms, independent control of front and rear bottoms, as well as rollover plows. Case developed the CH wheel-type plow with spring hitch release if an obstruction was hit. The CH and MT also offered spring release trip bottoms that would flip up if the

The standard for pull-type plows in the 1950s and '60s was the Case Model A. The A was known for its large trash capacity.

plow point hit a rock, the operator then had to back the plow up to reset the bottom. The S semi-mounted plow of the 1960s featured independent hydraulic control of front and rear bottoms from the tractor, this feature allowed the farmer to plow even furrows right up to the headlands. When the front bottoms got to the end, the operator could raise them up with the hitch and when the rear bottoms got to the end, he could raise them independently with a remote cylinder. The two-way rollover plow, like the 200, was popular in irrigated or contoured fields because it did not leave a dead furrow.

The 1970s

In the 1970s Case shifted to large semi-mounted plows because of the increasing popularity of much larger two-wheel-drive tractors and 3-point hitches on four-wheel-drive tractors. Increased maneuverability became essential with the larger plows. The 1970s also ushered in the 3300 Powr-Set hydraulic reset plows. No longer was it necessary to stop and back up to reset the bottoms after they had tripped, now they would hydraulically reset themselves once they had cleared the obstruction. The best feature of the 3300 Powr-Set was that the hydraulic pressure could be varied with a

The Case Model S semi-mounted plow featured independent hydraulic control of front and rear bottoms which allowed the farmer to plow evenly up to the headland with all bottoms.

With the Powr-Set plow bottom, one bottom could clear a rock 5 inches above ground while the others continued to plow 7 inches deep.

The two-way rollover plow was popular in irrigated or contour fields because it did not leave a dead furrow.

This Case Model 3300 Powr-Set plow was equipped with an on-land hitch to avoid having to run the right side dual tractor tire in the furrow.

valve setting for different soils. One bottom could clear a rock 5 inches above ground while the others continued to plow 7 inches deep. The Powr-Set plows were equipped with a gas accumulator that absorbed the surge in the system when the plow hit a rock. Special attachments were available like the NT mulcher that would till and mulch in one pass or the on-land hitch that became popular with the increased use of tractor dual rear wheels and the problems associated with running the outside dual in the furrow.

The moldboard plows of the 1970s were the 2000, 3000, 5000, 7000, and 8000. The 2000 series had the largest throat opening of 6 2/12 inches for trash clearance, they had a shear bolt trip and offered four to eight 16-inch bottoms. The 3000 series was the Powr-Set version of the 2000 and had a 29- x 26-inch throat. The 5000 was the Turnover Plow, offering three to five 16-inch bottoms with shear bolt trip or trip beam safety protection. The 7000 and 8000 were the 18-inch bottom plows — the 7000 was the shear-bolt version and the 8000 was the Powr-Set version. The 7000 was available in 4, 5, or 6 bottoms, and the 8000 in 6, 7, or 8 bottoms. The 8000 was the first Case plow with rear wheel steering for increased maneuverability. These were the last Case designed-and-built plows until the Case IH era.

The 1980s

In the early 1980s Case continued to offer moldboard plows but they were purchased from "Short Line" manufactures until many of them went out of business in the mid-1980s because of the depressed agricultural economy. The plows of this era were the 308 series for the David Brown size tractors and the 400, 500, 600, and 700 series for larger plows than those of the 1970s. The 700, for example, offered 10 bottoms, the 500, 20-inch bottoms, and the 600 rollover was adjustable to 16- or 18-inch furrows.

Case IH was manufacturing plows in 1985 at the IH plant in Hamilton, Ontario, Canada. The moldboard plow was still offered by Case IH but the volume had dropped way off when the Farm Bill and Conservation Reserve Program were enacted. The emphasis was now on soil conservation practices that recognized the benefits of leaving some trash on top of the soil. The remains from the previous growing period reduced both wind and water soil erosion, it also did a better job holding moisture.

The chisel plows that took over for the moldboard plows used less fuel and covered more ground with the same size tractor — a necessity born of a troubled agricultural economy of the 1980s. Some farmers felt that in certain soil conditions it was still necessary to use a moldboard plow every two years to allow the moisture and fertilizer get deep enough into the soil for good root development. So in the 1980s and '90s Case IH offered two fully-mounted and one semi-mounted plow. The 750 was a 4-5 to 6-7 bottom semi-mounted plow with automatic or toggle-trip bottoms. The 420 was a 2-, 3-, or 4-bottom fully-mounted plow with spring trip. A 450 heavy-duty fully-mounted 3-, 4-, or 5-bottom automatic or toggle trip was also available. The clearance ranged from 27 inches on the 420 to 34 inches on the 7500. In two-way plows a 145 high clearance had a clearance of 32 inches on the hydraulic trip beam model and 30 inches on the rigid spring trip models. The 145 was available as a 3-, 4-, or 5-bottom model. The 165 heavy-duty on-land model was a 4-5 bottom model with rigid or spring trip and 30-inch clearance. In the trail-type models the 700 high-clearance (33 inches) was available with 7-8 or 8-9 bottoms and the 800 flex frame was a 9-, 10-, 11-, or 12-bottom model. Both the 700 and 800 were available with automatic or toggle trip bottoms.

The Model 145 was the first two-way plow offered by Case IH and was built at the IH plant in Hamilton, Ontario.

Chisel Plows

1960s and 1970s

The chisel plow was first introduced and used in the wheat fields of the prairie states and provinces of the United States and Canada because it left enough stubble to hold the soil. In the 1960s the chisel plow started to gain popularity in the corn belt. The Case CP 10 and CP 13 were typical of the '60s product. The CP 10 was a 10-foot, 10-shank model and the CP 13 was a 13-foot, 13-shank model. Both models offered extensions to 12 and 15 feet, respectively.

Not quite having found its niche in 1960, the chisel plow was advertised as: "worked deep it plows . . . worked shallow it cultivates." The depth was controlled with the wheels. A variety of spike teeth, sweeps, and shovels were offered in sizes from 2- x 5/16-inch chisel teeth to 18-inch furrower shovels. In 1964 Case designed the first factory-built Optimum Tillage (OT) chisel planter, the OT-250. The Optimum Tillage System was really ahead of its time, the idea was to cut farming costs by reducing the number of passes over the field with various implements to increase yields and save time and moisture. This is how how it worked:

One Pass, Two Crop Approach. In areas that had a long enough growing season, the farmer would go right in the stubble behind the grain combine and in one pass, with the OT chisel planter, work up the ground and then apply the seed, herbicide, insecticide, and fertilize with the planter that was built onto the rear of the chisel. The chemical and ammonia tank were mounted on top of the chisel and additional tanks could be mounted on the tractor. The field was reseeded right behind the last combine pass and was ready to start growing the second crop of the season.

In 1964 Case was the first major manufacturer to build the Optimum Tillage chisel planter. The OT-250 was ahead of its time, cutting farming costs by reducing the number of passes over the field with various implements, as well as increasing yields, saving time, fuel, and moisture.

One Season, One Crop Approach. The farmer would start in the fall by chisel plowing and fertilizing — after harvesting and shredding. The plowing would be done 7 to 15 inches deep. This depth allowed the soil and the stubble to mix together better and the stubble rotted faster. It also let moisture soak down into the root zone. In the spring, when the other farmers were fighting time and weather, the Case OT farmer would be chisel-planting about 4 to 7 inches deep and applying starter, insecticide, and herbicide all in one fast operation. The moldboard plowing and disking had been eliminated, there was less soil compaction and fewer weather worries.

In some areas the OT planter would go in right behind the combine and stalk chopper, applying the seed, herbicide, insecticide, and fertilizer in one pass.

The Case Optimum Tillage chisel planter had row spacings of eight 20-inch rows, six 30-inch rows, four 40-inch rows, or four 48-inch rows. The change between row spacings was the same as any tool bar planter.

The 1980s and 1990s

In the early 1980s Case had four chisel plows in its line: the 513 was a massive deep-running heavy-duty V-type subsoil chisel with 5 to 13, 30-inch shanks; the 1800 was a trailing model with 26- or 32-inch shanks in widths 10 to 18 feet; the SC soil controller had special slicer disk blades in front and chisel shanks in the rear; and the 1805 mounted chisel was used with David Brown size tractors in widths of 5 to 7 inches. Again these were purchased products and faded out by the mid-1980s. In 1985, with the acquisition of International Harvester, the picture changed. Case IH was producing its own chisels at the Hamilton plant and featured toggle trip shanks on the Model 14 subsoil chisel and a flat fold, as well as a double fold, on the 5600 chisel plow. The 6500 Conser-Till plow replaced the soil controller.

Field Cultivators

An implement with spring teeth mounted on a frame that provided a breaking, pulverizing action on the soil and tore up weed roots has been called a lot of things through the years — depending on the generation and the region of the country. If it had wheels, the people in southeastern Wisconsin in the 1930s probably called it a Quack Digger. If it didn't have wheels and the region was elsewhere in the country, it may have been called a spring tooth harrow. But after 1960 it was called a field cultivator, regardless of location. The field cultivator was developed during the 1960s and it was a lot more sophisticated than the spring tooth harrow. It was heavier and it didn't drift or bounce around like a spring tooth, each tooth was under positive spring pressure from a coil spring that let it ride over an obstruction and snap back. The Case field cultivator of the 1960s was a 32-foot folding wing type or a 10-/12- to 18-foot mounted or pull type. Even though the field cultivator was developed in the 1960s, its greatest popularity

The field cultivator of the 1960s was a 32-foot wide, folding-wing type. It was much larger and heavier than the previous spring tooth harrows it replaced.

The Case disk plows were produced at the Case plant in Stockton, California, primarily for the West Coast irrigated areas.

developed in the 1990s because it became more versatile. The Case IH 4800 Vibra-Shank, for example, was used for final seed bed preparation, light primary tillage, chemical incorporation, pasture renovation — not just for wheat country seed bed preparation.

Disk Plows

In 1947 Case purchased a plant in Stockton, California, to produce implements that were peculiar to the West Coast irrigated farming. The WP, WPA, and WPH disk plows were produced at Stockton until it closed in 1967. The 900 one-way disk plow with a seeder was popular in the Prairie States and Provinces as a once-over all-disking and seeding operation in the 1960s. It was available in 12- and 15-foot sizes with 3-1/2-foot flexible gangs.

Both mounted and semi-mounted plows were produced at the Stockton plant.

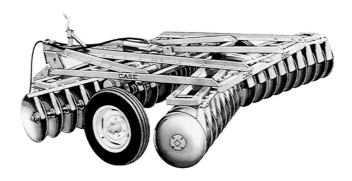

The Model S tandem wheel-type disk harrow featured a parallel lift for even disking.

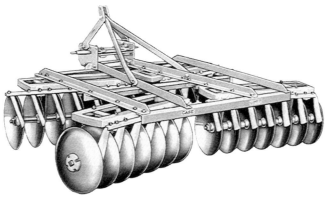

The SE mounted tandem disk was available in 7- to 9-foot sizes.

Disk Harrows

The 1950s

Prior to 1954 disk harrow penetration and leveling were controlled by changing the angle of the gangs. In 1954 Case introduced the first self-leveling wheel-type harrow. In 1960 the disk harrow was used pretty much as it had been since the horse-drawn days and that was chopping up the stalks or stubble before plowing so the plow would not plug up. Then in the spring it was used to break up and level the ground for planting. Case harrows such as the S tandem wheel-type with the parallel lift for even disking and was available in 7- to 17-foot sizes with 18- or 20-inch disks. The SE mounted tandem was available in 7- to 9-foot sizes with

16-inch disks and the RAH trailed tandem available in 7-, 8-, and 10-foot sizes with 18 inch blades.

The 1960s

By 1969, disks were still being used the same way but they were getting larger for the larger tractors. For example, the Case B tandem wheel type offered a semi-rigid design for leveling ridges and getting better penetration. With the larger size came the wing type for narrower transport like the Model WB that was 17 feet 10 inches to 21 feet 4 inches. The disk blade spacing on these disks was 7 inches.

By the late 1960s the disks were getting wider (21 feet) and heavier for the larger tractors.

With the tandem disks getting up to 31 feet wide, by the late 1970s the folding wing type became necessary for road transport or just for getting through the gate.

By the late 1980s and early '90s, as more government programs were tied to conservation plans, tillage options were needed to keep in compliance. The Case IH 4200 combo mulch finisher is a good example how the disk harrow and field cultivator were expanded to meet this need in high residue fields in one pass — by mixing, pulverizing and firming the soul, closing air pockets, killing weeds, while leaving residue on top to prevent soil erosion.

The 1970s

In 1970 the disks were not only getting larger, they were also getting heavier and the disk blade spacing was opening up. The Case E30, for example, was the biggest harrow at that time with a wide-wing hydraulic-fold tandem disk at 30 feet wide and weighing in at 11,774 pounds. In addition to the weight, Case also offered 9-inch disk-blade spacing on the E30 for increased penetration — these disks plowed! As fuel consumption became paramount during and after the oil embargo, instead of increased weight to gain penetration, a double offset tandem disk (DOT) was introduced. The DOT was a double offset tandem in the 31-foot size and was a popular disk because the offset, together with the 9-inch spacing, got excellent penetration and the double offset did a clean job and the disks pulled easier.

The Mid-1980s

The Case IH era brought Earth Metal® crimp-center disk blades. The Earth Metal® was an exclusive forging process designed to reduce fracturing. This process extended blade life by 20% while cutting shock resistance by up to 60%. The shallow concavity shape required less pressure to penetrate the soil compared to spherical or conical blades, this was important because it reduced drawbar pull by up to 50%. The Earth Metal® blades have proven very popular in the marketplace. Many farmers bought them from Case IH dealers and installed them on competitive harrows and improved their performance. The 1980s and '90s saw an increased demand for large blades and increased penetration even on the small 5- to 7-foot tandem harrows like the Case IH 122 offered with 18- and 20-inch blades and 7-1/2- or 9-inch blade spacing. On the large offset harrows like the 780 the blade sizes were up to 32 inches with 12-inch blade spacing.

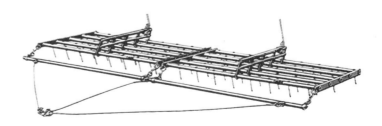

Seed bed tillage equipment didn't change much from the 1950s through the '70s, this Case RC spike tooth harrow is a typical example.

Machines like the 415 roller-mulcher are typical multiple-use seed bed tillage tools which are ideal for chemical incorporation and uniform germination.

The 4900 Vibra Shank® field cultivator can be used for seed bed finishing on fallow ground. The aggressive Vibra Shank® action is ideal for incorporating chemicals.

Seed Bed Tillage Equipment

The seed bed preparation tool is essentially used to break up crusts and clods prior to seeding to promote uniform germination. These tools haven't changed drastically through the years. From the 1950s through the 1970s, they consisted of the spike tooth harrows like the Case L, RC, RO, RF, and RLF models. Other popular tools were the Case T roller packer and the spring tine harrow. In the 1990s it was the 365 vibra tine mulcher cultivator, the 568 seedbed conditioner which was a different approach because it combined the spring-loaded Vibra Shank® tools with double-rolling mulchers all in one machine — the 415 roller mulcher and the 9-peg tooth harrow. Most of the machines from the 1990s were multiple-use machines which could be used for tillage and/or for incorporating chemicals.

The Earth Metal® blades used on the Case IH tandem and offset harrows have a unique crimp-center design that are stronger than conventional blades and reduce drawbar pull for improved productivity and fuel economy

Crop Production

The Case Model 200 pull-type planter was a hill-drop plate planter of the 1960s. The hill-drop technology was a carryover from the 1940s and dropped several kernels in one drop — the philosophy was safety in numbers.

The evolution of machines that planted corn, soybeans, beets, vegetables, cotton, and peanuts involved more than just getting the seed into the ground. The challenge was to accurately place these seeds at a uniform depth for a maximum seedling emergence. Farmers had enough to worry about — like the weather for 60, 90, or 120 days — without worrying about how well the seeds were put in the ground.

The 1960s

The Case planters of the 1960s were the 200, the 400, and the 434. The 200, a hill-drop plate planter, carried over technology from the

The planters of the 1970s, like this four-row planter, were getting more versatile in offering narrow row spacing (30-inch rows). They could work in min-till, no-till, and ridge-till planting practices and offered all the fertilizer and herbicide attachments.

1940s and '50s as it dropped several kernels in one drop. The philosophy was safety in numbers. The 400 planter was transition technology. It offered hill drop and check row for those who were slow to change and had the time to lay out the check wire at the end of each row. They also needed patience to cross cultivate for weed control once the crop emerged. The 400 also offered drill planting because farmers were finding out that drilling offered higher yields than checking with hybrids and fertilizer. The 434 pull-type planter featured speed and safety with the ability to hill drop at 140 hills per minute or drilling speed at 5 miles per hour. The 434 also offered either a dry or liquid fertilizer attachment, as well as a pre-emergence spray attachment as mechanical weed control was being replaced by chemicals.

The 1970s

In 1969, the planters reflected the trend away from the traditional 38- to 40-inch row spacing as the TC 46 offered four 40-inch rows or six 30-inch rows. The TC 64 offered six 40-inch rows or eight 30-inch rows or add a rear toolbar and plant 20-inch rows. The TC planter advertising spoke of the versatility it allowed the farmer to follow any tillage or planting practice as well as any row spacing. The TC planters also offered

The Cyclo Air planter offered large single or dual hoppers which greatly reduced fill time, regardless of planter size. The Cyclo Air 900 series is the fourth generation of the world's finest planters.

insecticide, herbicide, liquid, granular, or anhydrous attachments. This was also a popular era for the Case OT planter (see the Chisel Plow section of this book). The late 1960s and early 1970s were a transitional time as min-till, no-till, and ridge-till farming practices were really starting to demand versatility in planters. This also was one of the last years Case advertised and sold planters as their primary focus shifted to large tractors until 1985.

The Cyclo Air Planter

The first major breakthrough in planter technology came in the 1960s with the introduction of the 400 Cyclo planter by IH. The Cyclo planter was revolutionary because it was the first drum planter. This new concept allowed very accurate planting of irregular sized and shaped seeds which ultimately reduced the price of hybrid seed corn because ungraded seed corn could be used in the Cyclo planter. The Cyclo also offered a single large hopper that reduced fill time. It continues to be the leader in the industry because it

The Cyclo Air metering system has only three moving parts; the seed drum, the seed cut-off brush, and the seed released assembly.

has been constantly upgraded. The 400 Cyclo was replaced by the upgraded 500 Cyclo which was upgraded to the 800 and 900 Cyclo Air planter design.

How The Cyclo Planter Works

The Cyclo Air seed-metering system has only three moving parts: the seed drum, the seed cut-off brush, and the seed release wheel assembly. The seed drum is ground driven and revolves any time the planter is moving forward in a planting mode. Seed from the large hopper enters the revolving seed drum through a seed delivery chute. The seed drum contains a row of holes for each planter row. Each hole is indented from the inside of the drum to form a seed pocket. A hydraulic-driven blower provides air pressure to the seed hopper as well as to the seed drum through an air director. The hopper pressure is slightly higher than the drum pressure to insure that seeds move from the hopper to the drum. The seeds are held in the pockets of the drum by the air escaping around the seeds through the holes in the drum. As the seeds are being carried to the top of the drum, the cut-off brush removes the excess seeds which leaves only one seed in a pocket. Seed release wheels contact each seed pocket which stops the escaping air and releases the seed from the pocket. The released seed then drops into a seed discharge manifold and is carried to the row unit.

The Early Riser Planters

In 1980 IH introduced the Early Riser planters. These planters offered the farmer a choice of a plate or a Cyclo Air drum-type planter that matched a variety of tillage practices, acreages, and terrains. The plate-type planter offered trailing-rigid, mounted vertical-fold, and mounted rigid type in either 4, 6, 8, or 12 row with 30-, 36-, 38-, or 40-inch row spacing. The Cyclo Air offered a trailing-rigid frame, a semi-mounted rigid frame, a semi-mounted vertical-fold frame, a semi-mounted rigid frame corn/soybean special (an 8-row corn convertible to 13-row narrow soybean), and a trailing horizontal rear-fold frame which offered a 16-row narrow in addition to the 12-row narrow and 12-row wide. There were 4-, 6-, 8-, and 12-row sizes with row spacing from 30, 36, 38, and 40 inches in all types. Not only did the Cyclo Air offer a single hopper that reduced fill time, but both the plate type and the drum type made major changes in the furrowing planting and covering mechanisms.

How the Early Riser Planter Works

The Early Riser planter was very effective in its planting technique. The staggered double disk openers cut the narrowest furrow possible by placing one disk slightly ahead of the other to permit a narrower opener angle — the narrower the seed trench, the more precise the seed placement. The thin edge of the leading disk also penetrated hard-packed soil and sliced through

For operations that required the plate planter, Case IH offered the same advance techniques in the furrowing, planting, and covering mechanisms as the Cyclo Air.

heavy trash more effectively. Front-pulled equalizing gauge wheels were connected through linkage that maintained equal pressure on both gauge wheels at all times. As one wheel moved up over a clod or root crown, the other wheel was forced down. This equalizing action reduced opener movement to half the height of the obstacle and resulted in more uniform depth control and better seed placement, especially in rough or untilled ground. The grooved gauge wheel also trapped soil brought up by openers and placed moist soil back in the bottom of the seed trench. The patented firming point provided a well-defined V-shaped seed furrow. Conventional disk openers left a W-shaped seed trench that often affected control and spacing accuracy, resulting in uneven germination. The clean bottom assured that every seed was placed at the same depth. Twin inverted staggered covering disks closed the seed trench and provided good soil/seed contact in a wide variety of soil conditions. Inverted covering disks precisely closed the seed trench with moist soil in

conventional tillage and aggressively sliced trash in minimum-till and dense no-till sod conditions. Cheveron-tread press wheels gently firmed up the soil placed by the covering disks over the seed to eliminate moisture-robbing air pockets. A center rib on each press wheel provided a cracking slit so young plants could emerge easier in crusty soil conditions. In 1988 *Fortune* magazine picked the Early Riser planter as one of the 100-best American products.

Seed Flow Monitors

The ultimate in planting confidence was the development of the Early Riser monitor. It was a microcomputer-based monitoring system which could be mounted in the cab of the tractor in easy view and reach of the operator. The monitors (the hopper air pressure, the hopper seed level, the seed spacing by row or by planter average) gave the operator both an audible warning and provided word messages on the screen if a problem occurred. The Early Riser monitor also computed and displayed the total area covered, the immediate acres being covered, and the true ground speed. A more basic monitor, the Seed Flow II, was also offered and was an excellent accompaniment for the farmer with a Case or Case IH tractor with an Intelligence Center. The combination of the Intelligence Center and the Seed Flow II monitored total area covered, acres per hour, true ground speed, as well as seed population and hopper level. These monitors were made for Case IH by Dickey-john in Auburn, Illinois.

The Early Riser monitor was a microcomputer-based monitoring system that monitored hopper air pressure, hopper and seed level, seed spacing by row or by planter average, and gave both an audible and word message warning.

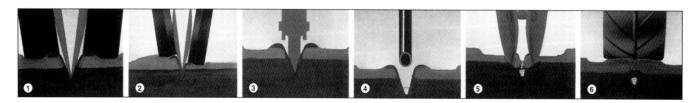

The Early Riser furrowing, planting, and covering mechanisms: 1. Staggered double disk openers. 2. Front pulled equalizing gauge wheels. 3. The grooved gauge wheel also placed moist soil back in the bottom of the seed trench. 4. Patented firming point. 5. Twin inverted staggered covering disks. 6. Chevron-tread press wheels.

Th Case Model D plain grain drill only sowed grain, as opposed to a fertilizer grain drill which sowed both fertilizer and grain.

Grain Drills

The design of grain drills was influenced by the operating environment rather than by the seeds they were going to sow. Through the years Case has offered plain grain drills which were for diversified areas in 6-, 8-, 10-, and 12-foot sizes to sow small grain, peas, soybeans, and alfalfa. The Case D was a typical plain drill. A fertilizer grain drill was essentially the same as a plain drill but it also applied fertilizer. The addition of applying fertilizer with the seed became popular in the 1950s. Both the fertilizer grain drill and the plain drill offered disk openers standard for the 7-inch spacing and hoe openers for the dry areas and wider spacing. The Case DF was a typical fertilizer grain drill. Another grain drill, the Case D press grain drill, was designed for dryland farming areas to sow small grain and press dirt over the seed to conserve moisture and accelerate germination.

Yet another type of grain drill was the Case D plow press grain drill. It was available in 4-, 5-, or 6-foot sizes and could be attached to the rear of a plow or land packer or it could be hitched directly behind a tractor. Similar to the press drill, the Case D plow press grain drill pressed the soil over the seed to conserve moisture.

The final grain drill was the Lister press grain drill. The Case Lister press drill was available in 8-, 11-, or 14-foot widths designed for large-scale grain producers in dryland areas. The Lister press drill sowed small grains on tilled soil in furrows between ridges which protected the seed from wind and collected the needed moisture.

Progress Is Always Amazing

One of the interesting things was the use of grain drills to sow soy beans in the 1930s and '40s as a hay crop. As beans became more profitable harvested as a seed crop, farmers changed to row-crop planters to plant their beans. Now they have changed back to drills and again sow their soy beans, but this time for seed crop. Progress never stops! Case was out of the drill business from 1969/early 1970s until 1985.

Late 1980s and Early 1990s

Between 1985 and 1990 Case IH came out with eight drills. The most interesting technology change in drills has been the 8500 which is an air hoe drill and the 8600 which is an air disk drill. The air drills offered a large single hopper for easy filling and propelled the

The Case plow press could be attached to the rear of a plow or directly to a tractor.

The Case Lister press drill sowed small grains on tilled soil in furrows between ridges which protected the seed from the wind and collected moisture.

The 8500 air hoe drill was a Western wheat country drill and was available with seeding widths from 33 to 45 feet. The air drill offered a large singe hopper capacity of 146-bushes of grain.

seed and fertilizer by air to the feed cups. The 8500 and 8600 were Western wheat country drills — a place where large four-wheel-drive tractors and large drills were used. The 8500 had a hopper capacity of 146 bushels of grain, it came in either a 33- or 44-foot size and weighed up to 21,460 pounds with the hopper empty. The 8600 was slightly smaller than the 8500.

Cultivators

Horse Sense

There must have been times when the farmer had his doubts that the early front-mounted tractor cultivator was a step up from the horse drawn or "sulky" cultivator. After all, it wasn't as difficult to hitch the horses up to the cultivator as it was to struggle getting the cultivator frame hooked up to the tractor. Once the horses got going, the farmer could tie the reigns to the lift lever and let the rhythm of the harness slapping lull him off to a quick nap in the heat of afternoon. If the team was good, they would go straight down the row and stop at the end and wait for the farmer to lift the cultivator out of the ground, then turn and go exactly the right number of rows over for the next pass. The tractor was supposed to be faster, but after the operator got the wheels spaced out and the cultivator mounted — well maybe, but he had to stay aware and count his own rows!

The first Case tractor that offered a mounted cultivator was the CC. Before the advent of preemergence chemicals and herbicides, the cultivator had to be mounted in the front of the tractor because the farmer wanted to cultivate close to the plant and also have maximum visibility.

The air disk drill was designed to work in Western wheat country, but it was also designed to work in more of a trash condition with the disk openers. The air disk drill was available in seeding widths of 30 feet. The air hoes and disk drills were designed to cover acreage quickly, while providing accurate and gentle seed distribution so that the seed was ready for germination.

The front-mounted cultivator was designed before the preemergence chemicals and herbicides, so the farmer had good visibility to cultivate close to the plant and control weeds. The only problem — it was a "bear" to put it on and off.

By the 1970s chemicals had made it unnecessary to cultivate close to the plant and the less cumbersome rear-mounted cultivator took over. The rear-mounted cultivator grew with the larger tractors and by the early 1980s were 32 feet wide.

By the mid-1950s Case had developed a cotton and corn 2- and 4-row drive-in cultivator for the 300 and 400 series tractors. These cultivators, as well as the 400, 600, and 700 cultivators, were designed so the gangs pivoted forward. The operator could then drive between the gangs, use the built-in jack to raise the gangs, and then swing the gangs into position for fastening. These cultivators were adjustable from 18- to 48-inch row spacing. In the early 1970s, as more emphasis was placed on roll-over protection by the OSHA standards, the tricycle front end with its vulnerability to roll over began to fade from the scene and with it the front-mounted cultivator. By this time chemicals had made it unnecessary to cultivate close to the plant and front-mounted cultivators were more cumbersome with the wide fronts, so the rear-mounted cultivator took over.

By the 1990s, field cultivators like this 1830 could handle up to 16, 36- to 40-inch rows.

In the 1970s and early '80s the rear-mounted cultivator got larger — 8 to 12 rows, 32-feet wide, and the extra-long gangs permitted generous tool spacing to allow free trash flow on the Case 180 and 188 cultivators. The operator didn't worry about scanning the rows like he did with the 2- and 4-row front-mounted cultivators, he didn't have time!

In the Case IH era of the mid-1980s and '90s, the rear-mounted cultivators that were offered included the 183 rigid or folding wing for 4 to 16 rows and the 146 cotton and corn cultivator for 6 and 8 rows. Later the 1820 and 1830 were added for the narrow 28- to 30-inch rows.

Rotary Hoes

The Case IH 181 rotary hoe, one of the better-selling seed bed preparation tools, got bigger over the years until it was up to 41-feet working width. In the 1990s the rotary hoes, like the 181 minimum-till and 184 min-till cultivator, were no longer just used as crust busters for young crops. Changing practices have shed new light on an old standby. Rotary hoes provide a low-cost way of getting rid of young weeds that may have survived the reduced use of chemicals or weeds that have gotten away because of weather or timeliness of chemical applications. Rotary hoes work well because they can control weeds in heavy residues. The front-mounted cultivator is even making a comeback with California vegetable growers since it keeps the soil loose, and as a result, the soil stays warmer.

Rotary hoes like this 181 grew to working widths of 41 feet by the 1990s.

Hay and Forage Equipment

The Early Case Balers

Loose hay was still the most popular way of storing or "putting up" hay as late as the early 1930s, even though the hay baler was developed in the mid-1900s. From the mid-1930s to the post World War II era, the baler had a meteoric rise in popularity due to the large demand for food and the limited storage space. Baled hay required only about 1/5*th* the space of loose hay. Baled hay was also easier to feed.

The serious entry into the hay equipment business occurred for Case with the purchase of the Emerson-Brantingham Company in 1928. Early Case balers were stationary and were hand-fed from a stack or from piles that were raked up in the field with a sulky or dump

This 14- x 18-inch big capacity baler was being fed from a stack and was well-suited for stack baling.

rake. These balers were horse or tractor drawn and were powered by a stationary engine such as the Case RC engine. The stationary baler was offered in either a 14- x 18-inch or 17- x 22-inch bale size and was a wire-tie baler. They offered some unique attachments, such as the signal bell which consisted of a notched wheel that was turned by the bale as it was pushed through the bale chamber and when the bale was of the desired length a projection on the wheel released the hammer which struck the bell. The operator then twisted the two wires to secure the bale. The stationary baler baled hay, cornstalks, straw, and waste paper. These balers were popular into the 1950s. The pick-up balers, available in 14- x 18-inch and 17- x 22-inch sizes, became popular in the mid-1930s. These pick-up balers looked a lot like the stationary balers with a conveyor that picked the hay up from a windrow.

The Case System-Baler and Slicer-Baler

In the late 1930s Case began to dominate the pick-up baler market with a 14- x 18-inch baler that was lightweight, fast, and reliable. It was known as the Case System-Baler. The System-Baler was the "only baler" of that era (1930s and '40s) and was pulled by every color

The early Case stationary balers (and some pick-up balers) were powered by the Case Model RC tractor engine.

This bell was an attachment used for signaling the operator or feeder when it was time to drop the division block and twist the ends of the wires.

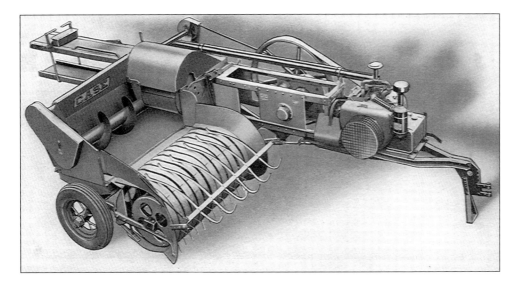

This Case Slicer-Baler, Model NCM, picked up the air-cured windrow and formed it into wire-bound sliced bales. This was the most popular hay baler on the market until the early 1950s when it was replaced by the automatic twine-tie balers.

of tractor on the market. In 1940 Case introduced the first Slicer-Baler which sheared off a slice of hay with each plunger stroke. These sliced bales made feeding hay to animals much easier. When the wires were cut and opened the individual slices slid apart like a deck of cards. The farmer didn't have to fight separating the accordion folds of the conventional bale.

The System-Baler and Slicer-Baler were wire-tie balers that required two operators or "tyers." The operator on the flywheel side of the baler placed a bale divider in a spring-tensioned drawer-like mechanism that inserted the divider into the bale. This same operator fed two wires into the divider and through the bale. The operator on the other side of the baler tied or twisted the wires together. Wires were available in two options — the straight end type which had to be twisted or the loop type which had a loop on one end and a head (similar to a rivet head) on the other and the two ends could be simply hooked together rather than twisted. A good tyer on the twist side always kept a handful of wires about a foot long bent around the "grab bar" so if the bale started to get too long for the normal wire he could always splice it rather than have a broken or untied bale. After a long day in the sun these splices were sometimes used to keep the person loading the bale wagon "on his toes" by tying him

The sliced bale was much easier to feed to animals because when the wire was cut, the slices fell apart. No more fighting to separate the accordion folds of the conventional bale.

"a really long one" that was awkward and heavy to handle.

The original System- and Slicer-Balers were powered by a four-cylinder Wisconsin air-cooled engine. In the early 1940s a PTO version was introduced called the NCT and the engine-driven version was then renamed the NCM. These balers totally dominated the market until a wire shortage during World War II and then New Holland introduced an automatic twine-tie baler that did not require operators. In the 1950s and '60s Case introduced several new balers, but none ever dominated the market like the System- and Slicer-Balers.

The bale tyers sat on either side of the bale chamber. The tyer on the right (in this picture) inserted the bale divider and fed the wires through the divider. The tyer on the left (in this picture) twisted or tied the wires together.

The bale divider was inserted behind the spring loaded device in this picture. The tyer pulled the handle back, inserted the divider and wires behind the spring-loaded device which kept tension on the divider, thereby forcing it into the bale.

NAP-2 and NAP-3 Balers

Around 1950 Case introduced the NAP-2 baler — a heavy-duty pick-up baler that was rated as a 17- x 22-inch machine that made bales up to 46 inches long. The NAP-2 was a semi-automatic baler that required only one operator to twist the wire ends. The wire was threaded by three needles mounted on a mobile carriage bringing the wire (from a wire spool rack) through the bale chamber and around the bale. The NAP-2 was replaced by the NAP-3 in the late 1950s. The NAP-3 was a fully automatic wire-tie baler.

NT and NCMT Twine-Tie Balers

The NT and the NCMT were the first Case attempts at an automatic twine-tie baler which were based on the NCM chassis with a purchased knotter and the needle-threading concept similar to the NAP-2. The NT had a lot of bugs and was not very successful. The NCMT was a redesigned model of the NT and was a good machine but by its introduction in 1953, Case had less than 5 percent of the market.

When the PTO version of the Case System-Baler was introduced, model numbers were added. The engine-driven model was the NCM and the PTO-driven model was the NCT.

The NAP-2 was a wire-tie baler driven by the Case SE engine and required only one operator (a wire twister) because the wire was threaded automatically with three needles.

The NT baler was essentially the NCT chassis with a purchased twine knotter.

The 130 Baler

In 1955 Case introduced what they termed "The Baler for the Family Size Farm" or the Model 130 baler. The 130 was a 14- x18-inch baler, but compared to the NCM and NCMT it was a compact baler. The pick-up was 20 inches narrower (47 vs. 67 inches) and the overall length was 5 feet shorter than the NCM-NCMT and the overall height was almost 2 feet lower. It was a low-cost baler for the small farm. The 130 had a newly redesigned Case knotter. The 130 was unfortunately very sensitive to varying hay conditions,

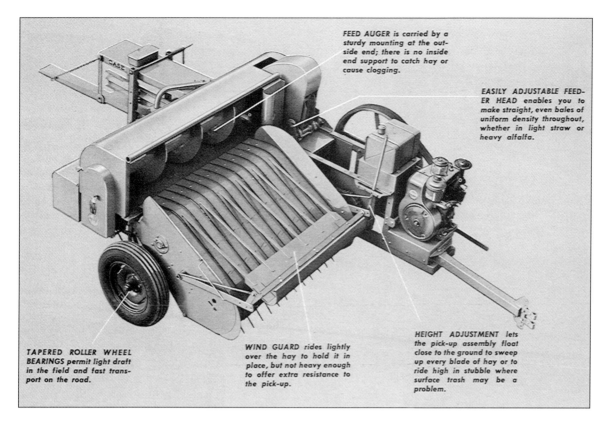

FEED AUGER is carried by a sturdy mounting at the outside end; there is no inside end support to catch hay or cause clogging.

EASILY ADJUSTABLE FEEDER HEAD enables you to make straight, even bales of uniform density throughout, whether in light straw or heavy alfalfa.

TAPERED ROLLER WHEEL BEARINGS permit light draft in the field and fast transport on the road.

WIND GUARD rides lightly over the hay to hold it in place, but not heavy enough to offer extra resistance to the pick-up.

HEIGHT ADJUSTMENT lets the pick-up assembly float close to the ground to sweep up every blade of hay or to ride high in stubble where surface trash may be a problem.

The Model 130 baler was a small baler designed for the family-sized farm. It differed from previous Case models as it had a Case-designed knotter and a feed auger that moved the hay from the pick-up to the bale chamber.

as were several other baler manufactures of that era. In preparing the Operator's Manual the ink on one version of the "Timming Instructions" would hardly be dry before another version was coming in from the field test crew. The 130 was only produced for two seasons and was then replaced by the 133 which was produced until 1961.

The 135, 140, 160, and 177 Wire-Tie Balers

From 1956 to 1959 Case produced three wire-tie balers and at one time, all three were being produced simultaneously. The 135 was produced at the Main Works in Racine, while the 140 and 160 were produced at Bettendorf, Iowa. The 135 was a wire-tie version of the 133 which was also produced at Racine. In addition to the wire twister, the 135 had a Flo-Director in front of the feed auger for hard-to-handle crops. It was available with either a PTO or engine-driven model.

The 140 and 160, introduced in 1956, were essentially the same size physically except the 140 produced a 14- x 18-inch bale and the 160 produced a 16- x 18-inch bale, each had a 16- to 45-inch bale length capacity. The

135 had a 12- to 48-inch length capacity. All three had 52-inch pick-ups. The 160 was replaced by the 177 in 1959 which was a larger baler, producing a 17- x 22-inch bale from 36 to 48 inches and weighing up to

The 135 wire-tie baler used the Flo-Director, located just in front of the feed auger, which helped increase capacity by providing a smooth, uniform flow of materials into the bale chamber and reduced wrapping around the auger with rank crops, as experienced with just the auger on the 130.

The Balers of the 1960s and 1970s

In late 1959 Case introduced the 200 baler which was the compact baler that would eventually replace the 133. The 200 was a 14- x18-inch baler that could produce a 10-inch longer bale than the 133 and it had 56-inch pick-up. A few unique design features were added to the 200. For example, the knotter was mounted on top of the bale chamber, out of the chafe and dirt rather than the side of the chamber; and it had a horizontal sweep arm at the top of the pick-up rather than an auger to move the hay into the bale chamber. In 1969 and during the early 1970s Case was producing three versions of the 200: the 230, the 330 twine-tie (a heavy-duty version of the 230), and the 330 wire-tie baler. The 200 was produced in France after Case got out of the baler business in the United States in the early 1970s. The French production ended in the late 1970s when the demand for loader backhoes required extra plant capacity. As a result the 200 had to be dropped.

The Balers from 1985 to 1990s

After Case announced the decision to discontinue baler production (except for the 200 baler production in France) in 1972, they did not offer a baler until 1985 and the IH acquisition. IH had sold their hay and forage tool business to New Idea, so for the first few years after the acquisition Case IH marketed

From 1956 to 1959 Case produced the 140 baler which made a 14- x 18-inch bale. They also produced the 160 which made a 16- x 18-inch bale. Both balers were manufactured at the Case plant in Bettendorf, Iowa.

175 pounds. The 177 also incorporated some of the features of the 135, such as the Flo-Director and the feeder head. By this time the Racine baler production was in the process of being moved to Bettendorf, Iowa, and in the consolidation several of the balers were phased out.

The Model 330 baler was a heavy-duty version of the Model 230. The 330 was available in either a twine-tie or wire-tie version.

One unique feature of the Model 200 and 230 series balers was that the knotter was mounted on top of the bale chamber rather than on the side, as previous balers had been. The idea behind the top-mounted knotter was to move it out of the dust and chafe that caused knotters to get out of time with the plunger.

Another unique feature of the 200/230 series balers was the sweep fork that replaced the feed auger and flo-director. The sweep fork was very successful because it worked in most crop conditions

The Model 200 baler's success was only exceeded by the NCM. The 200 was in a popular size and price range, plus its reliability was unequalled by any other Case baler until that time.

The 8580 was introduced in the early 1990s and was the largest square baler in the Case IH line. The 8580 made bales up to 9-feet long and weighing up to 2,200 pounds. The baler controls were automatic and electronic.

balers built by New Idea, a division of Allied Industries. This arrangement was not satisfactory, so in October of 1987, Case IH formed a joint venture with Hesston called Hay & Forage Industries. The joint venture produced the 8520, 8530, and 8545. They were 14- x 18-inch balers which featured a straight-through-design square bale with the pick-up under the front of the bale chamber rather than to the side. Hay & Forage Industries also produced the 8420, 8430, 8445, 8465, and 8480 round balers which produced bales from 550

pounds to 2,200 pounds and from a 4.5 foot diameter to a 6.25 foot diameter. Both square and round balers featured automatic and electronic controls.

Mowers To Windrowers

Space will not allow us to cover each and every model, so we will attempt to cover the evolution of these machines by decades.

The 1950s and 1960s

The decade of the 1950s and '60s witnessed some major changes in the way farmers handled the harvesting of hay and forage crops with the introduction of rotary mowers, windrowers, forage harvesters, and flail harvesters.

Mowers. The stalwart of Case mowers in the 1950s and '60s was the Model 10 offered with a choice of 5-, 6-, or 7-foot cut. The 10 was available as a Trail-Type (T-10), rear semi-mounted (10), or fully-mounted (M10). The Model 10 featured close trailing for fast square corners and outstanding maneuverability for high-speed cutting (6-7 mph). It also had a swing-back safety release to protect the cutter bar. The 1950s also saw the development and rise in popularity of the rotary mower or cutter like the Case 400 rotary cutter. The ability to control the cutting height from 1 1/2 to 15 inches, its ruggedness, and not having to bother with sickle sections were very appealing and heavily impacted the sickle mower popularity. Both types of mowers were offered as late as 1969.

Rakes. This era saw the biggest change in rake design although the conventional side-delivery rake

This 8555 shows the concept of the center-line design common to all the Case IH square balers. The center-line design moves the hay in a straight line, from the pick up all the way to the bale chute without twists or corners. It provided a smooth, gentle crop flow and less leaf loss for greater bale nutrition. The center-line design eliminated the need for all of the auger feeds, flo-directors, and sweep forks that baler engineers struggled with through the 1950s and '60s

The Model 10 sickle bar mower was the stalwart of the Case mowers in the 1950s, '60s, and '70s. The E10 (shown here) was best known for fast square corners and maneuverability.

The Model 170 side-delivery rake was a conventional cylindrical rake available in either the high-wheel Model F170 (shown here) or a low-wheel Model L170.

The first big change in side-delivery rakes came with the Model 281. The 281 had a parallel reel that was designed to gentile rake at 5 to 8 miles per hour with a minimum of leaf shattering by moving the windrow a shorter distance.

In the late 1950s one of the first Case windrowers was the PTO-driven Model 720.

like the 170 was still offered in 1960. Some changes had been made over the years, like offering the 170 in either a high-wheel model (F170) or the low-wheel model (L170). The first big change came in the 281 side-delivery rake. It was designed with a parallel reel rather than the longtime design of the cylindrical reel of the past. The new reel design was intended for faster (5 to 8 mph compared to 4 to 5 mph) gentile raking with a minimum of leaf shattering by moving the windrow a shorter distance. The side-delivery rakes were all ground driven. The last innovation in the side-delivery rake was the wheel-type rake designed to operate at 15 mph. Side-delivery rakes were offered as late as 1969.

Windrowers. In the 1960s the windrower started to change the way the hay crop was handled. Mower and rake popularity had peaked and was replaced by windrowers which both cut and windrowed the crop in one operation. Windrowers were not new to North America, they were developed in South Dakota as early as 1904 and later expanded into Canada. Initially windrowers were used for grain harvesting because the growing season was too short for the standing grain to ripen. Windrowed grain ripened faster than shocked grain. It was the 1960s before windrowers became popular with the U.S. hay regions. Case offered a pull-type windrower, the Model 720 (PTO driven), in 12- or 16-foot cut. Case also offered the original 840 machine

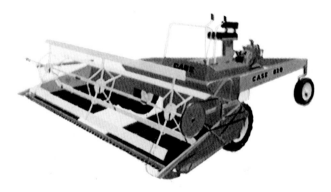

The 820 self-propelled windrower was a low-cost windrower sold in the 1960s.

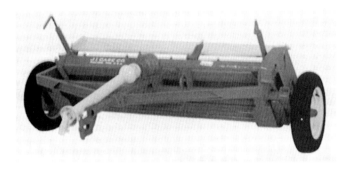

The Model 222 was the first Case hay conditioner and was introduced in the 1960s. It was soon replaced by the mower conditioner.

in 1957. Then the updated 850, a heavy-duty self-propelled machine and the 820 low-cost self-propelled machines were offered in 1960 — both had a choice of 10-, 12-, 14-, or 16-foot headers. These machines were powered by the Case A-125 air-cooled four-cylinder engine. These self-propelled machines had variable speed drive, power steeling, hydraulic header, and reel control.

Hay Conditioners. The introduction of the hay conditioner in the 1960s, like the Case 222, crimped and crushed the hay from the windrow to increase drying and baling time by 40 to 50 percent. The hay conditioner was soon replaced with the mower conditioner.

Forage Harvesters. Along with the development of the glass-lined oxygen-free silos and the bunker silos of the 1950s and '60s came the increased popularity of the forage harvester. The Case 200 series forage harvester, introduced in 1953, was representative of this era. The 200 was a multipurpose machine offering the farmer three choices of base units: the economy Model 210, the heavy-duty Model 200, and the Model 225. The economy Model 210 was a PTO-driven unit with a four-knife cutter wheel. It had a knife wheel speed of 850 rpm and cut lengths of 1/2, 1, and 2 inches. The heavy-duty Model 200, also a PTO-driven Case unit, offered a six-knife cutter wheel at speeds of 550 and 850 rpm with lengths of cuts from 1/3 to over 3 inches. The Model 225 was the same base unit as the 220 except it was engine driven. All three base units offered the following attachments: row crop, a corn harvester

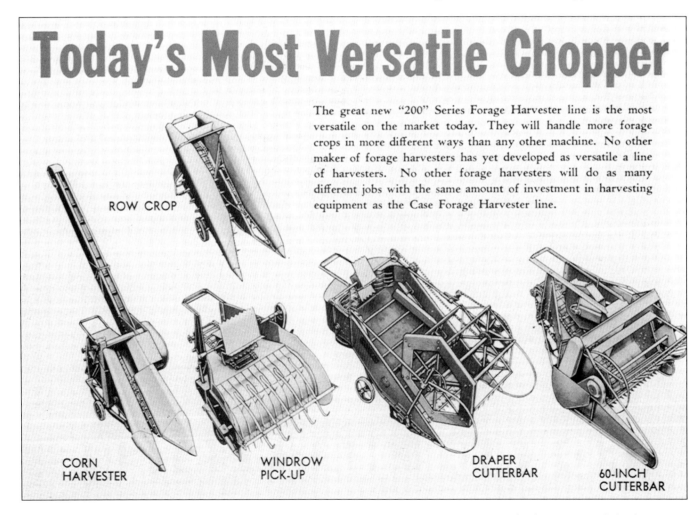

Today's Most Versatile Chopper

The great new "200" Series Forage Harvester line is the most versatile on the market today. They will handle more forage crops in more different ways than any other machine. No other maker of forage harvesters has yet developed as versatile a line of harvesters. No other forage harvesters will do as many different jobs with the same amount of investment in harvesting equipment as the Case Forage Harvester line.

ROW CROP

CORN HARVESTER

WINDROW PICK-UP

DRAPER CUTTERBAR

60-INCH CUTTERBAR

The Models 200 and 225 engine-driven, as well as the Model 210 PTO-driven, were the base units of the forage harvesters. All models offered these five attachments.

windrow pick-up, a draper cutter bar, and a 60-inch cutter bar.

No history of forage equipment would be complete without the mention of the forage blower that blew the chopped forage into the silo. Case offered the 421 starting in the 1950s and '60s, it featured a two-speed conveyor, torque limit clutch on the conveyor, 42-inch six-blade fan, and a replaceable liner in the fan housing. The 421 was available as either a belt-driven model or a PTO-driven model. The 421 was replaced by the 100 blower which was PTO-driven only and had a 54-inch fan and an agitated hopper.

Flail Harvesters. Dairy farmers of the 1950s felt that feedlot-style feeding would allow them to handle a larger herd. They just needed to chop the standing green hay and bring it to the lot every day rather than pasturing the animals. The most economical machine to accomplish this task was the flail harvester. The 640 Case was a typical flail machine, with a 60-inch cut, was PTO driven, and could be operated at 4 to 5 mph — an economical flail harvester.

The 640 flail utility harvester.

The 1950s and '60s also bred other types of forage machines, like the stalk-shredder and the clipper-mulcher, which were used to shred corn and cotton stalks before they were plowed under. The idea was to control the insects that lived in the stalks and also the shredded stalks decomposed faster. These machines were also used to top beets and potatoes. The Case machines of this era were the V stalker-shredder and the 645 clipper-mulcher. The V-12 was a big 12-foot shredder with 48-cup-type flails and the rotor was V-belt driven. Many V's were pulled in tandem with disk harrow to chop and mix trash.

The 1960s and 1970s

During this decade the Case commitment to the hay and forage products was beginning to soften because technology was rapidly changing. For example, the hay conditioner was incorporated into the windrower. Changes of this nature required a major financial commitment to engineering and development, as well as capital expenditure. Unfortunately the market share and pay back were just not there. This resulted in products such as the windrower being purchased from an outside supplier like Hesston until it was eventually phased out all together.

Mowers. The 10 series mower was still a popular sickle bar machine with the E10 rear-mounted and the

T10 trail-type mower. The 400 rotary-cutter was replaced with the 66 rotary-cutter which offered either a fully mounted option or a wheel type.

Rakes. The 281 side-delivery rake was replaced by the 400 rake which featured a floating reel and rubber-mounted teeth. It boasted raking an 8-foot swath at 10 mph. The Model 400 rake was the last side-delivery rake Case offered. By the time they were back in the hay and forage equipment business (after the IH acquisition) the side-delivery rake had been replaced by windrowers.

Windrowers. After 1960, the Case windrowers were manufactured by the Hesston Corporation and included four self-propelled and two pull-type models. The 1255 was the first hydrostatic drive model, powered by the Case 188 diesel with 12- and 14-foot headers and a 10-foot pea special. The 1155 was powered by either the Case 188 diesel or the Case 159 gas engine with a variable speed drive with 12-, 14-, or 16-foot headers. The Model 955, available with 10-, 12-, 14-, and 16-foot headers, was the replacement for the 820. The 655, a new small family-size farm unit with an 8-foot header, was also introduced.

Several types of pull-type machines were available. The 9-foot Model 555 had a drum-type reel with folding fingers and a 110-inch conditioner. The 575 pull-type was a 12-foot machine with an 81-inch conditioner. A lighter pull-type machine for grain windrowing only, the 755, was available with a choice of 12-, 16-, and 18-foot cuts. The 755 pivoted down to a 9-foot transport width.

The Model 66 rotary cutter offered a fully-mounted option or the wheel-type shown here.

The 400 side-delivery rake replaced the 281 and featured a floating reel and rubber teeth for raking a 12-foot swath at 10 miles per hour. This model is the drawbar-mounted version.

The 650, and later the 655, windrower was available with an 8-foot header targeted for the family-sized farm.

The 950/955 was a replacement for the 820 with a choice of 10-, 12-, 14-, or 16-foot headers and was powered by the Case A125 air-cooled engine.

The 1150/155 windrower was a variable speed drive and was powered by either a Case 188 diesel engine or a Case 159 gasoline engine. Either 12-, 14-, or 16-foot headers were available.

Forage Harvesters. The 300 was a replacement for the 200 forage harvester. The 300 cut slices as short as 13/64 inches or as long as 2 1/8 inches. The 300, like the 200, was a dual-purpose machine with a 2-row and a 1-row corn head (rather than just a single row like the 200), a 61-inch windrow pick-up, and a 90-inch draper cutterbar.

After 1972, mower and forage harvester production were phased out at Case. The windrower agreement with Hesston had been unstable since 1963 when Hesston wanted to concentrate on producing windrowers for the markets west of the Mississippi. Hesston also wanted Case to take their first year production units, Case had previously only taken enough first-year units to test and started buying production quantities the second year, so windrowers also started phasing out.

1985 to the 1990s

As with the baler, from 1985 to about 1988, IH was buying the rest of the hay and forage equipment from New Idea. The Hay & Forage Industries venture of 1987 produced as many as nine different models of mower conditioners: three models of self-propelled windrowers, four models of flail-type windrowers, and two models of forage harvesters.

Mower Conditioners. The mower conditioners featured intermeshing rubber on steel or TICOR conditioning rolls, conventional PTO-driven models, center-pivot models with hydraulic header drives, and sickle bar or disc mowers for cutting. The disc-mower design consisted of sickle sections mounted on several discs and captured the best of both worlds with the simplic-

The 300 forage harvester replaced the 200 series and was also a dual-purpose machine. It offered both a 1-row and a 2-row corn harvester, a 61-inch windrow pickup, and a 90-inch draper cutter bar.

This Case IH 8380 mower conditioner was a center-pivot model with a hydraulic header drive that gave the operator the capacity and maneuverability of a self-propelled windrower.

This 8840 windrower was a heavy-duty commercial hay harvester with heavy-duty beam construction, two-speed hydrostatic drive, and a hydraulic header drive.

ity of the rotary mower and the smooth cut of the sickle. The disc mower was especially effective in cutting wet fields, dense hay, or tangled grass.

Windrowers. The self-propelled windrowers of this era featured larger diesel engines from 70 to 98 horsepower. These units also had two-speed hydrostatic propulsion drives and hydraulic header drives. The pull-type units featured double swath windrowing and steerable tail wheels for improved maneuverability.

Forage Harvesters. The forage harvesters were available with a 72- or 90-inch windrow pick-up, two-row crop unit (adjustable for narrow or wide), and a three-row 30-inch crop unit.

The PTO-driven 781 forage harvester was available with either a 72- or a 90-inch windrow pickup. Row units were also available in a two-row unit that was adjustable for narrow or wide spacing or a three-row unit for 30-inch spacing.

Harvesting Equipment

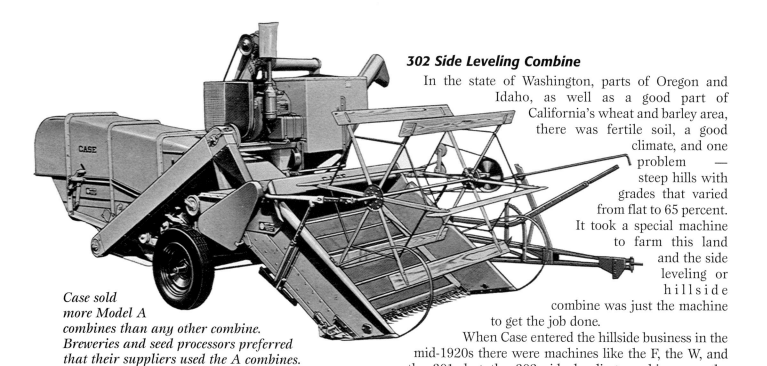

Case sold more Model A combines than any other combine. Breweries and seed processors preferred that their suppliers used the A combines.

Case Combines (1955 to 1972)

The Model A, built from 1938 until 1956, was the most popular and certainly the largest number of any model Case combine ever sold. The Model A, or A-6 as it was sometimes called, was a pull-type combine with a 6-foot header. The secret to the A's success started at the winged-tooth feeding auger located ahead of the cylinder. The auger wings on the side fed the crop to the center of the two-winged tooth beater. This beater fed the grain "heads first" to the 27-inch wide cylinder in a smooth stream of even thickness. Another part of the Model A's success was the extra-long straw walker (111 inches) which provided a long stream (over 9 feet) of straw which moved steadily through the machine eliminating bunching and "dead spots" that caused clogging and waste grain. This, together with a "Bottom Bouncing" agitation, assured complete separation of seed and straw. Seed crop processors and breweries used the A as a standard by which all combines were judged. The grain or seed from the A was always clean and definitely less cracked than other combines.

302 Side Leveling Combine

In the state of Washington, parts of Oregon and Idaho, as well as a good part of California's wheat and barley area, there was fertile soil, a good climate, and one problem — steep hills with grades that varied from flat to 65 percent. It took a special machine to farm this land and the side leveling or hillside combine was just the machine to get the job done.

When Case entered the hillside business in the mid-1920s there were machines like the F, the W, and the 301; but the 302 side leveling combine was the machine of the 1950s. Introduced in 1957, it was built for several years. The trick of hillside combining was to

The Model 302 side leveling combine was introduced in 1957 and replaced the 301.

124

The leveling of the Model 302 was done with a double swing frame and a rack-and-pinion arrangement on the drive axles, so when one wheel went down, the other came up at the same time and distance.

keep the threshing part of the machine level while the header followed the contour of the field. The machine leveling was done with a rack-and-pinion arrangement on the drive axles and a double swing frame, so that as one wheel went down, the other wheel came up at the

The operator kept the machine level by watching two level gauges, one on the front of the grain tank for fore-and-aft level and another in front of the steering wheel for side-to-side leveling. The leveling lever was located under the steering wheel.

same time and to the same distance to keep the combine level. A master cylinder on this same wheel or axle swing frame tilted the header to match the slope and keep the header parallel to the ground. The operator had two level gauges to keep his orientation as to what was level, one in front of the steering wheel for cross level and one on the side of the grain bin for fore-and-aft level. He kept his eye on the ball and his hand on the leveling lever, trying to keep the ball in the center of the gauge.

SP 800 and SP 1000

In 1959 Case introduced the SP 800 and SP 1000 self-propelled combines. The 800 was a replacement for the SP 150 and the 1000 was a new larger addition to the combine line. The 800 had a 32-inch cylinder and offered a choice of 10-, 12-, or 14-foot headers. The 1000 was a 42-inch machine offering a choice of 12-, 14-, or 16-foot headers. Both machines were powered by the Case 284-cubic-inch 4-cylinder Powerdyne gasoline engine — the same engine was used in the 30 series tractors. These combines had variable-speed belt-reel drives, power steering, and a concave drop pin that let the operator clear the cylinder without leaving the seat. The cylinder speed could be adjusted on the go (from 500 to 1,300 rpm) and featured a tachometer on the platform that indicated cylinder speed. Concave clearance could also be adjusted on the go. Both machines also offered two-row corn heads, but while the 1000 operated very well in most grains, it did not perform well in corn and rice.

The 600

The 600 combine was introduced in 1962 and was probably the most successful self-propelled combine Case ever produced. The 600 was available in a choice

The Model 1000 combine was a 42-inch cylinder machine with variable-speed belt-reel drives, power steering, and a concave pin drop to let the operator clear out the concave without leaving the platform. Cylinder speed and concave clearance could be changed on the go.

The 600 and 660 combines were the most successful self-propelled combines Case produced. They had a 40-inch cylinder with 4,440 square inches of separating area plus 2,663 square inches of cleaning area.

of either 10- or 13-foot headers and it had a 40-inch wide cylinder with 4,480 square inches of separating area, plus 2,663 square inches of cleaning area. The 600 was priced at $5,956.50. It had 53% more cylinder width, 32% more separating area, 35% more cleaning area, at almost $1,000 less than most of the leading combines in this size class. The 600 was powered by he

Two-row corn heads were also available on the 600 and 660 combines.

same diesel engine used in the 430 and 530 tractors. In 1967 the 600 was upgraded to the 660 and offered a 14-foot grain header, as well as two-row corn heads. The Case 201-cubic-inch gasoline engine was standard with the 188 diesel as optional on the 660. Both the 600 and the 660 offered two-row corn heads and were built at the Case plant in Bettendorf, Iowa.

The 700 and 1010 Combines

In 1963 Case introduced the 700 and 1010 combines. The 700 filled the gap between the 600 series and the 1000 or 1010 series. The separating area on the 700 was increased to 4,640 square inches from the 4,480 on the 600 and 660 with the long straw walker return pans that increased cleaning shoe efficiency. The 700 also had a larger engine — a 225-cubic-inch Chrysler slant six at 70 horsepower. The 700 had a 40-inch cylinder and offered 10-, 13-, and 14-foot headers, as well as a two-row corn head. The 700 was replaced by the 900 in 1964 and the separating area was increased to 5,080 square inches. In 1969 the engine horsepower was increased to 85 and a choice of two- or three-row corn heads were added. At that time the model number was changed to 960.

The Model 1010 was an upgrade of the 1000, as it kept the strengths of the 1000 and eliminated the weaknesses. It duplicated the 600's popularity. The 1010 was

The 700 combine was introduced in 1963 to fill the gap between the 600 series and the 1000 series. The 700 had a 40-inch cylinder but more cleaning area (4,640 square inches). The 700 was powered by a 70-horsepower Chrysler slant six gasoline engine.

The 660 was powered by a Case 201 gasoline engine as standard but the 188 diesel engine was an option.

an excellent machine and had all the operator conveniences of the 600 including the tralings check that was right on the platform at the operator's elbow. The 1010 had a 42-inch cylinder with 5,754 square inches of separating area and offered 12-, 14-, 16-, and 18-foot headers, as well as a two- or three-row corn head. The 1010 standard power was a Hercules 293-cubic-inch gasoline engine. Optional power was a Case 284 gasoline or LP gas engine or a 301 Case diesel engine. In 1967 and 1968 the 1010 was replaced by the 1060 grain combine and the corn special combine. They were an upgrade to machines with a more powerful Chrysler V-8 gasoline engine with 318 cubic inches and 88 horsepower as standard equipment. The Case 284 and 301 engines were still offered for the grain machines. A new operator's compartment

with a suspension seat, telescoping steering wheel, and a more comfortable cab were also offered. The 1160 corn special had a new corn head featuring three narrow rows for 28- to 30-inch spacing or four narrow rows (28 to 30 inches) or four wide rows (36, 38, or 40 inches) along with an LP gas 318-cubic-inch V-8 engine (the Case 301 diesel was also available). The 1060 grain combine also introduced an 18-foot grain head at that time (1967).

The 1060 combine was an upgrade of the 1010 with a more powerful Chrysler V-8 engine that had 318 cubic inches and 88 horsepower. The Case 284 and 301 engines were still offered as an option for the grain machines.

The 1660 grain combine and the 1665 Corn Special were the largest combines Case ever built with 52-inch cylinders and 90- to 100-bushel grain bins. The design had been pushed too far and in 1972 Case announced they were getting out of the combine business.

The 1660 Grain Combine and the 1665 Corn Special

The 1660 grain combine and the 1665 corn special were the largest combines Case ever built. The cylinders were 52 inches wide and the grain bins were expanded from 90 to 100 bushels. But in 1972 Case announced it was getting out of the combine business. Their combine designs were more than 10 years old and the company's market share was less than 7% — the payback on a new

design would take too long at these low volumes. It was a tough call — on the one hand the 1660 and 1665 were proof that the design was out of date, they did not perform to expectations. On the other hand, by dropping combines Case ceased to be a full-line company. Many predicted Case would have to return to a full-line status to survive — they were right. It took 13 years but Case returned to a full-line company in 1985 and in the process acquired the best combine on the market, the Axial-Flow combine from IH.

In 1985 Case acquired the best combine on the market, the Axial-Flow combine from IH. The Axial-Flow system featured a single in-line rotor with an impeller on the front of the rotor and a stationary rotor housing, with concaves and separating grates.

Axial-Flow Combines

1958 to 1990s

Time For Change. Starting in the late 1950s and through the '60s and '70s, the pressure for greater combine capacity was relentless. The cylinders kept getting wider, the straw walkers were getting longer, the engines had more horsepower, and grain bins were getting bigger. All of these factors meant that the combines were larger and heavier. As a result, these combines were harder to transport and could get stuck easier. All manufacturers faced the same problems with the farm economy growing, exports booming, and bankers encouraging farmers to invest in machinery and land. Larger machines were the demand.

By the early 1970s the conventional threshing methods were becoming overloaded and the straw walkers were the first to feel the brunt of it. Grain losses became unacceptable, plugging was unbearable in tough crop conditions, and larger grain bins began to compete for space with the threshing mechanism. It was a losing battle from a design standpoint and it was time to start with a clean sheet of paper. That's just what IH did. It took 15 years of development and a million man hours to design, build, and test, but in 1977 IH introduced the 1440, 1460, and 1480 Axial-Flow series of combines.

The Axial-Flow system featured a single in-line rotor with an impeller on the front of the rotor and a stationary rotor housing with concaves and separating grates. This simple system replaced the cylinder, rear beater, and straw walkers of the conventional combine design. The impeller on the front of the rotor drew the crop in and accelerated it to threshing speed prior to its contact with the rotor, rub bar, and concave. This technique allowed the crop to enter the rotor with less impact than a crop entering the cylinder, rub bar, and concave on a conventional machine. The single longitudinal rotor threshed and separated the crop as it rotated through the stationary rotor housing between the rotor, rub bar, and the housing. The grain moved around the housing with a centrifugal force 40 times greater than the gravity used on straw walkers of conventional machines which gave the Axial-Flow a cleaner product with less damage in one pass than a conventional combine that ran the grain through several times. The grain dropped out of the housing and augers moved the grain to the cleaning sieves. Opposed-action adjustable sieves removed the chafe from the grain. A cleaning fan with a variable speed drive removed any chafe and foreign material that remained. This simple, gentle, highly-effective threshing system was proven to be the best at harvesting quality grain.

The 1440 and 1460 Axial-Flow combines had 24-inch rotors that were 9 feet long, the 1480 had a 30-inch rotor of the same length. The 1400 series were powered by the IH 466 engine, the various horsepower ratings were achieved with naturally aspirated turbocharged and turbocharged/intercooled versions. The horsepower and grain tank size were: the 1440 — 135 horsepower and 145 bushels; the 1460 — 170 horsepower and 180 bushels; and the 1480 — 190 horsepower and 208 bushels.

It took 15 years and a million man hours to design, build, and test, but in 1977 IH introduced the 1440, 1460, and 1480 Axial-Flow series of combines.

This 1400 series combine had a pick up header. The 1400's were powered by the IH 466 engine: the 1440 at 135 horsepower, the 1460 at 170 horsepower, and the 1480 at 190 horsepower.

The Second Generation Axial-Flow Combines (1985-1990s)

In 1985, under the Case IH logo, the second generation Axial-Flow combines were introduced with higher horsepower, increased elevator capacity, and a new feeder reverser. The Series 1000 corn and grain heads were also introduced and were designed specifically for the Axial-Flow machines with increased cutting speeds to match the larger combines. The Second Generation machines also had increased horsepower: the 1640, which replaced the 1440, went from 135 to 150 horsepower; the 1660, which replaced the 1460, went from 170 to 180 horsepower; and the 1680, which replaced the 1480, went from 190 to 225 horsepower. The 1620 was a new machine with a 20-inch rotor at 124 horsepower and had a 125-bushel grain tank. In 1985 the Navistar engines were still being used, but by 1989 they had been replaced with increased horsepower Consolidated Diesel engines (the joint

venture of Case and Cummins Engine Company). For example, the 1620 increased to 145 horsepower, the 1640 to 160 horsepower, the 1660 to 190 horsepower, and the 1680 to 235 horsepower. By 1993 the 1644 was up to 180 horsepower and the 1688 was at 260 horsepower.

The Axial-Flow combine, in addition to having fewer moving parts and fewer problems, had many excellent design features, such as:

- A three-section concave that one man could quickly change if he wanted to harvest corn in the morning and beans in the afternoon.
- A rear-mounted engine that provided more balance and serviceability. The large roomy service deck provided easy access to the engine, hydraulic reservoir, and fuel tank. A folding rear deck ladder gave access to the deck.
- A shaft speed monitor checked nine functions: (1) the clean grain elevator; (2) the tailings elevator; (3) the cleaning fan; (4) the rotor; (5) the shoe sieve; (6) the straw chopper; (7) the straw spreader; (8) the feeder; (9) the rotary air screen. Should the shaft speed of any of these components slow down to 70% of its normal speed, an audible and visual alarm would alert the operator.
- As the grain and crop residue passed through the rotor, the grain loss monitor had four electronic sensors that generated electronic signals. It distinguished grain from residue and

The Case IH 1600 series were the second generation of Axial-Flow combines and were powered by CDC engines. A new, smaller version was also added to the line — the 1620.

This Model 1640 combine was equipped with a flexible cutterbar header. The 1640 and 1644 had a 24-inch rotor, 9-feet long and a 145-bushel grain bin. The 1644 was powered by a 359-cubic-inch 180-horsepower CDC engine.

This Model 1660 combine was equipped with a 6-row corn head. The 1660 and 1666 had a 24-inch rotor, 9-feet long and a 180-bushel grain bin. The 1666 was powered by a 505-cubic-inch 215-horsepower CDC engine.

This 1680 combine was equipped with a pick up header. The 1680 and 1688 had a 30-inch rotor, 9-feet long and a 210-bushel grain bin. The 1688 was powered by a 505-cubic-inch 280-horsepower CDC engine.

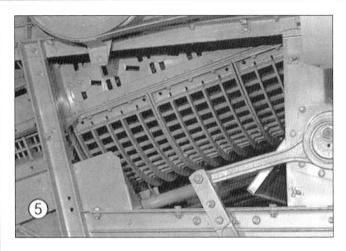

The Axial-Flow combine was equipped with a three-section concave that one man could quickly change — so he could be harvesting corn in the morning and beans in the afternoon.

The rear-mounted engine provided more balance to the machine and easier serviceability for the operator. The large deck provided easy access to the engine, hydraulic reservoir, and fuel tank.

The feeder reverser allowed the operator to avoid serious plugging. If a heavy slug entered the feeder, the operator simply stopped the combine and reversed the feeder to clear the slug.

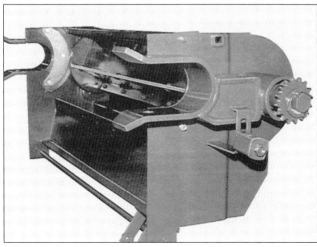

The rock trap allowed the operator to cut closer to the ground in rock-infested fields. Located between the feeder and the rotor, a powerful beater knocked the rocks out of the incoming material. The trapped rocks could be removed at the operator's convenience.

The shaft speed monitor (left) checked nine different functions. Should the shaft speed of any of the nine functions slow down to 70% of its normal speed, an audible and visual alarm would alert the operator.

The grain loss monitor (right) had four electronic sensors that distinguished grain loss from residue and gave a digital readout of any grain loss.

the cab-mounted monitor gave a digital readout of grain loss.

- The feeder reverser allowed the operator to stop the combine and push a button to reverse the feeder and clear a slug if one should enter the feeder.
- The rock trap, a powerful beater located between the feeder and rotor, knocked rocks out of the incoming material, allowing close-to-the-ground operation.
- The stone retarder drum helped retard other foreign objects from entering the combine.

The most efficient combine on the market, the Axial-Flow combine, truly overshadowed its conventional counterparts as the most efficient combine on the market. It could be operated at the fastest practical ground speed and still turn out cleaner grain, have less grain damage, fewer fines, and still be easier to dry. The Axial-Flow combine simply squeezed out more bushels per acre.

In 1988, *Fortune* magazine chose the Axial-Flow combine as one of America's 100-best products. The Axial-Flow combine was manufactured at the Case IH plant in East Moline, Illinois.

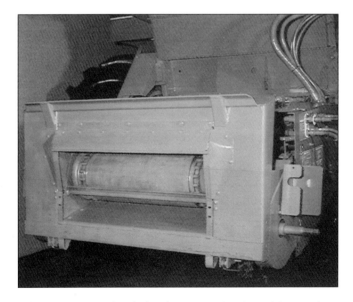

The stone retarder helped prevent foreign objects other than rocks from entering the combine.

The 1644, 1666, and 1688 were the family of Axial-Flow combines of the mid-1990s.

Hillside combines, like these 1670's, have come a long way since the Case 302. Electronics, microcomputers, and hydrostatic drives have simplified the operation tremendously.

Specialty Combines

Case IH offered three specialty combines in the Axial-Flow line: the 1682 pull-type combine, the 1670 hillside combine, and the 1680E European combine. The 1682 was designed to work with 130+ PTO horsepower tractors and had a 245-bushel grain tank. The 1670 hillside combine, with a 145-bushel grain tank, was equipped with a 235-horsepower CDC engine and was designed to level the separator on slopes as steep as 48 degrees. The 1670 also offered two- and four-wheel hydrostatic drive. The 1680E, an Axial-Flow rice combine, was also available with a specialty rotor and either flotation tires or a track drive. The 1680E was targeted for the European market which had to meet certain EEC directives such as sound levels, rotating beacons at the front and rear of the machine, as well as many other regulations.

The 1682 was a pull-type combine designed to work with a 130+ PTO horsepower tractors.

Case Cotton Harvesters

In August of 1927, the Case Board of Director's authorized an investigation into the possibilities of building a cotton harvester. Little more is recorded of these efforts except that in the collection of machines at the Case Museum there is a Case-built cotton picker which must have been a prototype.

In 1969 a new brush cotton stripper was introduced with a choice of either a trailer model or a basket model. The brush design had nylon brushes and rubber paddles that stripped the cotton from the plants. The basket had a capacity of 435 cubic feet and dumped hydraulically to the front. The stripper was produced at three different plants, first Anniston, Alabama, then at Burlington, Iowa, and finally at Bettendorf, Iowa, where production was discontinued in 1972.

In the early 1950s Case dealers in the Memphis, Tennessee branch area started selling the Rust cotton strippers mounted on DC tractors. By 1954 they had convinced Case management to buy the rights to the Rust cotton stripper from Ben Pearson who was probably better known for his archery skill and ability (like splitting an arrow shaft stuck in a target with another arrow in a Robin Hood movie) than cotton strippers. In 1954 Case was selling the Case Model 201 cotton stripper that could be mounted on Case DC, SC, or IH Farmall M tractors. The 201 was a two-row stripper designed for 40-inch row spacing. In 1955 Case adopted the 201 to the Case 400 series tractors as well as adding the Farmall H, Super M, and MD; the Oliver 77; and the Massey Harris 44 to the adaptable tractor list. A pair of stalk rollers were also offered for use where cotton was not firmly rooted. The rollers were attached under the stripping rolls, but turned in the opposite direction pulling down on the uprooted cotton stalk preventing it from entering the stripping unit and lodging in the augers.

This Model 201 cotton stripper was mounted on a 400 tractor. Case purchased the rights to the Rust cotton stripper in the early 1950s and manufactured them until 1972.

Model "201"

2-Row

CASE

COTTON STRIPPER

...for storm-resistant tight-locked cotton varieties

135

This Case basket model brush cotton stripper was mounted on a 930 tractor. These Case cotton strippers were also adapted for the Farmall H, Super M, and the MD; the Oliver 77; and the Massey Harris 44.

Case IH Cotton Pickers

1985 to 1990s

In 1985 Case IH offered two cotton picker models — the two-row 1822 and the four-row 1844 for 38- and 40-inch rows, respectively. The 1822 and 1844 were powered by the Navistar 466 engine. One of the most significant features of these machines was power-meter unloading. Instead of simply tipping the basket to unload, the basket was raised straight up and the basket door opened. The door acted as a spout and the conveyor system metered out the cotton without spilling or having to get up in the basket and manually fork the cotton out. If the operator was topping off a container when it was full, the door simply closed in the middle of unloading and the picker moved to another container. In an uninterrupted cycle, one person could lift, unload, and return to the field in 40 seconds with one hand and a single lever. The basket could be lowered to 12 feet 6 inches for transport.

The XPE Cotton Express

In 1990 the 1822 picker engine horsepower was increased from 150 to 160 horsepower and the 1844 picker remained at 215 horsepower with increased fuel

In 1985 Case IH offered two cotton picker models — the 1822 two-row and four-row and the 1844 (shown here) for 38- and 40-inch rows. The 1822 and 1844 were powered by Navistar 466 engines.

One of the most significant features of the Case IH cotton picker is the power-metered unloading system. Instead of simply tipping the basket to unload, the basket is raised straight up and the door opens and acts like a spout.

economy as a result of the installation of the CDC engine (XPE is eXtra Power and Economy). The automatic lubrication of the picker bar and bearing caps was also introduced in 1990. The automatic lubrication system was controlled by an onboard computer that could be programmed to the operating cycle based on drum cycle. Therefore, if the operator was operating at speeds less than full speed, he could program in a longer time between lube cycles. The lube cycle programming could be done according to the number of row units. For example, the recommended time for a four-row machine was 8 minutes after the alarm went off. The operator stopped the machine, activated the drum bypass switch, and pressed the drum lube switch — the grease pump operated and provided grease to the picker bar and bearing caps.

The 30-Inch Narrow Row Breakthrough

In 1991 Case IH introduced the 2055 Cotton Express®, a four- or five-row narrow cotton picker that would pick cotton planted in 30-inch wide rows. For well over 20 years farmers had been experiencing improved yields from narrow row spacing in corn and soybeans. Until the 1990s cotton farmers were limited to the traditional 38- and 40-inch row spacing because

Once the door is open, the conveyor system meters out the cotton without spilling or necessitating the operator to get up in the basket and fork the cotton out. If the operator is topping off a container and it becomes full, he can simply close the door in the middle of unloading and go to the next container.

137

Twelve Case IH 2055 five-row cotton pickers owned by a single operator working in the field.

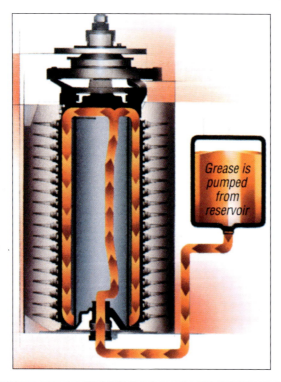

The automatic picker bar and bearing cap lubrication system on the XPE Cotton Express was controlled by an onboard computer that could be programmed to the operating cycle based on drum operating speeds. If operating at less than full speed, a longer time between cycles could be programmed.

Grease is pumped from reservoir

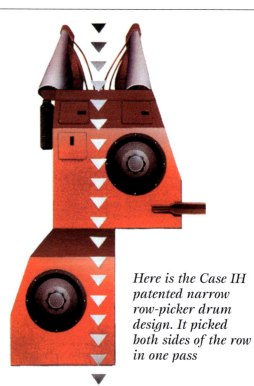

Here is the Case IH patented narrow row-picker drum design. It picked both sides of the row in one pass

The Cotton Express® pickers had an operator presence system which stopped the drum rotation any time the transmission was in neutral and the operator left the seat. A tether switch stored in a drum allowed him to slowly rotate the drum for inspection.

there were no pickers that could handle rows that narrow. The introduction of the 2055 gave them the best of both worlds as it was designed to pick four or five 30-inch rows or four 38- or 40-inch rows. Deere and Co. introduced their 9960 narrow row cotton picker in 1990 with a picker that had two drums per row (one following the other), but it only picked from the right side of the row. Case IH engineers decided to pick cotton the proven and most efficient way. In all conditions it was most efficient to pick from both sides of the row with one drum following the other. The

narrow spacing was achieved by completely changing the design of the drum drives from sprockets and chains to a more compact and efficient gear drive.

The second generation Case IH Cotton Express® pickers were the 2022, which was a two-row unit designed for conventional row spacing of 38 or 40 inches, and the 2055. These new machines introduced some interesting new features, such as the operator presence system which was designed to enhance safe operation without interfering with the field operation or maintenance. It stopped the drum rotation any time the transmission was in neutral and the operator left the seat. This feature allowed the operator to slowly rotate the drum for inspection and maintenance with a momentary tether switch stored in a drum. The power on the 2055 was increased to 260 horsepower from 215 horsepower on the 1844.

Case IH also offered the 1800, a four- or six-row self-propelled cotton stripper. The 1800 featured the power-metered unloading system and hydraulically-driven stripper units rather than drive belt and shafts. The Case IH cotton pickers were manufactured at the East Moline, Illinois plant.

Corn Pickers (1955 to 1960)

Corn pickers were phasing out in the 1950s and '60s do to the popularity and safety afforded by corn combines. Case produced the single-row Model P pull-type and the two-row mounted 425 corn picker. Corn pickers lost their popularity for several reasons. The trend in the late 1960s was away from dual front wheels on tractors and focused more on an increased use of adjustable front axles which made pickers impossible to mount. Another reason for their loss in popularity was the inability to quickly put the picker on or take it off. This could "tie" up the tractor in very busy seasons and was not desirable. The Model 425 was the last corn picker produced by Case.

This Model 425 corn picker was mounted on a 730 tractor.

139

Agricultural Material Handling Equipment

The problem of feeding and also cleaning up after livestock grew as there were fewer farmers feeding more livestock. In the beginning it was very simple, the livestock were moved to the feed and the waste took care of itself. As demand increased, however, the process was speeded up and the whole approach had to change. In the 1950s as "lot-type" feeding was growing in popularity, the material handling of these products was changing so that the "fewer farmers" could do more — and more efficiently. Prior to this time, farm wagons hauled the feed in and manure spreaders hauled the waste out. In the beginning of the decade the Case VW-S farm wagon with steel wheels and a horse pole

In the 1950s the Model VW-S steel wheel farm wagon was still available with an optional horse pole or a tractor tongue.

was still offered but as the decade progressed the VWTA and the G-20 wagon came in offering rubber tires with taper roller wheel bearings. With these new wagons, wheel tread increased to 66 inches and the bolster stakes went from 38- and 42-inch box sills to 46- and 50-inch sills.

By the end of the decade Case had teamed up with Helix to produce a new breed of wagon — the 90- to 125-bushel T100 and the 110- to 140-bushel T200 auger unloaders. They automatically filled the feeders and feed bunks. The G portable hammer mill ground grain or hay and blew it directly into the auger unloaders. Case-Helix also promoted an "Erector Set" type build up where the farmer could start with a 100-bushel grain box on a farm truck, then add a conveyor floor, add extension sides and beaters, and finally a bunk feeder. The result was that the wagon grew with the farmer's needs.

Farm Loaders. The typical farm loader of this era was the 150 which was built at the Case plant in Rockford, Illinois. The manure spreaders had grown from the 50- and 75-bushel spreaders to the 105- and 125-bushel spreaders, PTO-driven spreaders, and 75- to 95-bushel, ground-driven spreaders. All models had chain-driven beaters.

The VWTA was one of the early farm wagons to offer tapered roller bearing wheels in the mid-1950s. The farm wagons were manufactured at the Case plant in Burlington, Iowa.

STANDARD TREAD IN 4 MODELS
1. "VWTA-S," has tapered roller bearing disk wheels with 6.00 — 16, 4-ply implement tires and tractor hitch, steel clevis type.
2. "VWTA," has tapered roller bearing disk wheels, 6.00 — 16, 4-ply implement tires and horse pole.
3. "VW-S," has 28 x 4-inch plain bearing steel wheels with tractor hitch, eye bolt type.
4. "VW," has 24 x 4-inch plain bearing steel wheels and horse pole.
(See Specifications — Back Cover)

CASE

MODEL "VWTA-S"

Illustrating below the extreme short turning of a Case Farm Truck. A minimum inside turning radius of 8 feet is unusual in a farm truck.

STANDARD TREAD IN **4** MODELS
for All Farm Hauling

One of the innovations of spreaders in the 1960s was this V-belt driven beater. It was smoother and put less strain on the beaters and shafts, especially in cold weather.

As bunker feeding allowed fewer farmers to do more, the auger unloader like this Case Helix Model T-100, became popular with the livestock farmers of the late 1950s/early 1960s. The T-100 had a 125-bushel capacity.

The 1960s

Manure Spreaders. The manure spreaders grew in the 1960s as the Case line now included 100-, 115-, 135-, 140-, and 180-bushel machines, all PTO driven. This era also produced another Case first, the V-belt driven beaters that were smoother and applied less strain on the beaters and shafts.

Farm Loaders. The Rockford-built farm loaders of the 1960s were the 190, 393, and 295. The 190,

The farm loaders of the 1960s, like this 190 designed for the 430 and 530 series tractors, had 2-inch single-acting cylinders and a 40-inch bucket.

intended for the 430 and 530 tractors, was a light-duty loader with 2-inch single-acting cylinders, a 40-inch bucket, and a dump height of 8 feet. The 393 loader had 2-1/2-inch cylinders and was also used by the 430 and 530. The 295 loader was intended for the 730 and 830 tractors with 3,000 pounds of break out and a dump height of 9 feet.

Elevators. The elevators of the 1960s were the A50 double chain 21-inch elevator, expandable from 26 to 62 feet. The Model 55 auger elevator had a 1,200-bushel-per-hour capacity with a 6-inch auger and was expandable from 27 to 52 feet.

Farm Wagons. The farm wagons from the 1960s were the 8,000-pound RW4 with a 62-inch tread and the 12,000-pound RW6 with a 72-inch tread.

The typical farm loader of the mid-1950s was this Case Rockford-built 150 farm loader shown here loading a 105-bushel spreader.

By 1960 farm wagons capacity increased to 12,000-pounds with a 72-inch tread like this Model RW6.

The 393 farm loader was one of the last Case-produced loaders. The 393 was designed for the 430 and 530 series tractors. Great Bend Manufacturing produced the farm loaders for Case after July of 1970.

The Model A50 double-chain elevator was 21 inches wide and expandable from 26 to 62 feet long. The A50 was produced in the 1960s.

The 1970s

After the Case Rockford plant closed in July of 1970, the 70 series loaders were built for Case by the Great Bend Company of Great Bend, Kansas. The 70 loaders could lift 1,950 pounds up to 10 1/2 feet and had 4,000 pounds of break out with 2-1/2-inch lift and tilt cylinders. The 70 series fit the 1175, 1170, 1070, 970, 870, 770, 570, 470, and all the 30 series tractors. The 75 high-lift loader, which lifted to 16 feet, was available for loose or baled hay. The David Brown tractors used the David Brown loader made at the plant in Leigh, Lancashire, England.

In 1969 Case acquired a line of skid steer loaders known as the Uni-Loader from Universal Industries in Hudson, Iowa. The Uni-Loader gained popularity as a material handler on the farm because it was surefooted in slippery yards and pens and could get in and out of places where other farm loaders couldn't operate. In fact, it could turn 360 degrees in its own tracks. In the early 1970s Case started marketing the 1737 and the 1740 Uni-Loader for agricultural use in addition to its already established construction equipment market.

A Model 70 loader on a 1070 tractor. The 70 series loaders were designed for the 30 series tractors, as well as the 470's, 570's, 770's, 870's, 970's, 1070's, 1170, and 1175 tractors.

For the large feed lot, the W14 Feed Lot Special articulated loader was ideal. It featured a 2-cubic-yard bucket with a hydraulic grapple and bucket teeth as standard and it also had a full power shift transmission with a torque converter. The W14 was an excellent choice for speed and capacity.

1980 to 1985

The material handling in the early 1980s consisted essentially of the same type as during the 1970s with some additions. The 1816 Uni-Loader was added and

The 1737 Uni-Loader was first marketed for agricultural use in the early 1970s. The 1737 and 1740 Uni-Loaders were very successful in this market because they could turn 360 degrees in their own tracks and could operate where other farm loaders couldn't.

The W14 "Feed Lot Special" was an articulated loader especially equipped for feed lots with a 2-cubic-yard bucket and a hydraulic grapple as standard equipment.

The 1816 Uni-Loader was an immediate success because it could go where only wheelbarrows had gone before — it was only 35 inches wide.

was an immediate success because it could go where only wheelbarrows had gone previously — it was only 35 inches wide and could go through 36-inch doors. The 1835 and 1845 were new models and had Case engines. The 1835 was 54 inches wide so it could maneuver through a 5-foot gate in a livestock shelter and work under the 7-foot roof. It could still work outside the shelter loading and unloading trucks with its 9-foot 2-inch lift height. The 1845 was the big capacity machine with a 1,700-pound lift capacity and the 9-foot 9-inch lifting height.

The 70 series and David Brown farm loader were replaced by the Case Quick-Attach loaders produced by Great Bend for Case from 1980 until 1985. The Quick-Attach meant that the loader and frame (with the control valve) could be attached or detached from the tractor in minutes and the mounting brackets were all that remained on the tractor. The 56L was used for the 1190 through the 1390. The 66L mounted on the 1490 and the 1690. The 90 Quick-Attach was mounted on the over-100-horsepower tractors, the 970 through the 1370.

1988 to 1994

Under the Case IH logo the farm loaders were manufactured at the Case IH plant in Hamilton, Ontario. Sixteen loaders fit all the Case and Case IH 94 series, Case IH and International 85 series Doncaster tractors, Maxxum, Magnum Case and Case IH 90 series, Case IH 96 series, International 66 and 86 series, International 88 series, and Case IH 235, 245, 255 compact tractors.

The Uni-Loader models were produced in the Burlington, Iowa plant. The 1818, 1825, 1835c, 1840, and 1845C Uni Loaders had bucket dump heights from

The 66L Quick-Attach loaders fit on the 1490 and 1690 tractors. The Quick-Attach loaders could be taken on and off of the the tractor quickly because the control valve stayed with the loader on all that was left on the tractor was a compact bracket. The hydraulics were attached to the tractor remote couplers with the quick disconnects.

The 90 L loaders were designed for 1896 and 2096 tractors and produced at the Case IH plant at Hamilton, Ontario, Canada. The 90L was replaced by the Model 96 loader.

The Case Ih Model 1580 manure spreader was the largest capacity spreader in the line with a capacity of 318 bushels.

96 to 116 inches. By the mid-1990s Case IH was offering six models of Uni-Loaders for agricultural material handling ranging from 18 to 60 horsepower.

Model	Gross Hp	Operating Load (lb)	Dump Height at Hinge Pin (in.)
1818 gas	18	550	96
1825 gas	25	800	98
1825 diesel	25	800	98
1835C gas	47	1,200	110.5
1840 diesel	54	1,350	110.5
1845C diesel	60	1,700	116.75

Forage Blowers. The Model 600 was the forage blower of this era and had a 60-inch rotor to efficiently blow haylage and corn silage into the tallest silos. The 600 had automatic air inlet control to help prevent pipe plugging.

Manure Spreaders. The 1500 series manure spreaders of the 1990 to the mid-1990s era came in six different models with heaped capacities from 148 to 318 cubic feet. It also carried a lifetime original owner warrantee on the steel fronts and sides. They had a reinforced 6-inch channel steel hitch A-frame through the cross members and side panels. A tough polyethylene bonded floor was designed to ensure good cleanout under the most adverse conditions.

Model	Heaped Capacity (cubic feet)
1530	142
1540	189
1550	196
1560	230
1570	279
1580	318

Bale Processor. The Model 8610 bale processor was new for the 1990s and could shred as many as 10 big round bales per hour and would distribute it to low bunks or to the ground.

Grinder Mixers. Two Model 1300 grinder mixers were available in 105- and 150-bushel sizes that could grind up to 120,000-pounds of shelled corn per hour.

The Case IH bale processor could handle most any size and weight bale — round bales up to 6 1/2 feet in diameter, as well as small round bales, rectangular bales, and loose hay.

The Case IH grinder mixers came in two sizes, 105 and 150 bushel, and could grind up to 120,000 pounds of shelled corn per hour.

Outdoor Power Equipment

Case entered into the compact tractor market in November of 1964 with the purchase of Colt Manufacturing, who made two models of garden tractors and some implements. Colt started in Milwaukee, Wisconsin, in 1962 making one of the first hydraulic-drive compact tractors which was introduced in 1963. Colt moved to Winneconne, Wisconsin, in 1963. From 1964 until mid-1966 the compact tractors were distributed through the Colt distribution system under both the Colt and Case brand names. This distribution system was ineffective and unsuccessful, so in 1966 Case dropped the Colt line and bought out the former stockholders and directors. At this point Case began concentrating on signing up their agricultural dealers to handle the distribution.

The first Case models were the 130, a 10-horsepower tractor, and the 180, a 12-horsepower tractor. Both the 130 and the 180 used Kohler four-cycle air-cooled engines and had Case-designed Hydra-Static drives. The pump was driven directly from the engine and the hydraulic motor was mounted on the side of the

From 1964 until mid-1966, the garden tractors were distributed under both Case and Colt brand names (as shown here). The tractors essentially looked the same except the Case tractors were painted Desert Sunset and Flambeau Red and had the hallmark Case black stripe on the hood side. Case dropped the Colt line in 1966.

In 1964 Case purchased Colt Manufacturing Company of Milwaukee, Wisconsin, who made two models of garden tractors and offered some purchased implements like this front-end loader.

This Model 222 Case garden tractor was equipped with a Case-made 44-inch dozer blade. The styling was changed in 1968 to the square front hood and grille cap with the headlamps in the upper grille.

and the 444 high clearance at 14 horsepower. A 50-inch mower was also added.

In 1969 Bill Schlapman, who had been instrumental in the marketing development of the Case loader backhoe, was made General Manager of Garden Tractor Design, Manufacturing, and Marketing. Two new 7-horsepower models were announced, the 107 was a mechanical transmission version and the 117 was a hydrostatic drive version. The styling more resembled the larger 70 series agricultural tractors, including a unitized hood and grille for more convenient servicing. The colors on the entire line of compacts (which was now up to six) were changed to Desert Sunset and Power Red. A 34-inch mower was also added. Many quality improvements were made in manufacturing, for example each tractor received a dynamometer test to insure consistent performance. The distribution system was also being expanded. The outdoor power equipment was becoming a mature, quality product.

transmission case. There were no belts or pulleys to adjust. The appearance of the tractor was similar to the Colt design except for the Desert Sunset and Flambeau Red paint, with the hallmark long black Case stripe on the hood side and the Case eagle on the front grille cap. The rear fenders were squared up in the late 1960s from the original half moons. Case manufactured the rotary mowers in 38- and 44-inch sizes, a dump cart, a hydraulic rotary tiller, and a 44-inch dozer blade. A host of purchased attachments were also available.

In 1968 the hood and grille, along with the head lamps, were changed to a more squared-off appearance. Four models were introduced: the 220 at 10 horsepower, the 222 at 12 horsepower, the 442 high clearance at 12 horsepower,

This 444 high-clearance tractor was rated at 14 horsepower and was equipped with a rototiller.

This Model 107 was a 7-horsepower model with a mechanical transmission. A Model 117 with hydrostatic drive was also introduced in 1969 and the sheet metal resembled the 70 series tractors being built in Racine.

During 1972, the 7-horsepower models were increased to 8-horsepower Briggs and Stratton engines and the 244, a low-profile 14-horsepower model, was introduced. The 600 series was also introduced in 1972, it was a loader/tractor and a loader/backhoe

aimed at the needs of landscapers, nurseries, public works departments, building and public works contractors. These units were impressive and were designed from the ground up. Each had a special integral welded steel frame, a heavy-duty front axle, power steering, tapered roller front wheel bearings — and the hydrostatic transmission was ideal for loader work. The 600 series were powered by 18-horsepower Onan engines with a dual range transaxle. The loader bucket was 44 inches wide with a 600-pound lift capacity. The backhoe had a digging depth to 7 feet 9 inches and the digging radius was 9 feet 3 inches from the swing pivot.

In 1974 compact or garden tractors, as they were sometimes called, became a division of Case — the Outdoor Power Equipment Division.

The Mod 80 riding mower was released in 1977. This unit had a rear-mounted 8-horsepower Briggs and Stratton engine and a mechanical drive transmission.

1978 to 1983

During the next five years Case made many improvements and innovations in the outdoor power equipment line. These improvements included: hydrive and the Case open-hydraulic system for remote controlling attachments from a common transmission hydraulic system; the rear discharge mower; the double-action log splitter that mounted on the back of the tractor — the tractor hydraulics split logs on both the inward stroke as well as the outward stroke; incorporating tilting hoods for service; and the rubber

This 648 loader/backhoe was powered by an 18-horsepower Onan engine and was aimed at the needs of landscapers, nurseries, public work departments, as well as building and public works contractors. The bucket was 44 inches wide and the backhoe had a digging depth of 7 feet 9 inches.

The Mod 80 riding mower was introduced in 1977 and was equipped with an 8-horsepower rear-mounted Briggs and Stratton engine and had a mechanical transmission.

In the late 1970s and early 1980s changes gave the operator more visibility and greater safety from moving belts with protective covers and shields. The colors were also changed to Power Red with white wheels.

engine Iso mounts to suppress vibration for a smoother ride. Several styling changes included: more visibility for the operator, added safety from moving belts with covers and shields, easier mower removal, and a color change from Desert Sunset to all Power red with white wheels and black decals. The Outdoor Power and Equipment Division remained successful and profitable until it was sold by Case to Ingersoll Equipment Company in 1983.

In the 1960s and '70s just about every farm equipment manufacturer was in the compact tractor business — but by the mid-1980s they were all disappearing. Allis-Chalmers was gone, Ford was gone, Massey Ferguson was gone, International Harvester had sold Cub Cadet, and Case sold their modestly profitable Outdoor Power and Equipment Division to Ingersoll Equipment Company. With the ever-shrinking number of agricultural equipment dealers in the depressed agricultural economy of the 1980s, the farm equipment manufacturers distribution system for compact tractors was also shrinking. No one could obtain an adequate share with so many active competitors with larger distribution systems like Sears, discount stores, and hardware stores. These larger distribution systems had the advantage of economies of scale in the compact tractor business.

In 1983 Case sold the Outdoor Power and Equipment Division to Ingersoll Equipment Company.

Construction Equipment

It Started With Steam

Case's involvement in the construction equipment industry dates back to the 1800s and the days of the steam engine. The road machinery line began with steam rollers and road graders. After the steam, however, the line expanded to include crawlers and tractor loaders, towing tractors for baggage carts and aircraft, as well as engines for Gallion graders and tractors, and engines for Caterpillar. In November of 1947, marketing of products for the construction industry became a separate division of the Case Company called the Industrial Division. The new division marketed Case tractors equipped with various attachments made by outside suppliers, such as sweepers, snow plows, and front-end loaders. They also sold a line of products manufactured by Case, such as highway mowers, towing tractors, stationary engines, and industrial tractors.

The Model VAIW, a small-wheeled industrial tractor, was one of the few models Case produced during World War II for warehouse and airport use. The VAIW was produced from the early 1940s until 1953.

By 1954 Case had designed and developed a loader, called the Powerloader, that was an integral part of the tractor rather than an add-on, as had been sold earlier. The 30, 40, and 50 Powerloaders were designed and

In the late 1940s Case sold the Model CI tractor to Gallion to power their motor graders.

150

In the late 1940s Case marketed tractors equipped with attachments made by outside suppliers like this VAI tractor equipped with a broom.

acquisition of the American Tractor Corporation (ATC) — a manufacturer of small and medium size crawler loaders, crawler dozers, backhoes, crawler fork lifts, trailers, and scarifiers. This acquisition forever changed the Case Company. With the acquisition of the American Tractor Corporation completed in early 1957, Case made a substantial commitment to the construction equipment business. During the next 20 years Case acquired eight new product lines:

1964 — Macarr concrete pump from Macarr Company of Los Angeles, California. This pump was capable of pumping up to 35 yards of concrete per minute.

1968 — Drott Manufacturing of Wausau, Wisconsin. A line of hydraulic excavators, cranes, and straddle carriers.

1968 — Davis Manufacturing of Wichita, Kansas. Crawler and rubber-tired trenchers, boring equipment, line lying equipment, and tilt bed trailers.

1968 — Beloit Woodlands of Ashland, Wisconsin. Log Skidders.

built by Case using either the SI, DI, or 500 diesel tractors as the chassis. The Powerloaders were 1/2-yard, 3/4-yard, and 1-yard bucket machines designed with a parallel lift toggle. This feature made them good material-handling machines because it provided automatic crowding action, as well as automatic bucket leveling through to full raise. These machines had good clearance under the lift arms (10 feet 6 inches) and a dumping clearance of 8 1/2 to 9 feet at a 40 degree bucket angle.

In 1956 the Case Board of Directors hired Morgan Stanley to conduct a study of their business. The study was conducted in March and April of 1956. One of their recommendations was that as a long-range consideration Case should look at diversification to smooth out the up-and-down cycles of the agricultural business and also utilize their substantial excess manufacturing capacity. On September 6, 1956, Case approved the

The Powerloaders were the first attempt by Case to develop a loader that was an integral part of the tractor. The Model 30 Powerloader (shown here) was powered by the SI tractor.

Case eagle logo (the beginning).

Once the Industrial Division, Now the Construction Equipment Division

In 1965 the Industrial Division name was changed to the Construction Equipment Division (CE). During its growth and maturity the Industrial/Construction Equipment Division prospered under several flags or logos: first "Old Abe" with the block Case, the wheel and track, the black metal tread or chip, and the newer Case logo. The IH logo was never associated with the Construction Equipment Division and the CE products. Case felt that its name and logo in the 1970s and '80s was stronger and had greater recognition in the construction industry than IH, especially since IH had sold off their construction equipment division several years prior to the acquisition.

New Case logo with yellow accent (1990s).

Black Case metal chip logo (1970s and '80s).

Wheel and track logo (1960s).

The Model 40 Powerloader (shown here) was powered by the DI tractor. The Powerloaders were introduced in 1954.

*The Model 50
Powerloader was
designed around the
LAI tractor, but by
the 1954 introduction
it was introduced with
the 500 diesel tractor.*

1969 — Universal Industries of Hudson, Iowa. Two models of skid steer loaders and 39 attachments.

1970 — Losenhausen Mashinenbau AG of Dusseldorff, West Germany. Rollers and vibrating plate-type compactors (Vibromax).

1972 — Calsa of Zaragosa, Spain. Spain's leading wheel loader manufacturer.

1977 — 40% of Poclain SA, LePlessis of Bellville, France. The world's leading manufacturer of hydraulic excavators. Case purchased the rest of Poclain in 1986.

By the 1970s the Case construction equipment line had grown to over 50 models and more than 10 different product lines.

The Macarr pump line was purchased from the Macarr Company in 1964.

In 1968 Case purchased a line of excavators, cranes, and straddle carriers from Drott Manufacturing.

The Davis line of trenchers, boring equipment, line lying equipment, and tilt bed trailers were purchased in 1968.

A line of log skidders were purchased from Beloit Woodlands in 1968.

Two models of skid steer loaders (Uni-Loaders) were purchased from Universal Industries in 1969.

The compaction line of products was purchased from Losenhausen Mashinenbau in 1970.

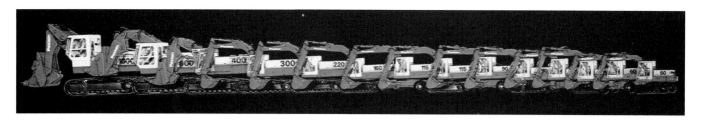

The Poclain family of excavators ranged from under 30,000-pound capacity to over 95,000-pound capacity. Forty percent of Poclain was purchased from Poclain SA in 1977 and the remainder of the company in 1986.

In the quest for a four-wheel-drive loader that could fill the need for a digging machine in the European market, Case purchased Calsa in 1977.

"Growing" Customers

In order to better understand the events that took place after the construction equipment acquisition binge of the 1960s and '70s and why some products were successful and others were not, it is important to understand the Case construction equipment customers. They are "grown" from the finance arm of a wholly-owned Case subsidiary, the Case Credit Corporation and its lease rental program ("Rent To Own"). The Credit Corporation began in 1957, but it wasn't until May 1966, that they announced a construction equipment short-term rental program — the first in the industry! At the time it essen-

tially covered loader backhoes, but in the tight money of 1968, the program was expanded to cover most of the remaining products.

To this day nobody equals Case when it comes to a similar program for growing customers. For example, it usually starts with someone who has been an operator for about 10 years and is looking for more — like owning his own business. This individual scrapes up enough cash to come into a Case CE dealer with the first month down and a security deposit to rent a loader backhoe (in the early days) or a Uni-Loader (in today's economy). Together with his pick-up truck and a small trailer behind it, this customer could be in the landscaping business . . . or snow removal business . . . or the pool contracting business. There are a lot of ways someone can make a living with a Uni-Loader and a pick-up truck. Six months later, he's got enough money or equity to transfer the rent contract into a buy. Three years later he's got three Uni-Loaders, a 580 loader backhoe, and a 550 crawler. Another three years later he's got an excavator as well as a wheel loader to go with it.

Case has been building customers through this process for over 30 years and building them better than anyone else in the world. Financing is the key. Case has cultivated its customers this way for many years and as long as there are products that fit the growth of these customers, it has worked well. Products outside of this growth area have not been as successful, as some of

The 580 loader backhoe has been "growing" Case construction equipment customers for over 30 years.

Many Case customers have started out renting a Uni-Loader and together with a pickup truck and a small trailer, have gotten into the landscaping business — or snow removal business — or pool contracting. Six months later they have enough money or equity to transfer the rent contract into a buy — and they are on their way, soon owning more Case equipment.

these products were discontinued or sold. But now let's take a look at the products that propelled the Case Construction Equipment Division and Case into one of the worlds leading agricultural and construction equipment manufacturers.

Loader Backhoes

The First In The World!

In 1957 Case created the first integral loader backhoe to be designed, manufactured, sold, and warranted by the same company. Previous to the Case design, farm equipment dealers picked up backhoes from various suppliers and mounted them on farm tractors with loaders. Some makes were even mounted on the 3-point hitch, but they were too light and it took a lot of creative plumbing that constantly leaked and required a "heap" of maintenance.

In 1956, at the time of the acquisition, Case was participating with American Tractor in a product display in the ATC parking lot in Churubsco,

Indiana. A few of the ATC people were looking at the Case 300 tractor and thought their backhoe would fit on it. That night they tried it — they "whomped" the backhoe on the 300. The next day the Case people weren't too happy with what they had done to their tractor, but they got over it. That winter, at the 1957 Chicago Road Show, American Tractor put the wheel tractor with the backhoe in a back corner for the first day. It drew so much attention, however, that the second day they moved it to the front of the display. The rest is history! For almost 40 years Case has remained the largest producer of loader backhoes in the world.

Why has the Case loader backhoe remained number one in its field? In one word, productivity. The productivity of Case loader backhoes has increased with every new model since 1957. Case did this by constantly improving the design to give the tractor the ability to do more things, to work in more conditions, and above all to constantly strive to provide the operator with more comfort and safety. The major design changes enhancing productivity were:

Mechanical Shuttle. When the 310 and 320 were introduced in 1957, they had a 148-cubic-inch Case gasoline engine, a 4-speed spur-gear transmission, and a dry friction clutch, as well as a mechanical synchronized shuttle. By eliminating complicated shift patterns when "quick shifting" from forward to reverse, the mechanical shuttle was able to speed up the forward/reverse operation.

This machine started Case in the loader backhoe business — the "whomped up" 300 tractor with an American Tractor Company loader backhoe in 1956.

The 310 was sold through the agricultural dealers which retained the ag. sheet metal and the ag. colors and did not have a self-leveling loader. The 320, however, did have a self-leveling loader and was sold through the Case industrial dealers and was painted yellow.

Torque Converter. The torque converter with an 8-speed transmission was introduced in the 420 in 1958. The torque converter drive, as it was called in the 420, was similar to the Case-O-Matic drive as introduced in the 400 agricultural tractor. The torque converter made the loader operation even more efficient because it prevented the engine from lugging down and kept the hydraulic pump operating at full capacity at all times for positive, fast response.

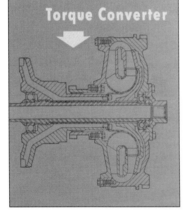

The torque converter with an 8-speed transmission made the loader operation more efficient. It kept the engine from lugging down and the operator having to shift gears so often.

Extendable Boom and Extendahoe. In 1963 Case introduced the Extendable Boom for increased reach and depth on the 530 Construction King. In 1966 Case introduced the 580CK and a new concept in backhoe design, it

had a totally enclosed box boom. This design offered a mechanical extendahoe that could increase dig depth by 2 feet, thereby providing the ability to work in more conditions.

Power Shuttle. In 1965 the power shuttle was combined with a Twin Disc Torque Converter on the 580. The power shuttle speeded up the loader operation by eliminating the need for clutching when shifting back and forth from forward to reverse.

Flat Operators Platform. In 1976 the operator's platform was made completely flat on the 580B so the operator didn't have to step up to operate the hoe and then step down to move the tractor or operate the loader. The seat simply swiveled around which caused a lot less operator fatigue and was safer.

Componentized Drive Train. From 1957 until the 580C in 1976, the power train for the loader backhoe was a tractor chassis (complete with wheels and tires) shipped from the tractor plant in Racine, Wisconsin. Starting with the 580C, the trans axle came from the Case transmission plant in Racine, the power shuttle and torque converter were from Borg Warner, and the engines came from the Case Rock Island plant. These components were shipped to the Case Burlington, Iowa plant where they were assembled into a frame made at Burlington and the loader and backhoe (also made there) were mounted on the frame. This unitized construction allowed more flexibility and innovative design in power trains, hydraulic systems, operator compartment, and engines, as well as hoe and loader mounting.

The extendable boom increased the reach and depth capabilities of the backhoe.

Case introduced a new concept in backhoe design, the Extendahoe®, in 1966. This design could increase dig depth by 2 feet.

The power shuttle combined with a torque converter to speed up the loader operation by eliminating the need for clutching when shifting back and forth from forward to reverse.

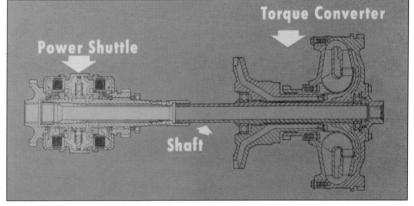

The flat platform introduced on the 580B in 1976 increased productivity because the operator simply had to swing the seat around to operate the backhoe rather than getting off one seat and onto another to operate it.

Over-Center Backhoe. Prior to the 580C, all backhoes hung way out behind the tractor in the transport position, which made it difficult to load on trailers or come up out of a basement. So Case designed an over-center backhoe that allowed the boom and dipper stick to fold back over center, toward the tractor, instead of being straight up and parallel with the back of the tractor. The over-center design made the backhoe much more maneuverable.

Four-Wheel Drive. The addition of mechanical front drive axle (MFD) in 1978 made the loader backhoe just about a "go anywhere" machine. It certainly filled the productivity criteria of giving the tractor the ability to do more things and work in more conditions.

From 1957 until 1976, the power train for the loader backhoe was shipped from the tractor plant in Racine, Wisconsin, to the Case plant in Burlington Iowa, where the hood, grille, platform, and the loader backhoe were added.

Engines. Putting a lot of horsepower along with a lot of capacity to get more productivity out of the same size package was the byword in the 580-size machine. Since 1957 the horsepower increased 20 horsepower from 47 in the 320 to 67 in the 580K — all in the same size package. The Case 148 gasoline engine, the 188 diesel engine , the 207 diesel engine, and the Case/Cummins joint venture Consolidated Diesel 4-390 engine were used.

The above changes are by no means all of the alterations the Case loader backhoes have experienced since 1957, they are simply milestones. Many hundreds of changes have occurred in hydraulic systems, loader structure and function, backhoe structure and design, ROPS, cabs, operator controls,

In 1976 with the introduction of the 580C, the power train was componentized with the trans axle shipped from the Racine transmission plant and the engines shipped from the Case Rock Island, Illinois plant, to the Burlington plant. This design allowed for more flexibility and innovation in the design of loader backhoes.

show the percent increase in cubic yards of material moved on a 2- by 4- by 100-foot trench. For example: the 580 SL T shows a 128% increase in productivity over the 580B, 115% over the 580C, 93% over the 580D, 71% over the 580SE, 41% over the 580L, 38% over the 580K, and 22% over the 580SK. These units were equipped with a standard backhoe and a 24-inch trenching bucket. Productivity numbers for the 580L through 580SE were obtained in 1994.

The over-center backhoe design allowed the boom and dipper to fold back over center instead of being straight up and parallel with the back of the tractor. It made the loader backhoe more maneuverable.

comfort and convenience, serviceability, and even styling that let the operator become more efficient — that is why Case remains the leader in the industry.

Productivity

Here are some examples of productivity increases over a 23 year period starting with the 580 in 1971 to the 580 SL T in 1994. The numbers in the chart below

Case Backhoe Productivity Improvement from the B-Series to the L-Series

	580B	580C	580D	580SE	580L	580K	580SK
580 SL T	128%	115%	93%	71%	41%	38%	22%
580 SK T	87%	78%	59%	40%	16%	13%	—
580K	65%	57%	40%	24%	3%	—	
580L	61%	53%	37%	21%	—		
580SE	34%	27%	13%	—			
580D	18%	12%	—				
580C	5%	—					

How Big?

Looking back through the years it seems that the world of the loader backhoe was not much larger than

The addition of the mechanical front drive axle (shown here) made the loader backhoe a "go anywhere" machine.

The Case 188 gasoline and diesel engines were used in the 580s. Putting a lot of horsepower with a lot of capacity has been the byword in the 580-sized machines.

The start-up of the first Consolidated Diesel (CDC) prototype engine occurred in May 1979.

The 580E was the first product to use the CDC 4-390 engine.

the 580 or possibly the 590. When it got bigger than that, the customer started to separate the digger from the loader and the question of "should it be a larger loader backhoe or a smaller excavator" was answered. The Case 680 and 780 loader backhoes are a good example. This size machine, regardless of what company made them, struggled to find a home in the marketplace comparable to the 580 size machine. The 680 was introduced in 1966 had a 90-horsepower engine with a 1-1/2-cubic-yard bucket that could dig to 20 feet 7 inches. The 780, introduced in 1971, was a 112-horsepower machine with a 1-3/4-cubic-yard bucket that could dig to 22 feet.

How in the World?

Loader backhoes are used throughout the world except in Japan and to some extent in Germany (because the excavator is the dominant construction machine in these two countries). The Case loader backhoes are manufactured in Burlington, Iowa ("The Loader Backhoe Capitol of the World"); and Vierzon, France; as well as Brazil and Australia, and are shipped worldwide. In 1980 Case-France celebrated production of its 10,000th Model 580 loader backhoe. That same year, the Burlington, Iowa plant and Case celebrated their 25-year anniversary of worldwide loader backhoe leadership and the production of 200,000th loader backhoe unit. To commemorate the occasion Case produced a special limited anniversary edition of seven-hundred and fifty 580 loader backhoes, finished in silver and black. In 1988, *Fortune* magazine listed the 580K as being among the best products built in the United States. In the 1990s the 580 L series has continued to keep Case on top as the world's leading manufacturer of loader backhoes.

The world of the loader backhoe, it seems, was not much larger than the 580 or 590. Larger machines like this 680H have struggled to find a home in the marketplace comparable to the 580s.

The 580 loader backhoes were built at the Case plant in Australia and shipped worldwide.

This 580G with a side shaft backhoe was produced by the Case plant in Vierzon, France. In 1980 the Vierzon plant celebrated production of its 10,000th loader backhoe.

In 1980 Case produced 750 limited-edition 580 loader backhoes painted silver and black. They commemorated the production of the 200,000th loader backhoe from the Burlington, Iowa plant

The first 500 Uni-Loaders, like this 1537, were produced for Case by Universal Industries in Hudson, Iowa.

In March of 1973 the 1816 went into production and was an immediate success. It was only 35 inches wide and 6 feet 4.5 inches high — it could go through a 36-inch door as easy as a wheelbarrow.

Skid Steer Uni-Loaders

In 1969 Case bought the design and manufacturing rights to a skid steer loader called the Uni-Loader from Universal Industries. Two models were available in the Uni-Loader. Universal Industries, located in Hudson, Iowa, produced the first 500 units and put the Case decal on them. The first Case production started in the plant in Rockford, Illinois, and then moved to the Burlington, Iowa plant when Rockford was closed in 1970. Case struggled with these original machines because they required high maintenance, mostly due to the variable-speed drive power train.

The 1830 was the second of a new design of Uni-Loaders that went into production in March of 1974, just one year after the 1816.

In 1971 two new models were introduced, the 1737 and the 1740. The 1737 was designed with the Case 148-cubic-inch gasoline engine and the 1740 had the 188-cubic-inch diesel engine. The Uni-Loader was also one of the most successful Case construction equipment products.

The New Beginning

In May of 1972 management approval was given to design a new line of Uni-Loaders. Nine months later, in March of 1973, the 1816 went into production, the 1830 followed one year later (March 1974), and by March of 1975 the 1845 was in production. Three new models in 36 months and in one-year increments!

The 1816 was a new market approach — a machine only 35 inches wide and 6 feet 4.5 inches high that could go through a 36-inch door or gate as easy as a

The 1740 Uni-Loader was one of the first Case-produced machines and used the Case 188-cubic-inch diesel engine.

In March of 1975 the 1845 went into production. Case had designed and produced three new models in 36 months.

wheelbarrow. The 1816 used a hydrostatic-type power train with a chain drive to the wheels. The transmission had two variable displacement pumps. The Tecumseh engine was a 16-horsepower, air-cooled, gasoline engine and the loader had a lifting capacity of

1,025 pounds. The 1830 was powered by a water-cooled, gasoline 30-horsepower Renault engine and had a lifting capacity of 2,130 pounds. The power train was hydrostatic with a two-stage chain drive to the wheels, the transmission had two variable displacement pumps and two fixed displacement piston motors. The 1845 had the same power train as the 1830, and was powered by either a Case 159-cubic-inch gasoline or a 188-cubic-inch diesel engine at 45 horsepower. The lift capacity of the 1845 was 2,920 pounds.

Changes to the Uni-Loaders in the 1980s

The goal for Uni-Loaders in the the 1980s was to design and manufacture machines that were the easiest to maintain, were the most rugged, and had the best power train combination to make them high performance machines. The horsepower of the 1816 was increased from 16 to 18 horsepower with a new Onan gasoline engine and the addition of a Kubota diesel engine. The model number was also changed to 1818. Serviceability was greatly enhanced with a swing open door for routine engine checks and a forward tilt ROPS. The tilt was assisted by a gas strut and provided unobstructed access to the engine, hydraulic hoses, pumps, and motors for fast easy servicing. The power train was upgraded to a hydrostatic that had a single stage chain drive to all wheels and two variable displacement gear-

In the 1980s serviceability was greatly enhanced on the Uni-Loader. Two smaller models, the 1818 and the 1825, had a forward tilt ROPS. The tilt was assisted by a gas strut and provided unobstructed access to the engine, hydraulic hoses, pumps, and motors for easy servicing.

All of the Uni-Loaders of the 1980s featured a swing open door for the frequent and routine service checks — like checking the engine oil level.

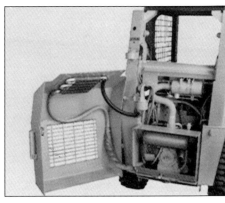

The larger models, like the 1830, 1835, and 1845 featured a roll out ROPS instead of the tilt ROPS for easy servicing.

The Uni-Loaders of the 1980s and '90s were (from left to right) the 1818, 1835C, 1845, 1818, and the 1838 (not shown here).

type charge pumps and two fixed displacement motors. The lift capacity on the gasoline loader was 1,100 pounds and 1,300 pounds on the diesel.

The 1825 was the new 25-horsepower model. Two engines were available: a Nissan gasoline and a Kubota diesel. The power train was the same type as the 1818. The 1825 had the swing open door and the tilt ROPS. The lift capacity was 1,600 pounds.

The 1830 was upgraded to the 1835 series which offered the 44-horsepower Teledyne gasoline engine or the 42-horsepower Teledyne diesel engine. Serviceability enhancements were also designed into the 1835 series, like the swing open door and the 1835 featured a roll out ROPS instead of the tilt ROPS, which could be slid forward for easy access to the engine, hydraulic system, and power train. The lift capacity of the 1835 was 2,350 pounds.

In 1986 the Case engine was replaced with the Case/Cummins joint venture Consolidated Diesel Corporation 4-390 diesel engine at 60 gross horsepower on the new 1845. Serviceability enhancements were also incorporated in this model. By the 1980s the 1845 had become the entry-level machine in the Case customer "Rent to Buy" program. The 1845 was also beginning to replace the small crawler loader in many applications.

An 1835C Uni-Loader was rated at 48 horsepower and had a 1,200-pound operating load.

The 1845 was beginning to replace the small crawler loader in many applications.

The 1845 Special, designed for fertilizer plants, had special paint protection of several coats of primer covered with vinyl paints. The paints were were especially formulated for corrosive environments.

Attachments

The Uni-Loaders had a host of attachments: a backhoe, manure forks, pallet forks, hydraulic grapples, scarifiers, and a wide range of buckets. There was even an 1845S — a machine designed for fertilizer plants that was produced with a special paint protection of several coats primer and vinyl paints especially formulated for corrosive environments. The Uni-Loaders are manufactured at the Case plant in Wichita, Kansas.

Wheel Loaders

The wheel loader is the only "home grown" construction equipment product in the Case line. In August of 1954 Case commissioned Davee, Koehnlein, and Keating market analyst to do a study to see if Case was justified in developing and marketing a package power-loading unit similar to the Hough "Payloader."

The study concluded that a unit loader like the "Payloader" would exhibit consistent market growth because of increasing construction industry labor costs.

167

The first unit-type loader produced by Case was the W-9 Terraload'r in 1957. The W-9 was a rigid-frame wheel loader.

The need for lower cost material handling was evidenced by a shift from wheel tractor mounted loaders to unit loaders, as well as a shift from crawler loaders to unit loaders. Competition would be severe, but Case would benefit from its dealer service organization. A good unit loader would act as a signal to dealers that Case was committed to maintaining

and expanding the Case franchise in the industrial machinery market.

The strategy was to continue to market the present tractor-mounted loader until the unit loader made it unprofitable. The project was approved and the first unit loader, called the W-9 Terraload'r, went into production in 1957 at the Main Works in the old "Wheel Shop" which later became known as the "Loader Building."

The "W" Line: 1957 to 1968

The early models of the "W" line, those produced prior to 1968, were rigid-frame machines with a steerable rear axle. The W-5, the smallest machine, started out using the Case 164-cubic-inch gasoline engine and later switched to the 188-cubic-inch diesel engine. It used the 300 tractor transmission and mechanical shuttle with a torque converter as its power train. The steering axle was similar to the Racine-built 420 and 425 industrial tractor front axle. The W-5 was a 1-yard machine with a carrying capacity of 3,000 pounds and was designed for fertilizer plants, coal yards, foundries, and stockpiling. The W-5 had 12:00 x 24 front tires and 7:00 x 16 rears.

The W-9, W-10, and W-12 used the larger Racine-built engines starting with the 251-cubic-inch gas (only the W-9 used this), all the way to the 451-cubic-inch Case Powrcel diesel. The Allison 3-speed powershift transmission was used in the W-9, W-10, and W-12. Wisconsin planetary axles were used with the front being a non-steerable and the rear, a steerable axle using a Rzeppa ball joint for a shorter turning radius.

The W-7 was a little different as it used a Clark transmission and axles. The steerable axle used a

The original "W" line was produced from 1957 until 1968. They were all rigid farm machines with a steerable rear axle and a non-steerable front axle. They were all four-wheel drive except the W-5 (in the upper right). The W-5 transmission was a Case transaxle which powered the front wheels.

All of the original "W" line loaders used a Rzeppa joint steering axle except the W-7 shown here which used a constant velocity joint steering axle.

and this also made it easier to open cab doors at any time — whether the loader arms were up or down. These machines were first built at the loader building in Racine, Wisconsin, and then moved to the Case plant in Rockford, Illinois.

The "W" Line: 1968 to 1988

The "W" line between 1968 and 1988 consisted of the W-11, W-14, W-18, W-20, W-24, W-26, W-30, and W-36. They were all articulated machines using non-steerable axles with the chassis pivoting in the middle. The operator compartment was located in front of the pivot, so he was always moving in the same direction as the bucket. These loaders were powered by Case engines (except the W-36, which used a Detroit Diesel 6V-53) until the mid- and late 1980s when they were replaced by the Consolidated Diesel Company engines. The first articulated loader produced was the W-26 at the Case plant in Terre Haute, Indiana. These units had 3- and 4-speed powershift transmissions. The loader linkage was a parallel design which made them good material-handling machines, but they were never recognized as digging machines. The bucket capacities ranged from 1 cubic yard for the W-11 to 4 cubic yards for the W-36 in 1/2- and 3/4-cubic-yard increments.

From the beginning the "W" line was a solid machine in the government bid business — local, state, and federal governments. Thousands of machines were sold to the United States government, in fact there were times in the 1980s when a lot of the Case plants were running at 40% capacity and the Terre Haute plant was building "W" line loaders and running at 85% of capacity. The Government Sales Department and the "W" line loader business virtually kept the wolf away from the door!

constant velocity-type joint rather than a Rzeppa joint. The W-7 was a maximum 2-cubic-yard machine and the W-9 was a maximum 2-1/2-cubic-yard machine at 5,500 pounds. The W-10 was a maximum 2-7/8-cubic-yard machine at 6,500 pounds, and the W-12 was a maximum 3-1/2-cubic-yard machine at 9,000 pounds. The large units were designed so that the rear wheels carried 37% more weight than the front wheels for safer steering with a full bucket down steep grades and over rough terrain. The loader arms used parallel linkage and featured self leveling which made them good material handling machines. The loader arms pivoted at the front of the operator cockpit rather than at the rear. As a result the arms were not constantly moving on both sides of the operator like competition

The "W" line from 1968 to 1988 were articulated machines with the operator compartment in front of the articulation hinge. The loader linkage was a parallel design which made them good material-handling machines.

The concept for the W-11 loader origi-nated from the design of the MC 4000 articulated rough-terrain forklift Case developed for the U.S. military.

The first articulated loader Case produced was the W-26 at the Terre Haute, Indiana plant.

All of the "W" line machines, except the W-36, used Case engines. The W-36 used a Detroit Diesel 6V-53 engine.

These MW-24 loaders were ready for shipment.Over 2,000 MW-24 loaders were sold to the U.S. military

The Super 1500 loader, made by Calsa, was a good digging loader and filled the need for Case in the European market.

Zaragosa, Spain and Wheel Loaders

Since the "W" machines were material handlers and not digging machines, Case bought Calsa, a wheel loader manufacturer located in Zaragosa, Spain, to fill their European need for a high-quality four-wheel-drive loader that could work as a digging machine. The original 1500 series were good machines, but the following series, the 700 series, were not. As a result Case decided on a new approach, known as the "World Loader."

The 21 Series – A World Loader

The 621, introduced in 1988, was the first 21 series wheel loader. The 621 was developed under what Case called the Product Definition Release System which established a rigid product definition from extensive market surveys. It also got the affected groups, such as engineering, manufacturing, purchasing, finance, marketing, service, and technical publications, involved from the beginning and kept them involved through the whole process so the commitments could be kept. For example, the manufacturing group was involved in building engineering prototypes so the real thing could be tested. This process cut the development to introduction time from the traditional 6 years to only 30 months. Only the Uni-Loaders were completed in a shorter time period.

Following the 621, was the 721 in 1989, the 821 in 1990, and the 921 in 1991. This new line of wheel loaders were digging machines as well as material handlers. The loader linkage was the more rugged Z-bar design and the operator compartment was located in a more traditional location behind the articulation pivot so the operator wasn't jostled around as much. The engine power for the 621 was the CDC 6-830, the 721 and 821 used the CDC 6-T 830, while the 921 used the larger Cummins LTA-10 6-cylinder engine. The transmission was a 4-speed forward, 3-reverse full powershift, with an electric twist grip range selector located on the steering column. The rest

At the time Case acquired Calsa, they also made a rigid frame four-wheel-steer farm tractor. The farm tractor was discontinued shortly after the acquisition.

171

The 621, the first of the work loaders, was introduced in 1988 and developed under what Case called a Product Definition Release System. In 1993 the 621B replaced the 621 and offered optional extended reach lift arms (the 621B XT). The 621B was a 2.25- to 2.75-cubic-yard machine.

In 1989 the 721 was released for production. It was replaced by the 721B in 1993 which was also offered with optional extended lift arms (the 721B XT). The 721B was a 2.50- to 3.25-cubic-yard machine.

In 1990 the 821 was released. The 21 series placed the operator in a more traditional location — behind the articulation pivot so the operator wasn't jostled about so much. The 821 was replaced by the 821B in 1993. The 821B was a 3.5- to 4.0-cubic-yard machine.

All of the 21 series offered low effort controls, panoramic visibility, operator comfort, and optional ride control to enhance productivity.

The last and largest of the 21 series was introduced in 1991. The 921 was a 4.75- to 5.0-cubic-yard machine. All of the 21 series were equipped with high-quality features such as automatic return-to-dig, return-to-travel, and height control. All features shortened the work cycle.

of the operator's cab was quite unique also, with low effort servo loader controls with a wrist rest, a suspension seat, analog gauges, liquid crystal bar graphs to alert the operator to the status of various functions, and a low noise cab. Service was fast access and was easy. The bucket capacity ranged from 2 3/4 cubic yards on the 621 to 5 cubic yards on the 921.

The 21 series were originally built in the Case plants in Wausau, Wisconsin, and Zaragosa, Spain, but in 1992 production was consolidated at the Case plant in Fargo, North Dakota. The Fargo plant specialized in manufacturing all the Case articulated machines for both the agriculture and the construction industry and all Case wheel loaders were also built there.

Rough Terrain Forklifts

Simple and Reliable

The Case rough-terrain forklift has been the unsung hero in the Case construction equipment product line for almost forty years. There is nothing magical about forklifts. They are simple, they never break down, and they work . . . and work . . . and work. Case is the only major U.S. manufacturer remaining in this market. The rough-terrain forklift is a derivative of the agricultural tractor and loader/loader backhoe technology.

For Case, the forklift began in 1957 with the M-3 that was designed by the American Tractor Corporation for a small crawler equipped with a torque converter. The

The W-5 Terraloader with its torque converter and shuttle transmission was the first Case conversion to a rubber-tired forklift — the MW-5. The MW-5's most popular use was in a concrete products yard or a lumber yard.

M-3 was designed to smoothly handle materials over rough, muddy terrain in the building trades industry. It didn't take long after the acquisition of American Tractor for Case to figure out that a rubber-tired rough-terrain forklift would be more versatile, so they went to work. One of the simple applications was to mount the forklift on a W-5 loader chassis — creating the MW-5. With a torque converter and a shuttle transmission, it was a natural fit.

The 310 and 420 Forklifts

The next step in Case's quest for a rough-terrain forklift was to increase the lateral stability by mounting the forklift on the rear of the 310 (ag/utility model) and the 420 (industrial model) loader backhoe chassis. This modification was a little more complex, since the operator platform and all the controls had to be reversed, the final drive had to be changed so there were more and faster speeds in reverse, and a counterweight had to be added. On the very early models, Harlo (located in Grandville, Michigan) built the turn around operator's platform

Rough-terrain forklifts got their start at Case with the M-3 crawler forklift made by the American Tractor Corporation which Case acquired in 1957.

After the MW-5, the next step in forklifts was to mount a forklift on the rear of 310 or 420 loader backhoe chassis. The controls and platform, as well as the final drive, had to be modified for the forklift application.

Current rough-terrain forklifts, like this 580 series, offer a four-wheel-drive option. Case is the only major manufacturer remaining in the rough-terrain forklift market.

and mast, but Case started to design and build their own in 1969. This was design time well spent, since this product has essentially remained in the line for almost 30 years with very few changes.

In the 1957 acquisition of American Tractor, Case acquired five models of crawler tractors ranging in horsepower from 34 to 62 horsepower.

Through the Years

The power trains and engines changed on the forklift as the loader backhoe power trains and engines changed. The models also changed like the loader backhoes — 310/420 to 30 series to 580 series. Lift capacities offered more variety like 4,000-, 5,000-, and 6,000-pound units, four-wheel-drive models were also offered, and there was a choice of 10-, 12-, 14-, 21-, and 28-foot masts. Because of economies of scale, Case is the leader in the market and in the 1970s private labeled their machines for Eaton Corporation in Cleveland, Ohio. The forklifts are still produced in the Case Burlington, Iowa plant.

Crawler Dozers and Crawler Loaders

In 1957, with the acquisition of the American Tractor Corporation, Case acquired a product line of five medium-sized crawler tractor models ranging from 34 to 62 horsepower. By 1958 the product line had pretty much settled in at four models and has remained at four over the years. Like most of the other products, the quest for more productivity in the same size package has increased the horsepower. In 1978 the range of power was 39 to 103 horsepower and by 1989 it was 63 to 150 horsepower. The American Tractor crawlers had Continental engines, but all Case crawlers used Case engines until the late 1980s when they were replaced with the Case/Cummins joint venture CDC engines.

The mix of loaders and dozers has changed as the market for crawler loaders began to decline almost immediately. In 1958 there was a loader for every model of tractor, but by 1989 Case offered only three loaders, and by the 1990s only dozers were offered. Small excavators cut into the basement business of the large crawlers and the wheel loader cut into the material handling business. The skid steer Uni-Loader has been replacing the small crawler loader. The medium-size

This American Tractor Corporation (ATC) Model 600 crawler transmission was the first crawler transmission to offer both a power shift with a torque converter and the power turn feature.

ATC was also the first company to offer a counter-rotation feature in a crawler tractor. The crawler transmission offered counter-rotation in the Models 800 and 1000 crawler tractors.

crawler dozer fits the mold for Case's technique of growing customers and, consequently, has done well because they are great finish grading machines which fits into many of these customer's growth patterns. The transmission and dozer hydraulics really made these machines unique.

The First Powershift Crawler Transmission

In the mid-1950s, American Tractor Corporation hired a company called Transmission and Gear from Detroit, Michigan, to design a powershift transmission with a torque converter for their 600 crawler. It became the first crawler tractor in the industry to feature a power turn. Previously, steering the crawler tractor was done with the brakes — the operator would apply the brake on one track and keep power applied to the opposite track, the tractor would then pivot around the track being held by the brake. The only flaw was that the operator became very fatigued, working the brake steering all day. The power turn was a new concept. Instead of a standard clutch and a gear transmission, the 600 crawler transmission was designed with multiple-disc hydraulic clutches. To power turn, the operator simply shifted one track speed control lever into low while the other was in high and the tractor would power turn in the direction of the slower track.

The Counter-Rotation Transmission

During the design of the powershift transmission for the 800 and 1000 crawlers, Marc Rojtman, President of American Tractor Corporation, had an idea for a

counter-rotating transmission. He talked to Chris Gerst of Transmission and Gear about it on a Friday, Gerst drew up the plans over the weekend and Rojtman approved them. The 800 and 1000 crawler tractors were the first crawler tractors in the industry to offer the operator three ways to turn or steer the crawler tractor: a power turn, a traditional break turn, or the new revolutionary counter-rotation turn. The counter-rotation turn was an excellent feature when working in confined areas or when grading. It allowed the operator to be more productive by pushing dirt in both directions instead of backing up empty. To make a counter-rotation turn, the operator simply shifted one track into forward and the other into reverse and the tractor pivoted 360 degrees in its own length.

Both of these transmissions, the powershift and the counter-rotation powershift, were way ahead of their time. As a pioneer, growing pains always exist — especially when the design occurred over the weekend!

The 800 and 1000 crawlers were the first in the industry to offer the operator a choice of three ways to steer a crawler tractor — (from left to right) the traditional brake turn, the power turn, and the counter-rotation turn.

The Case-designed power shift crawler transmissions (from left to right) used in the 850, 1150, and 450 crawlers.

After the acquisition of the American Tractor Corporation, Case bought back many of the 800 and the 1000 crawlers. The transmission design responsibility was moved to the Transmission Design Group at the Racine tractor plant who cleaned up the Gerst design. A new industrial torque converter was used rather than the automotive type, heavier drop housings and final drives were added, they beefed up clutch packs and then redesigned the brakes and improved clutch modulation, plus many other improvements. The new transmissions were first available in the Model 601 powershift version and the Model 593 in the power-shift/counter-rotation version. The first Case-designed crawlers that used these new transmissions were the

850 (which replaced the 800 and 750), the 450 (which replaced the 600), and the 1150 (which replaced the 1000). All three crawlers were an immediate success. The 601 and 593 transmissions were first produced by Case at their Rock Island plant and then later at the transmission plant in Racine, Wisconsin.

All but two Case crawlers, the 310 and 1550, have used the 601 or 593 transmissions with some variations, such as the 1450 which required planetary final drives at that horsepower. The 310, the smallest crawler with 30 drawbar horsepower, used a Clark transmission with 3-speeds forward and 1-reverse, and had planetary steering. In 1970 a Borg Warner mechanical shuttle and a torque converter were added to the 310 and the model number was changed to 350. The 1550, the largest crawler, had 150-net-engine horsepower and used a hydrostatic transmission.

The First Power Tilting Dozer Blade

The first crawler-mounted dozer blade that could be hydraulically tilted or tipped from the operator's seat was introduced on the 800 crawler. Prior to the power tilt blade, the operator had to stop the tractor, get off, and "wrestle" a big heavy blade into tip or tilt position by hand. The power tilt blade made the operator more efficient when cutting ditches, crowning roads, and breaking through hard ground. The operator could drop either corner of the blade 14 inches or tip the blade fore and aft 10 degrees while in motion. Caterpillar wanted to buy this patent and Case finally agreed to sell it to Caterpillar in 1969 for $30,000 with a limited right to use this patent only on dozers over 150 horsepower.

Wet or oil bath brakes were added to the 601 transmission for the 1450 crawler. This 601 transmission was used on both the 1150 and the 1450 crawlers.

This Model 310, the smallest of the crawler tractors, used a Clark transmission with three-speeds forward and one reverse. The 310 had a planetary steering system.

177

A hydrostatic drive was used in the 1550 crawler dozer. It was the largest crawler at 150 horsepower.

The hydrostatic transmission was used in the 1550 crawler dozer.

Case was the first in the industry to offer a power tilting dozer blade on a crawler. The power tilting blade could be tilted from the operator's seat. Prior to the tilt blade, the operator had to stop and get off the tractor and "wrestle" the heavy blade into a tilt position. In 1969 Case sold Caterpillar a limited right to use this patent only on dozers over 150 horsepower. Caterpillar paid Case $30,000 for these rights.

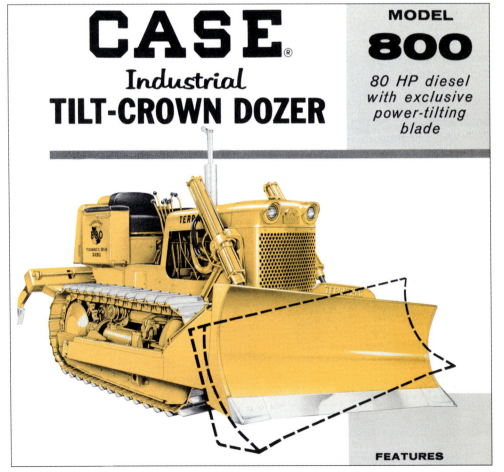

CASE®
Industrial
TILT-CROWN DOZER

MODEL
800
80 HP diesel with exclusive power-tilting blade

FEATURES

Track Technology

Case is a world leader in track technology. For example, they were one of the first to have automatic track lubrication with built-in track reservoirs that maintained a constant head of grease on each roller. They were also the first to have hydraulic track adjustment that allowed track tension to be increased with a grease gun. Case was also the first with the sealed track to reduce wear to external track bushings and they had the first automatic track tensioner — the track that adjusts itself. Case also developed the special application rubber track. It was not a high-speed track but it let the crawler drive across a sidewalk without damaging it.

The Case crawler tractor has matured into a high-quality well-accepted product. The 450 and 550 are excellent entry-level machines and fit the Case plan to "grow" customers into the 850, 1150, and 1450. The Case crawlers have been produced in the United States in plants in Burlington and Bettendorf, Iowa, and in Wausau, Wisconsin. Overseas they have been produced in Seoul, South Korea, as well as Leeds and Redruth, England.

Trenchers and Cable Layers

Case entered the trencher and cable layer business in November of 1968 when they acquired Davis Manufacturing of Wichita, Kansas. Davis made crawler and rubber-tired mounted trenchers, cable laying equipment, hydra-boring equipment, and tilt trailers. Davis operated as a separate division of Case until 1981 when they were made part of the Construction Equipment Division. The product line of trenchers included:

• The walk-behind trencher was used for tight projects and smaller tasks in the landscaping area, such as yard lighting and sprinklers. The walk-behind trencher was only 31 1/2 inches wide, so it easily passed through yard gates and other narrow passages. This trencher was a popular rental yard product because of its simplicity with a 10-horsepower air-cooled engine with rope or electric start and a 3-speed transaxle. The walk-behind trencher could dig 24 inches deep and up to 6 inches wide.

• The compact crawler trencher, at only 41 inches wide and 85 inches long, was ideal for building contractors. A flush trencher attachment permitted digging a

Case entered the trencher and cable laying business in 1968 when they acquired Davis Manufacturing. The Davis line included this family of rubber-tired and crawler-mounted trenchers and cable laying equipment.

The walk-behind trencher was used for tight projects like yard lighting and sprinkler systems. The walk-behind trencher was only 31.5 inches wide, so it went through yard gates and other narrow passages. It could also dig 24 inches deep and 6 inches wide.

straight line footing trench against batter boards for precise foundation alignment. Plumbing contractors typically used it for centerline trenching and the ability to reverse directions and backfill. Nursery operators found that it could trench around a tree so it could be

lifted out with minimal disturbance to the roots and the earth ball. Another popular rental yard unit, it was powered by an 18-horsepower air-cooled engine and had a sealed hydraulic ground drive with variable speed ranges. This compact crawler trencher could dig to a depth of 66 inches and offered an optional Case hydra-bore attachment for boring under driveways, walks, and streets.

• The compact self-propelled cable plow was used for direct burial of cable and flexible pipe with minimal lawn and ground disturbance. It typically handled telephone, gas, cable TV, fiber optics, and electrical service, as well as irrigation and lawn sprinkler jobs. This cable plow was only 117 inches long and could pass through 36-inch gates, as well as direct-bury cable to 12, 18, or 24 inches. The compact cable plow was powered by a 33-horsepower water-cooled diesel and had a hydrostatic transmission. Case cable plows had a unique designed hinged drop chute with a removable gate that isolated plow vibration from the machine and the cable for more comfortable operation.

• The 30-, 40-, 50-, 60-, and 80-horsepower heavy-duty trenchers offered versatility for the utility,

Compact trenchers like this crawler was ideal for building contractors because it offered a flush trencher attachment that permitted digging a straight line footing against batter boards for precise foundation alignment.

The compact cable layer handled telephone, gas, cable TV, fiber optics, electrical service, as well as irrigation and sprinkler jobs.

Heavy-duty trenchers, like this HD 45 equipped with a trencher on the front and a cable plow on the rear, were designed to offer versatility for the utility, communication, or municipal markets. These heavy-duty trenchers could dig 5-, 6-, or 7-foot deep trenches dependent upon horsepower.

communication, or municipality markets with backhoe, cable plow, trencher, blade, and hydra-bore attachments. These heavy-duty trenchers could dig 5-, 6-, or 7-foot deep trenches based on their horsepower and could handle cable with a maximum diameter of 1 5/8 inches. These units all had hydrostatic drives.

Re-thinking Trencher Design

Until the mid-1980s all of the heavy-duty trenchers were articulated. In the '80s Case engineers began re-thinking the heavy-duty trencher design, based on the ever-changing customer needs and new technology. The engineers designed a rigid frame concept that used steerable planetary axles with four-wheel drive and four-wheel-selective steering. With this concept both the front and rear wheels steered — the front with the steering wheel and the rear with a control lever — and provided coordinated steering. The rigid frame concept used an electronic sensor to make the rear wheels track the front wheels and gave full power turns in a 21-1/2-foot circle for working around trees, buildings, and walls. Front-wheel steering was available for normal trenching. Rear/crab steer offered greater gripping power and stability on slopes for offset cable plowing or hillside trenching. Only Case four-wheel-selective steering featured automatic centering when switching

out of rear or coordinated steering. This steering feature was a proven system developed by Case for their large four-wheel-drive tractors in 1979. The steering wasn't the only change as the trencher drive was re-designed without clutches, belts, chains, or sprockets.

This 760 heavy-duty trencher was the first four-wheel-steer trencher produced in the industry. The 760 had a rigid frame design with four-wheel drive and four-wheel steer based on the Case-proven four-wheel-steer concept. The 760 was upgraded to the 860 in 1990.

The 660 trencher was the second generation of Case four-wheel-steer machines produced by Case. The 660 was a 60-horsepower trencher with a dig depths of 72 inches. This 660 was equipped with a trencher, blade, and a backhoe.

The Case family of trenchers for the 1990s were the 60 walk-behind, TF300 compact crawler trencher, maxi-sneaker compact cable plow, 360 (30 horsepower) heavy-duty trencher and cable plow, 460 (37 horsepower) heavy-duty trencher and cable plow, 560 (51 horsepower) trencher, 660 (60 horsepower) heavy-duty trencher, and the 860 (86 horsepower) heavy-duty trencher.

Serviceability was also enhanced. The operator's platform was mounted on rubber Iso mounts to help isolate vibration and reduce operator fatigue — another proven Case design. To top it off, Case offered a 2,000-hour or two-year warranty. The 760 was the first of the new trenchers introduced in 1986. It was then upgraded to the 860 and the 360, 460, and 560 were all introduced in the 1990s with the rigid frame four-wheel-steer design. The trencher really fit into the Case entrepre-

neurial spirit of growing their customers and it was also an excellent rental yard product. The trenchers were produced at the Case plant in Wichita, Kansas.

Hydraulic Excavators

Drott Excavators

Case entered the hydraulic excavator business in 1968 with the acquisition of Drott Manufacturing in

The Drott family of excavators in 1968 consisted of these five machines (from left to right): 45 Cruz-Air, 40 Cruz-Air, 30 crawler excavator, 40 crawler excavator, and the 50 crawler excavator.

Wausau, Wisconsin. At the time of the acquisition, Drott had five models of hydraulic excavators: two were rubber-tired four-wheel-drive, front-wheel steer models (the 40 and 45 Cruz-Air) and three were crawler models (the 30, 40, and 50 crawlers). Drott was an early leader in excavators, but lacked the distribution system which Case could provide.

During the next few years Case dominated the under 50,000-pound excavator market in the United States. Throughout this period excavators were sold under a dual distribution system. Excavators sold under the Case name had Case engines and those sold under the Drott name had GMC diesel engines. The Drott excavators were simple, straight-forward machines with a lot of horsepower and hydraulic systems. The American contractor got very used to these machines — check the oil, clean the windshield, and put it to work!

The rubber-tired units did well in the municipal markets for grading, precision sloping, and cleaning drainage ditches and trenches with the wrist-o-twist buckets (buckets that could be twisted or tilted clockwise or counter clockwise to shape the side of a bank or

ditch to acquire the desired slope). These units also could be driven from one job site to another and could work on a roadside without damaging the road surface. The rubber-tired units were also extensively used in the logging industry for loading logs at paper and saw mills where the loading area was paved.

The crawler units were very productive and versatile units in the general construction and logging markets. Drott was one of the most respected names in the woods, with the rubber-tired Cruz-Air Loggers and the crawler feller/bunchers that could grab a tree, shear it off, and stack it in a pile.

From 1968 until 1981, excavators were sold under both the Drott name and the Case name. Case excavators, like this 880, were powered by Case engines while Drott excavators were powered by GMC diesel engines.

The 45 Cruz-Air equipped with a wrist-o-twist bucket like this one were very popular in the municipal markets for grading, precision sloping, and cleaning of drainage ditches. They could be driven from one job site to another and could work on a roadside without damaging the road surface.

The Cruiz-Air with the raised cab was used extensively for loading and unloading logs at paper and saw mills.

The 1080 crawler excavator was a U.S.-built machine from the Case Wausau, Wisconsin plant.

This Model 600 was the second largest excavator built by Case. The Model 600 was used in the mining industry and was so large it had to be moved on a transport. The Model 1000 was the largest machine.

The 1187C feller/buncher was designed and built in Wausau for pulpwood harvesting in the late 1980s after the European excavators did not work out for tree harvesting. The feller/buncher would grab the tree and shear it off with a scissor-like action and lay the tree aside.

The Wide World of Excavators

In the late 1970s the Japanese caught on to this low-maintenance reliable-unit idea. The yen was cheap and the dollar was expensive, so they could do it cheaper while improving the technology. The Japanese had a vested interest in excavators since over one-half of the world's excavators were sold in Japan.

About the time the Japanese were entering the market, Case was looking for a way to increase their construction equipment distribution in Europe. They were talking (with Tenneco) to the French government, who had become involved with the leading hydraulic excavator company in Europe, Poclain S.A., located in Le Plessis-Belleville, France (just outside of Paris). Poclain was in financial trouble and the French government would only allow Tenneco/Case to acquire 40% of Poclain in France. However, Tenneco/Case did acquire 100% of the distribution system outside of France, as well as 100% of Poclain assets outside of France including a manufacturing facility in Brazil. By 1977, the deal was completed (the rest was purchased in 1986) and Case began selling the French-built excavators. Poclain produced excavators from under 30,000 pounds to over 95,000 pounds for the

After the tree was cut a Case crawler excavator equipped with a de-limber like this one would remove the limbs from the trees right in the woods.

In the 1980s and early 1990s the medium size crawler excavators were built in France. These machines (from left to right) were the 688, the 888, and the 1088. Case continued to build the medium size crawler for Europe into the mid-1990s.

commercial market, in addition to two large machines, the Model 600 and the Model 1000, used in the mining industry. The Case North American distribution system was never geared to handle the 600 and 1000. The European excavators of the 1960s and '70s were very sophisticated, with high-pressure systems designed for maximum hydraulic efficiency and European fuel prices. The Poclain excavators were too sophisticated for the North American market because the contractors in this market in the 1960s weren't as interested in hydraulic efficiency with fuel at 25-cents per gallon as they were in the labor-intensive maintenance costs these high-pressure hydraulic systems incurred. European customers were very maintenance

oriented, they retorqued the hydraulic fittings at the proper intervals and they invested in maintenance. As a result, the product would run forever and perform well. The American contractor, however, wasn't as maintenance oriented. He probably didn't own a torque wrench and wasn't about to use one. The Poclain excavator and the American customer were not a good match — Case bet on the wrong horse!

Case had a mix of Drott and Poclain excavators in the 1970s and '80s. Nine models were in Case's line, six were built in France: the 688 at 29,000 pounds, the 888

The large size crawler excavators of the 1980s and early 90s were (from left to right) the 125B, the 170B, and the 120B also made in France. These models were discontinued in 1991.

This 1187C was equipped with a tree saw that was used to harvest trees for lumber production. The saw was preferred for lumber production rather than thee feller buncher because it provided a clean cut rather than the crush cut of the feller buncher and yielded more usable lumber.

at 35,000 pounds, the 125 at 54,000 pounds, the 1088 at 45,000 pounds, the 170 at 72,000 pounds, and the 220 at 95,000 pounds. The 1085 Cruiz-Air, the 1086 Cruiz-Air Logger, and the 1187 feller/buncher were built in Wausau. Case tried using the French-built machines in logging but they didn't work out, so the 1187 was designed especially for tree harvesting with the 30 years of Drott logging experience behind it. By 1991 Case had decided to stop producing the large excavators (the 170, 220, and 125) and closed the plant at Carvin, France, but continued to produce the mid-size excavators for Europe at the Crepy plant in France.

Sumitomo Excavators

By 1990 the Japanese had the excavator technology, low prices, and ownership in the market. Their prices were driven by the exchange rates in the late 1970s and early '80s. That advantage eventually disappeared but so did the competition. Japanese excavators all used the same components and with 50% of the world's excavators sold in Japan, it gave them a volume and component base unlike any other. No real competition exists outside of Japan — the technology and components just can't be bought in the United States. That is why most American excavator manufactures now buy Japanese excavators and put their own engines in them.

The 1086 logger with the raised cab and a grapple fork was a standard in the logging industry of the late 1980s and early '90s for log stockpiling.

In 1993 Case announced a whole new line of excavators for the North American market. This line consisted of six models, the 9010 through the 9060, produced by Sumitomo — a Japanese excavator manufacturer. The new Japanese excavators had

The 90 series Sumitomo-built excavators were introduced in 1993 for the U.S. market. The 9010 series was a 27,500-pound machine.

The 9020 series was a 33,957-pound machine.

187

The 90 series machines offered dig depths from 18 feet 3 inches to 32 feet 1 inch. This 9030 was a 44,100-pound machine.

Case/Cummins CDC engines. The Japanese excavator has become very sophisticated and also very expensive. The next wave of excavators is coming but this time from Korea. The Korean excavators are entering the market at low prices, they aren't as sophisticated, but have solid quality — it's a continuing wave!

The Transient Products

Not all of the products Case acquired in the 1960s and '70s were successful. Some of these products did not fit into Case's scheme of "growing" customers and as a result these products fell by the wayside.

The Macarr Concrete Pump (1964 to 1975)

The concrete pump was designed to pump concrete to a building site that was inaccessible to a concrete truck. Normally the concrete would have to be moved to the forms by a wheelbarrow or cart. The concrete placer or pump was capable of pumping over level distances up to 500 feet and heights of 4 to 6 stories, at rates up to 35 yards of concrete per minute. The pump was first built at the Case plant in Stockton, California. In 1967 a separate Concrete Machinery Division was formed for the concrete placer and production was moved to Terre Haute, Indiana, and later to Waterford, Wisconsin. Case didn't have any other products in this line and it didn't fit the customer mold, so dealers did not know how to sell it. The concrete pump was discontinued in 1975.

All of the 90 series machines used Case/Cummins CDC engines. This 9040 was a 53,950-pound machine.

Largest of all the 90 series machines was the 9050 at 98,475 pounds.

The P-50 Case Hydra Placer concrete pump fell by the wayside because Case didn't have any other products in the concrete line and dealers didn't know how to sell it

This carrydeck crane was at work in a warehouse.

Drott Cranes and Straddle Carriers (1968 to 1988)

Drott manufactured three models of large hydraulic boom cranes called Cruz-Cranes and a small 6- to 7-1/2-ton carrydeck crane which all sold well under the dual distribution system. In 1981, however, Drott was consolidated into the Construction Equipment

This Travelift was transporting a structural beam.

The Case 2500 Cruz-Crane was erecting a storage silo.

Division and Case dealers did not know how to sell their cranes. The carrydeck cranes were sold to Shuttlelift, Inc., a subsidiary of Marine Travelift, Inc. in Sturgeon Bay, Wisconsin. The Cruz-Cranes were soon discontinued. The straddle carriers or Travelifts, which handled cargo containers and loaded them onto trucks and lifted large boats and sailing yachts out of the water, befell the same fate because they required erection crews and Case dealers were not equipped to handle this type of erection business. The Travelift straddle carriers were sold to Mi-Jack Products in Manitowoc, Wisconsin, in 1984.

This straddle-lift three-high stacker was handling cargo containers at a shipping port.

Log Skidders (1970 to 1976)

The entry into the log skidder market started with the purchase of the design and distribution rights to the Beloit log skidder in 1968, from Beloit Woodlands of Ashland, Wisconsin. The Case Beloit skidder was respectable, but it was simply placed with the wrong marketing group. The dual distribution system was used in 1968, where Drott products were marketed by both Case and Drott dealers. The Drott dealers were marketing the Cruz-Air Loggers and the feller/bunchers and the Case dealers were not marketing logging equipment. The log skidder was put

Case purchased the design and distribution rights to the Beloit log skidder in 1968 from Beloit Woodlands of Ashland, Wisconsin. Unfortunately this skidder was put in the wrong distribution system, and thus its fate was sealed.

This Case Vibromax plate compactor was used to compact soil prior to pouring concrete flat work.

into the Case distribution system. If it had been put into the Drott distribution system and sold by Drott dealers, the outcome could have been different. Drott was one of the best names in the woods, Erv Drott worked every wood show in the world without a skidder. Case dealers, on the other hand, had no products to complement the skidder, so it was finally discontinued due to lack of interest.

Vibratory Rollers and Compaction Equipment (1970 to 1992)

When Case acquired Losenhausen in 1970 and Losenhausen acquired Whilhelm Weller GmbH in 1972 it was a great acquisition for Europe. The right companies, right market — and compaction was every-

A Case 300 log skidder dragging logs out of the woods.

thing in Germany, Europe, and parts of the Middle East. The driving surface on the Autobahn in Germany is excellent even after more than 50 years. The reason — it was properly compacted before paving. Losenhausen had a line of compaction equipment and Weller was the largest supplier of medium-sized vibratory compaction equipment in Germany. The compaction line consisted of two rammers (the SL1 and SL2), five plate compactors (the AT 22, AT 40, Models 600, 900, and 1300), a walk-behind vibratory roller, as well as larger riding vibratory asphalt and compaction rollers.

The United States is not a compaction-oriented country: we dig a hole, fill it with gravel, and let cars drive over it all summer. When the cars start to bottom out, the city comes out and throws more gravel in it, and then black tops it. Every summer we tear them up, re-grade and re-pave them, and by the time 500 miles are done it's time to go back and start over. So again, due to lack of interest, Case sold most of its Vibromax compaction equipment business in Dusseldorf by April of 1992.

A walk-behind vibratory roller.

A 602 trash compactor.

A 752B asphalt roller.

The Case family of riding compactors.

A 1102 soil compactor.

Military Products

The 530 Air Force towing tractor enjoyed the longest military career of any Case product, spanning almost three decades. The 530 Air Force towing tractor was an offshoot of the Case-O-Matic drive design. The smooth start of the converter tractor made it ideal for towing ground support equipment for aircraft.

In the late 1960s products such as this 450 crawler were developed for helicopter transport for the U.S. Army. Other 450's were developed that could be dropped by parachute from an aircraft.

Products for the military services have been pivotal to the Case construction equipment business from the very beginning. In some cases the military business supported the commercial business. For example, when Case first entered the unit loader market with the "W" line in 1957, they would take a group of people from the Racine Clausen Works down to the Main Works and for 30 to 60 days a year build an inventory of loaders. Once Case got into the military business they boosted the loader line up to running two shifts for 12 months a year. As the commercial business grew, they began looking for additional space and moved the production first to Rockford, Illinois, and then to Terre Haute, Indiana.

In the late 1960s 1150 crawlers like this one were developed for the U.S. Marine Corps. with certified Detroit Diesel (GMC) engines.

The Early 1960s

The first military customer after World War II was the U.S. Navy who purchased the W-10 DS (the S stood for "Special"). These W-10's used Cummins engines because they were U.S. Government Certified which meant Cummins had supplied the government with an engineering drawing for every part of that engine, including vendor parts. This procedure standardized their inventories and gave the government the capability of making the part if necessary. It was a very costly process for a company and at that time Case did not have enough military business to justify certification of their engines. The W-10 DS also had special provisions for "deep water fording" which meant it had to operate in 60 inches of water. Case built about 500 W-10 DS's for the Navy.

The U.S. Air Force was also a customer in the early days of military products. The most popular product with the Air Force in that era was the towing tractor as discussed in the chapter on the Case-O-Matic drive. The Air Force also bought "W" line loaders.

Several Case products, such as this 580 loader/backhoe, were developed to ford 60 inches of water.

The Vietnam War Era

In the late 1960s the 450 crawlers were developed for the U.S. Army that could be dropped from an aircraft. The U.S. Marines used loader backhoes, crawlers, and pretty much the whole CE product line. In the late '60s the Marine Corps. purchased a large fleet of 1150 crawler loaders that were equipped with Certified Detroit (GMC) diesel engines. They were also required to run in 60 inches of salt water and survive—quite a task for a crawler. In 1969 Jerry Waite, head of the Case Government Sales Organization, was asked by

In 1969 Jerry Waite, the manager of Government Sales for Case, was asked to go to Vietnam to observe the construction of fire support bases. One of the recommendations was to replace hand digging of bases with equipment like the 450 crawler/dozer shown here working in Vietnam.

Military equipment was also built for our allies, like this MC 4000 fork lift supplied to the Israeli Army.

This M6K 6,000-pound forklift was developed for the U.S. Navy and was equipped for deep water fording.

This M4K articulated rough-terrain forklift was developed for artillery support as well as loading and unloading aircraft. This was the first Case venture into a strictly military vehicle.

This M4K was undergoing a field test. The M4K was used to rearm tanks since it could work in extremely rough-terrain conditions.

A M4K rough-terrain forklift in helicopter transport. About 4,000 of these machines were built for the U.S. military.

the military to go to Vietnam to observe the construction of fire support bases. He then made recommendations on better and more efficient ways to "dig in" and fortify these artillery installations, which were being dug by hand. The result was a contract of 450 crawler dozers and 580 loader backhoes for Case.

This same trip also uncovered the need for a 4,000-pound rough-terrain forklift, so Case developed the MC 4000 articulated rough-terrain forklift. This was Case's first venture into a strictly military vehicle. Case owned the design, tooling, and software — this machine was never put on the commercial market (but the concept was used to develop the W11 wheel loader). The first 425 MC 4000's went to the Marine Corps. The later version, the MK 4000, was sold to both the Marines and the U.S. Army. This was a unique machine for artillery support, it could load and unload containers from aircraft, and it could be used to rearm tanks since it could work in extremely rough-terrain conditions. About 4,000 of these machines were built for the U.S. military. This forklift was used to branch off into foreign markets like the Israeli Defense Forces, countries like Oman, as well as the United Nations.

6,000 and 10,000 Pound Forklifts

A 6,000-pound forklift, the M6K, was developed for the U.S. Navy and was a water fording machine. The M6K was built on the W14 wheel loader chassis. A number of these machines were also sold to the United Nations and ended up with our Allied countries. A 10,000-pound forklift, the M10K, was developed for the U.S. Air Force by modifying a W-20 wheel loader. The Air Force used these heavy-duty forklifts to pick up huge loads and move them in and out of the back of a C130 Hercules and C141 jet transport aircraft.

After the Drott acquisition the Military Products branched out with machines to build defenses for fortifications using cranes and excavators. A large number of cranes were sold to the military. Products for the military and state and local governments totaled 25% of the products sold by the Case Construction Equipment (CE) Division and it was always a welcome piece of business because many times it smoothed out the recession cycles occurring in the commercial markets.

This M10K 10,000-pound forklift was developed for the Air Force to pick up huge loads and move them in and out of C130 Hercules and C141 jet transports.

This Case Drott MC2500 crane was developed for the U.S. Marine Corps. to build defense fortifications.

This Case Drott Cruiz Air was another of the Drott products that helped Case branch out into the military products market.

These "W" line military loaders were ready for shipment from the Case Terre Haute, Indiana plant. Products for the military and state and local governments totaled 25% of the products sold by the Case Construction (CE) Division.

Product Support and the Future

From the very beginning Case has demonstrated its dedication to supporting its customer and products. Whether it was the founder, Jerome Increase Case, following up on a separator cleaning problem in Faribault, Minnesota, in 1884, or the concern of Leon Clausen, then Chairman of the Board, in a 1951 letter to the President, Vice Presidents, and the Service Manager of Case, "The more automatic a machine becomes, the more it complicates itself, and the urgent necessity for special training of the sales force . . . becomes of vital importance. If the program of education and training is thoroughly done, these machines can be put on the market successfully. If it is not done thoroughly, they will be a 'flop.' "

Service Training (1914 to 1960)

Service training formally began in 1914 when service schools were held in all branch territories by a branch service representative. In this era, each branch house had a classroom for regular dealer/mechanic training where small components and cut-a-ways of magnetos, distributors, pumps, and valves were discussed. The heavier hands-on training, such as splitting a tractor, was done in either a corner of the showroom or in the warehouse. Simple? Yes, but life was simple in those days and so was the product. When new products were introduced, the branch service representatives were trained at the factory by factory service representatives, engineers, and members of the Case main office service department. This system worked well while the company was small because all the field people knew the engineers, factory representatives, and service department people on a first name basis. When they had a field problem, they would phone each other direct and the results were very good.

Service Training (1960s and '70s)

With the acquisition of the American Tractor Corporation, the Industrial Division started its own central service training in Racine in 1959 and the Agricultural Division did the same in 1963. By this time the products were becoming more complicated and required full-time training instructors, mock-ups, and audio-visual teaching aids.

By the mid-1970s the Agricultural Training Group, in addition to the central training school, had three 18-wheelers that traveled around the United States and Canada with the teaching aids. They put on classes at local technical schools for several dealerships in the area. This worked well because instructors from the local technical schools sat in on the classes and got a first-hand idea of what was expected of the local dealership service personnel. Some Case dealers and technical schools even got together and sponsored training programs for new service technicians as a result of the exposure to the mobile service training. The mobile

Since 1914 hands-on service training has been the dedication of Case to customer satisfaction. Whether it was a simple chain drive transmission or a more sophisticated power shift transmission, the Case commitment has always been to diagnose it right and repair it right — the first time every time.

The Case Construction Equipment Division's customer center is located in the heart of Wisconsin's North Woods at Tomahawk, Wisconsin. It provides a facility where customers can operate a complete line of construction equipment. The facility has complete lodging and training facilities.

training concept was even expanded to countries outside of North America.

The construction equipment training group used a different approach by preparing a series of basic audio-visual programs with accompanying booklets that could be used to train new service personnel either at the dealership or at a technical school. The 1970s also saw the Technical Publications Group pioneer the preparation of sophisticated television training programs, called Vista Television Communications, for both service and sales personnel.

Service training on new products, like this 821B in 1993, as well as updates on older products are held year round in the Case Construction Equipment Training Centers.

Thousands of hours of update training on agricultural products like this combine are held every year in the service training centers on an on-going basis to keep Case dealer service technicians up-to-date so they can provide 100 % customer satisfaction.

Training in the 1980s and '90s

Training in the 1980s and '90s expanded to all phases of the dealership operation: The Vista programs now covered sales, service, and parts. A Parts Skills Institute was established to assist parts people on all aspects of serving a customer. A Customer Center for construction equipment was expanded in the heart of Wisconsin's North Woods in Tomahawk, Wisconsin. Regional training centers for total dealership training were built around the country so training could be customized to meet the needs of different regions. A new expanded training center was also completed in Racine, Wisconsin, in the 1990s. Case also had training facilities in France, Great Britain, Germany, and Australia.

A Parts Skills Institute was established to assist parts people on all aspects of customer service.

Need a manual or parts catalog?

Need a manual or a parts catalog for your Case, Drott, Davis, Vibromax, Case IH, or International Harvester (agricultural) product? Check with your Case or Case IH parts counter person. They have a Technical Publications Catalog at their counter which can help you find what you need, tell you the price, and order it electronically for you immediately — you may be surprised how far back they can go to fill your request. Yet another way Case supports its customer.

The Case parts person can help you find the right manual or catalog — and order it for you.

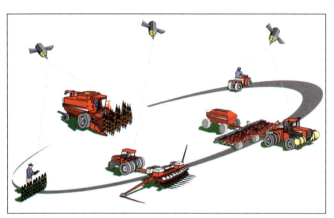

In the near future Case will enter the space age with its new Advanced Farming Systems, beginning with state-of-the-art yield monitoring devices that will use satellite technology to help farmers improve crop yields.

The Future

To look to the future with Case one must start in the late 1950s and "Look Back to the Future." The best vehicle for this is the Case logo:

• In 1956 the Case logo was Old Abe — the point where this book begins. Case was primarily a full-line agricultural equipment company with a few industrial products.

• In 1969 Old Abe was retired and the Case name stamped in metal treads became the logo. It was quite symbolic of the future. The eagle was not as well recognized in the construction equipment business as it was in the agricultural equipment business. Case business

shifted to 40% agriculture and 60% construction equipment in the 1970s through aggressive acquisitions. The Ag Division essentially became a producer of large tractors.

• In 1985 Case acquired International Harvester. Two logos were used: the Case stamped name for construction equipment and the Case stamped name and IH for agricultural equipment. Case was again a full-line agricultural equipment company and the Construction Equipment Division began to refine its product line into what fit the mold of "How Case Grows Customers."

• In 1994, the point at which this book ends, Case was back on the stock market again as a publicly traded company. The name JI Case had been dropped and a new company emerged — the Case Corporation. The new company announced a new logo in November of 1994. It was a simple Case and Case IH. The Case with

a yellow bar is the construction equipment logo and the Case IH with a red bar is the agricultural equipment logo. The business is now split 35% CE and 65% Ag. "Looking Back to the Future" is quite well summed up by a customer after a recent plant tour; "I went home feeling good about Case, I saw signs of long term commitment in the buildings, the products, and the people. I know they will be around for a long time."

The tractor of the future, in addition to all of the ergonomic enhancements, will be a total communication center with complete satellite-driven computer technology.

Tomorrow's 580 will enhance loader backhoe productivity beyond the greatest expectations of the past decades.

Specialized equipment like this Case corn harvester of the future, will use satellite weather technology to determine when the harvest yield will be at its maximum.

The next wheel loader may be totally robotic controlled.

Appendix

During the 1950s Case agricultural tractors were produced in Racine, Wisconsin and in Rock Island, Illinois. In 1961 agriculture tractor production ceased at Rock Island and was consolidated in Racine. In 1964 four-wheel-drive agriculture tractor production started in Racine and in 1965 was transferred to Rockford, Illinois. In 1971 production of four-wheel-drive agriculture tractors was returned to Racine. In 1972, with the acquisition of David Brown, agriculture tractors were produced in Meltham, England. With the acquisition of International Harvester in 1985 agriculture tractors were also produced at Neuss, Germany; St. Dizier, France; and Doncaster, England. In 1986 with the acquisition of Steiger, four-wheel-drive agriculture tractors were also produced in Fargo, North Dakota. Production of four-wheel-drive agriculture tractors ceased in Racine in 1987. Four-wheel-drive agriculture tractors were also produced in Brazil. David Brown ceased tractor production in 1988.

Serial numbers during this period were assigned in blocks to each plant each year by Corporate Standards. Because of various acquisitions, beginning in 1988 the serial numbers included three letters to identify the producing plant.

Serial Numbers of Tractors Produced in Racine and Rock Island

Year	Starting Number	Ending Number	Plant*	Year	Starting Number	Ending Number	Plant*
1955	8060001	8070464	R	1972	8691801	8712000	R
1955	6038001	6040300	RI	1973	8712001	8736600	R
1956	8080001	8087136	R	1974	8736601	8759600	R
1956	6050301	6068999	RI	1975	8770001	8796500	R
1957	8100001	8108600	R	1976	8797501	8809949	R
1957	6075001	6089800	RI	1977	8810601	8821441	R
1958	8120001	8131350	R	1978	8830001	8838826	R
1958	6095001	6115200	RI	1979	8840001	8851892	R
1959	8140001	8154999	R	1980	9901991	9909713	R
1959	6120001	6140000	RI	1981	9910025	9918560	R
1960	8160001	8165796	R	1982	9918830	9924694	R
1960	6144001	6158100	RI	1983	9924700	9931357	R
1961	8168801	8180843	R	1984	9931800	9938080	R
1961	6162601	6172550	RI†	1985	9938100	9941572	R
1962	8190001	8203550	R	1986	9941573	9945447	R
1963	8208001	8226500	R	1987	9945448	9949622	R
1964	8229001	8251840	R	1988	JJA0001501	JJA0009956	R
1965	8253501	8278502	R	1989	JJA0009957	JJA0020438	R
1966	8279001	8305500	R	1990	JJA0020439	JJA0031763	R
1967	8306501	8332100	R	1991	JJA0031764	JJA0040513	R
1968	8332101	8356250	R	1992	JJA0040514	JJA0046419	R
1969	8356251	8376150	R				
1970	8650001	8673000	R				
1971	8674001	8691756	R				

* R = Racine.
  RI = Rock Island.
† Production ceased.

Four-Wheel-Drive Tractors Produced in Rockford, Illinois*

Year	Starting Number	Ending Number
1964	9800001	9800037
1965	9800051	9802060
1966	9802101	9804411
1967	9804501	9806411
1968	9806601	9808274
1969	9808276	9810391
1970	9811301	9814980

* From 1964 through 1970 four-wheel-drive agriculture tractors were made in Rockford, Illinois, along with four-wheel-drive industrial loaders. Serial numbers were assigned from the block of serial numbers for the plant, so the serial numbers for four-wheel-drive agriculture tractors were not identified from industrial loaders.

Four-Wheel-Drive Tractors Produced in Racine, Wisconsin*

Year	Starting Number	Ending Number
1974	8762001	8764000
1975	8767001	8769800
1976	8792901	8796766
1977	8825001	8827150
1978	8827601	8829523
1979	8853001	8855468
1980	8855925	8858888
1981	8859025	8861308
1982	8861530	8863691
1983	8863700	8864150
1984	8864170	8866211
1985	8866225	8866970
1986	8866971	8867558
1987	8867559	8867690†

* 1971, 1972, and 1973 four-wheel-drive agriculture tractor production was transferred to Racine and is included in the block of serial numbers assigned to the plant. Separate block of serial numbers were assigned for four wheel drive agriculture tractors starting in 1974.

† Last tractor built in Racine.

North American Tractor Production – Rock Island Plant (1955-1961)

Model	1955	1956	1957	1958	1959	1960	1961
VAC14	1,279	–	–	–	–	–	–
VAI	563	7	–	–	–	–	–
VAO	137	–	–	–	–	–	–
VAH	175	–	–	–	–	–	–
300 Ser. Start 49		–	–	–	–	–	–
300	–	112	137	–	–	–	–
301	–	334	284	5	–	–	–
310	–	1,532	1,628	6	–	–	–
311	–	4,082	2,868	–	–	–	–
302	–	–	7	–	–	–	–
312	–	–	458	–	–	–	–
350	–	–	–	6	–	–	–
210 B	–	–	–	178	203	–	–
211 B	–	–	–	1,145	496	–	–
300 B	–	–	–	55	15	–	–
301 B	–	–	–	126	85	–	–
302 B	–	–	–	13		–	–
310 B	–	–	–	462	523	–	–
311 B	–	–	–	900	1,645	–	–
312 B	–	–	–	39	–	–	–
410 B	–	–	–	462	406	–	–
411 B	–	–	–	1,606	1,184	–	–
510 B	–	–	–	184	251	–	–
511 B	–	–	–	685	919	–	–
610 B	–	–	–	389	355	–	–
611 B	–	–	–	2,093	1,120	–	–
614 B	–	–	–	19	106	–	–
430	–	–	–	–	–	823	2,143
530	–	–	–	–	–	930	784
530 C	–	–	–	–	–	725	267
630	–	–	–	–	–	743	777
630 C	–	–	–	–	–	1,288	488
540 C Air Force	–	–	–	–	–		361
Chassis for Burlington (Loader/Backhoe)							
310	–	–	633	200	–	–	–
320	–	–	1,506	899	–	–	–
210 B	–	–	–	448	1,480	–	–
310 B	–	–	–	1,357	1,568	–	–
320 B	–	–	–	1	50	–	–
420 B	–	–	–	413	1,626	–	–
310 B-FL	–	–	–	–	275	–	–
420 B-FL	–	–	–	–	135	–	–
430	–	–	–	–	–	440	295
430 FL	–	–	–	–	–	126	141
530	–	–	–	–	–	2,068	1,508
W3	–	–	–	–	–	708	556

North American Tractor Production Racine Plant (1955-1957)

Model	1955	1956	1957	Model	1955	1956	1957
401	2,798	1,823	1,075	500	450	900	—
411	2,713	1,708	1,000	520	—	125	—
403	18	25	24	600	—	—	1,515
413	27	23	8	610	—	—	350
400	1,182	445	450	620	—	—	90
410	702	425	400	900 B	—	—	750
420	25	70	35	910 B	—	—	150
425	50	80	75				
402	81	—	—				
412	189	2	—				

North American Tractor Production Racine Plant (1958-1959)

Model	1958	1959	Model	1958	1959
701B	381	84	810	85	50
711B	320	660	702B	212	280
703B	6	24	712B	99	120
713B	8	11	802B	694	292
700B	60	83	812B	270	205
710B	45	99	725	—	16
801	3,250	1,799	831C	—	341
811	2,109	937	841C	—	101
803B	5	25	900B	1,850	3,040
813B	11	19	910B	355	495
800	145	110	920B	—	50

North American Tractor Production Racine Plant (1960)

Model	1960
730	10
731	20
732	25
741	55
742	15
730C	20
731C	130
732C	25
740C	20
741C	125
742C	520
830	15
831	145
832	45
841	80
842	15
830C	25
831C	469
832C	115
840C	25
841C	294
842C	75
930	1,062
940	548
W930	20

North American Tractor Production Racine Plant (1961-1972)

Model*	1961	1962	1963	1964	1965	1966	1967	1968	1969	1970	1971	1972
430	—	1,748	2,324	2,560	2,302	1,920	1,632	2,313	1,446	—	—	—
530	—	558	1,218	2,145	2,250	1,753	1,335	391	976	—	—	—
630	—	515	666	—	—	—	—	—	—	—	—	—
730	1,489	956	1,464	1,696	2,445	2,321	1,733	1,410	596	—	—	—
830	3,785	2,474	2,804	3,820	4,425	2,570	2,693	1,733	522	—	—	—
930	3,008	2,892	3,849	4,391	6,812	7,338	5,578	4,062	2,186	—	—	—
1030	—	—	—	—	—	3,408	4,464	3,891	2,000	—	—	—
540C	—	—	283	56	—	—	334	—	142	461	230	53
470	—	—	—	—	—	—	—	—	114	416	497	781
570	—	—	—	—	—	—	—	—	84	182	391	416
770	—	—	—	—	—	—	—	—	564	282	559	286
870	—	—	—	—	—	—	—	—	845	853	1,269	271
970	—	—	—	—	—	—	—	—	1,494	2,250	2,951	1,847
1070	—	—	—	—	—	—	—	—	1,714	2,193	2,530	1,124
1090	—	—	—	—	—	—	—	—	—	315	135	—
1170	—	—	—	—	—	—	—	—	—	844	972	—
1175	—	—	—	—	—	—	—	—	—	—	2	1,628
1270	—	—	—	—	—	—	—	—	—	—	4	1,090
1370	—	—	—	—	—	—	—	—	—	—	4	1,748
1470	—	—	—	—	—	—	—	—	—	43	795	485
2470	—	—	—	—	—	—	—	—	—	—	—	652
1200	—	—	—	322	533†	310†	309†	175†	392†	—	—	—

Chassis for Burlington (Loader/Backhoe)

Model*	1961	1962	1963	1964	1965	1966	1967	1968	1969	1970	1971	1972
430	—	580	289	459	430	428	—	—	—	—	—	—
530	—	2,190	4,352	4,621	5,125	4,751	—	—	—	—	—	—
430FL	—	125	101	243	406	247	—	—	—	—	—	—
W3	—	601	98	—	—	—	—	—	—	—	—	—
480	—	—	—	—	—	30	154	549	—	—	—	—
580	—	—	—	—	—	1,408	5,895	5,995	—	—	—	—
580L	—	—	—	—	—	34	374	412	—	—	—	—
Combined 480•580•580FL	—	—	—	—	—	—	—	—	7,216	9,173	10,030	10,976

* Reporting by series.

† Production started in Racine, was transferred to Rockford in 1965, and back to Racine in 1970. These are Rockford production numbers.

North American Tractor Production Racine Plant (1973-1978)

Model	1973	1974	1975	1976	1977	1978
870	1,266	598	—	—	—	—
970	2,286	1,880	2,648	1,740	2,187	1,130
1070	2,043	2,717	3,229	3,891	3,205	1,657
1175	1,539	1,197	956	1,270	1,074	676
1270	1,000	695	513	747	480	218
1370	2,254	2,911	3,855	2,938	2,686	1,017
1570	—	—	—	1,469	1,497	904
2470	1,503	1,351	1,393	1,670	812	242
2670	—	487	1,526	2,197	625	464
2870	—	—	—	47	656	261
480-580-580L*	10,976	7,844	7,819	—	—	—

* Burlington chassis. Starting in 1976 Burlington used components in place of complete chassis.

North American Tractor Production Racine Plant (1973-1994)*

Model	1979	1980	1981	1982	1983	1984	1985	1986	1987	1988	1989	1990	1991	1992	1993	1994
2090	3,213	2,133	2,366	1,427	1,261	—	—	—	—	—	—	—	—	—	—	—
2290	3,873	3,239	2,994	2,258	1,419	—	—	—	—	—	—	—	—	—	—	—
2390	2,357	1,816	1,959	1,283	338	—	—	—	—	—	—	—	—	—	—	—
2590	2,153	1,592	1,284	845	191	—	—	—	—	—	—	—	—	—	—	—
1896	—	—	—	—	—	759	314	254	—	—	—	—	—	—	—	—
2096	—	—	—	—	—	476	1,081	918	—	—	—	—	—	—	—	—
2094	—	—	—	—	1,060	338	—	—	—	—	—	—	—	—	—	—
2294	—	—	—	—	1,210	1,702	1,030	693	800	—	—	—	—	—	—	—
3294	—	—	—	—	54	839	143	—	—	—	—	—	—	—	—	—
2394	—	—	—	—	607	1,055	300	494	356	—	—	—	—	—	—	—
3394	—	—	—	—	—	—	93	620	806	—	—	—	—	—	—	—
2594	—	—	—	—	—	1,144	330	179	120	—	—	—	—	—	—	—
3594	—	—	—	—	—	—	154	742	721	—	—	—	—	—	—	—
2470	373	—	—	—	—	—	—	—	—	—	—	—	—	—	—	—
2670	601	—	—	—	—	—	—	—	—	—	—	—	—	—	—	—
2870	295	—	—	—	—	—	—	—	—	—	—	—	—	—	—	—
4490	398	944	870	845	396	—	—	—	—	—	—	—	—	—	—	—
4690	360	1,140	677	41	294	—	—	—	—	—	—	—	—	—	—	—
4890	381	858	720	666	91	—	—	—	—	—	—	—	—	—	—	—
4494	—	—	—	—	3	424	238	168	114	—	—	—	—	—	—	—
4694	—	—	—	—	3	209	214	210	—	—	—	—	—	—	—	—
4894	—	—	—	—	3	322	311	218	18	—	—	—	—	—	—	—
4994	—	—	—	—	3	221	—	—	—	—	—	—	—	—	—	—
7110	—	—	—	—	—	—	—	—	158	1,987	1,960	2,401	1,386	1,033	408	—
7120	—	—	—	—	—	—	—	—	160	2,499	3,070	3,388	3,186	1,746	1,128	—
7130	—	—	—	—	—	—	—	—	154	1,662	1,863	2,204	897	700	376	—
7140	—	—	—	—	—	—	—	—	143	2,210	2,803	2,579	1,822	1,127	606	—
7150	—	—	—	—	—	—	—	—	—	—	—	6	351	720	154	—
7210	—	—	—	—	—	—	—	—	—	—	—	—	—	—	208	853
7220	—	—	—	—	—	—	—	—	—	—	—	—	—	—	806	2,443
7230	—	—	—	—	—	—	—	—	—	—	—	—	—	—	247	763
7240	—	—	—	—	—	—	—	—	—	—	—	—	—	—	522	1,515
7250	—	—	—	—	—	—	—	—	—	—	—	—	—	—	168	922

* Four-wheel-drive tractor production was transferred to Fargo, North Dakota, with the acquisition of Steiger in 1987.

Nebraska Tractor Test Results*

Test No.	Model†	Year	Max. PTO Hp	Max. Dbr Hp	Weight (lb)	Engine	Cylinders	Bore & Stroke	Disp. (cu. in.)‡	Rated RPM	Fuel§
565	401Dsl	1955	49.40	43.82	6,582	Case	4	4 x 5	251	1,500	13.91
614	301 Dsl	1957	30.80	28.73	3,743	Cont.	4	3.375 x 4.375	157	1,750	12.77
678	711-B Gas	1958	52.19	46.64	6,420	Case	4	4 x 5	251	1,500	9.93
680	801-B Dsl	1958	54.42	50.14	6,935	Case	4	4.125 x 5	267	1,800	12.13
688	211-B Gas	1958	30.84	26.09	3,655	Case	4	3.125 x 4.125	126.5	1,900	8.88
689	411-B Gas	1959	37.12	30.67	4,349	Case	4	3.375 x 4.125	148	2,000	7.95
692	900-B Gas	1959	70.24	65.59	8,525	Case	6	4 x 5	377	1,500	13.77
736	831-C Dsl	1960	63.74	58.48	7,275	Case	4	4.375 x 5	301	1,900	13.20
742	731C Dsl	1960	56.50	50.64	7,095	Case	4	4.125 x 5	267	1,900	11.45
769	541C Gas	1960	41.26	37.14	4,345	Case	4	3.5 x 4.125	158.7	2,100	9.14
770	640-C Gas	1960	49.72	43.26	4,675	Case	4	3.8125 x 4.125	188.4	2,250	9.17
772	531 Dsl	1960	41.27	37.20	4,117	Case	4	3.8125 x 4.125	188.4	1,900	14.71
774	441 Gas	1960	33.11	29.39	3,620	Case	4	3.375 x 4.125	148	1,750	10.36
777	841C Gas	1960	65.64	59.81	7,325	Case	4	4.25 x 5	284	1,900	9.13
785	431 Dsl	1961	34.38	31.33	3,839	Case	4	3.8125 x 4.125	188.4	1,750	14.16
788	630 Dsl	1961	48.24	40.67	4,637	Case	4	3.8125 x 4.125	188.4	2,000	12.85
868	1200 Dsl	1964	119.90	106.86	16,585	Case	6	4.375 x 5	451	2,000	11.81
917	831CK Dsl	1965	64.26	58.68	8,070	Case	4	4.375 x 5	301	1,900	12.23
922	941GP LPG	1965	85.86	75.61	8,975	Case	6	4 x 5	377	1,800	7.04
952	1031 Dsl	1966	101.79	92.62	9,335	Case	6	4.375 x 5	451	2,000	12.01
1032	770 Pwrshft Gas	1969	53.53	47.99	—	Case	4	4 x 5	251	1,900	7.58
1030	870 Pwrshft Dsl	1969	70.53	63.80	9,390	Case	4	4.625 x 5	336	1,900	12.93
1006	1470 Trct King Dsl	1969	144.89	132.06	17,300	Case	6	4.625 x 5	504	2,000	14.39
1061	770 Man Gas	1970	56.32	50.09	8,810	Case	4	4 x 5	251	1,900	8.17
1037	970 Pwrshft Dsl	1970	85.31	74.48	10,335	Case	6	4.125 x 5	401	1,900	12.85
1062	1170 Dsl	1970	121.93	110.46	13,540	Case	6	4.375 x 5	451	2,100	13.09
1067	1070 Man Dsl	1971	107.36	91.45	11,410	Case	6	4.375 x 5	451	2,100	12.62
1076	870 Pwrshft Dsl	1971	77.92	67.47	10,230	Case	4	4.625 x 5	336	2,000	12.41
1078	970 Manual Dsl	1971	93.87	81.27	11,080	Case	6	4.125 x 5	401	2,000	13.26
1102	1370 Dsl	1972	142.51	123.01	15,290	Case	6	4.625 x 5	504	2,100	11.82
1103	1270 Dsl	1972	126.70	108.28	13,440	Case	6	4.375 x 5	451	2,100	11.55
1114	2470 Dsl	1972	174.20	154.24	20,485	Case	6	4.625 x 5	504	2,200	12.55
1160	1270 Dsl	1974	135.39	120.85	15,470	Case	6	4.375 x 5	451	2,100	11.49
1165	2670 Dsl	1974	219.44	193.65	20,810	Case	6	4.625 x 5	504	2,200	12.60
1209	1410 Dsl	1976	80.88	69.25	7,750	David Brown	4	3.94 x 4.5	219	2,300	14.38
1218	1570 Dsl	1976	180.41	152.96	16,290	Case	6	4.62 x 5	504	2,100	12.46
1241	2870 Dsl	1977	252.10	219.61	25,100	Saab-Scania	6	5 x 5.71	673	2,200	12.37
1296	2290 Dsl	1979	128.80	109.36	12,770	Case	6	4.62 x 5	504	2,100	11.73
1302	2390 Dsl	1979	160.72	143.37	15,590	Case	6	4.62 x 5	504	2,100	12.66
1303	2590 Dsl	1979	180.38	156.10	15,740	Case	6	4.62 x 5	504	2,100	13.03
1304	2090 Dsl	1979	108.74	94.93	11,910	Case	6	4.62 x 5	504	2,100	12.69
1328	4490 Dsl	1979	175.20	153.30	20,840	Case	6	4.62 x 5	504	2,200	12.52
1329	4690 Dsl	1979	219.62	195.60	22,310	Case	6	4.62 x 5	504	2,200	12.84

* Sources: *Farm Tractors 1950-1975* by Lester Larsen (1981) and *Farm Tractors 1975-1995* by Larry Gay (1995). Both books are published by the American Society of Agricultural Engineers in St. Joseph, Michigan.

† Dsl = Diesel.

‡ Disp. = Displacement.

§ Fuel economy data during a 10-hour run at 75% load, (hp hr/gal).

Nebraska Tractor Test Results*

Test No.	Model†	Year	Max. PTO Hp	Max. Dbr Hp	Weight (lb)	Engine	Cylinders	Bore & Stroke	Disp. (cu. in)‡	Rated RPM	Fuel§
1330	4890 Dsl	1979	253.41	224.81	25,750	Saab-Scania	6	5 x 5.71	673	2,200	13.27
1378	1190 Dsl	1981	43.09	36.21	4,620	Case	3	3.94 x 4.5	165	2,200	12.59
1379	1290 Dsl	1981	53.73	46.41	6,570	Case	4	3.94 x 4	195	2,200	12.90
1380	1390 Dsl	1981	60.59	52.16	6,620	Case	4	3.94 x 4.5	219	2,200	13.24
1381	1490 Dsl	1981	70.51	60.24	7,705	Case	4	3.94 x 4.5	219	2,200	13.00
1383	1690 Dsl	1981	90.39	78.08	8,755	Case	6	3.94 x 4.5	329	2,300	13.50
1525	2094 Dsl	1984	110.50	100.12	14,190	Case	6	4.62 x 5	504	2,100	12.93
1526	2294 Dsl	1984	131.97	116.38	14,390	Case	6	4.62 x 5	504	2,100	12.21
1527	2394 Dsl	1984	162.15	141.04	16,240	Case	6	4.62 x 5	504	2,100	12.71
1528	3294 Dsl	1984	162.63	143.68	17,915	Case	6	4.62 x 5	504	2,100	12.76
1529	2594 Dsl	1984	182.07	161.96	16,220	Case	6	4.62 x 5	504	2,100	12.94
1530	4994 Dsl	1984	344.04	303.78	31,315	Saab-Scania	8	5 x 5.51	866	2,100	13.87
1546	1594 Dsl	1984	85.90	73.54	9,345	Case	6	3.94 x 4.5	329	2,300	13.56
1548	1896 Dsl	1984	95.92	85.77	13,495	CDC-Case	6	4.02 x 4.72	359	2,100	13.65
1549	2096 Dsl	1984	115.67	101.40	14,180	CDC-Case	6	4.02 x 4.72	359	2,100	13.92
1583	3394 Dsl	1985	162.86	144.29	15,800	Case	6	4.62 x 5	504	2,100	12.48
1584	3594 Dsl	1985	182.27	163.52	17,590	Case	6	4.62 x 5	504	2,100	12.91
1604	685 Dsl	1986	61.02	53.81	5,835	Case IH	4	3.88 x 5.06	239	2,400	11.86
022	485 Dsl	1986	43.0	36.7	6,475	Case IH	3	3.88 x 5.06	179	2,200	12.64
023	885 Dsl	1986	73.0	62.4	7,130	Case IH	4	3.94 x 5.5	268	2,400	13.31
040	9110 Dsl	1987	168.4	149.21	20,160	CDC-Case	6	4.49 x 5.32	505	2,100	14.57
041	9130 Dsl	1987	191.2	175.47	21,080	CDC-Case	6	4.49 x 5.32	505	2,100	15.33
042	9150 Dsl	1987	246.1	229.83	26,000	Cummins	6	4.92 x 5.35	611	2,100	16.65
043	9170 Dsl	1987	308.1	282.07	33,970	Cummins	6	5.5 x 6	855	2,100	15.11
044	9180 Dsl	1987	344.5	311.16	35,570	Cummins	6	5.5 x 6	855	2,100	14.87
1609 & 049	7110 Dsl	1988	131.97	116.50	16,590	CDC-Case	6	4.49 x 5.32	505	2,200	13.35
1610 & 050	7120 Dsl	1988	151.62	137.99	16,605	CDC-Case	6	4.49 x 5.32	505	2,200	14.74
1611 & 051	7130 Dsl	1988	172.57	155.35	17,090	CDC-Case	6	4.49 x 5.32	505	2,200	15.00
1612 & 052	7140 Dsl	1988	197.53	180.72	17,565	CDC-Case	6	4.49 x 5.32	505	2,200	14.41
075	5120 Dsl	1989	78.2	65.2	10,540	Case	4	4.02 x 4.72	239	2,200	12.44
076	5130 Dsl	1990	89.9	74.3	10,670	Case	6	4.02 x 4.72	359	2,200	12.49
077	5140 Dsl	1990	97.0	81.4	11,055	Case	6	4.02 x 4.72	359	2,200	12.54
1649 & 087	9230 Dsl	1991	198.63	191.67	24,272	CDC-Case	6	4.49 x 5.32	505	2,200	14.18
1650 & 088	9240 Dsl	1991	200.53	190.31	28,380	CDC-Case	6	4.49 x 5.32	505	2,200	13.70
1652 & 097	9260 Dsl	1991	265.84	241.15	30,300	Cummins	6	4.92 x 5.35	611	2,100	14.53
1651 & 096	9250 Dsl	1991	266.01	240.68	30,225	Cummins	6	4.92 x 5.35	611	2,100	14.77
1663 & 121	7150 Dsl	1992	216.83	197.86	18,752	CDC-Case	6	4.49 x 5.32	505	2,200	14.45
142	5220 Dsl	1993	80.9	69.1	10,415	Case	4	4.02 x 4.72	239	2,200	13.13
143	5230 Dsl	1993	90.8	78.7	11,145	Case	6	4.02 x 4.72	359	2,200	12.80
144	5240 Dsl	1993	101.4	92.3	11,385	Case	6	4.02 x 4.72	359	2,200	13.37
145	5250 Dsl	1993	112.2	103.4	11,190	Case	6	4.02 x 4.72	359	2,200	13.86
1682 & 166	7220 Dsl	1994	156.00	138.69	17,514	CDC-Case	6	4.49 x 5.32	505	2,200	13.65

* Sources: *Farm Tractors 1950-1975* by Lester Larsen (1981) and *Farm Tractors 1975-1995* by Larry Gay (1995). Both books are published by the American Society of Agricultural Engineers in St. Joseph, Michigan.

† Dsl = Diesel.

‡ Disp. = Displacement.

§ Fuel economy data during a 10-hour run at 75% load, (hp hr/gal).

Bibliography

Gay, Larry. 1995. *Farm Tractors 1975-1995.* American Society of Agricultural Engineers: St. Joseph, MI.

Holmes, Michael, S. 1992. *J I Case The First 150 Years.* Case Corporation: Racine, WI.

Larsen, Lester. 1981. *Farm Tractors 1950-1975.* American Society of Agricultural Engineers: St. Joseph, MI.

Letter, 1951. L. R. Clausen to Johnson, Brown, Pearse, Kornwolf. Dated June 18, 1951.

Marsh, Barbara. 1985. *A Corporate Tragedy (The Agony of International Harvester Company).* Doubleday and Co.: New York.

Quick, Graeme and Buchel, Wesley. 1978 *The Grain Harvesters.* American Society of Agricultural Engineers: St. Joseph, MI.

Rupnow, John and Knox, Carol, Ward.1975. *The Growing of America, 200 Years of U.S. Agriculture.* Johnson Hill Press, Inc.: Fort Atkinson, WI.

Williams, Robert, C. 1987. *Fordson, Farmall and Poppin' Johnny (A History of the Farm Tractor and Its Impact on America).* University of Illinois Press: Chicago.

Additional Reading Available from ASAE

J. I. CASE
* *Full Steam Ahead, J. I. Case Tractors & Equipment Vol. 1.* David Erb and Eldon Brumbaugh.
* *Case Tractor Buyer's Guide.* Peter Letourneau.
* *Case Tractors 1912-1959 Photo Archive.*
* *Data Book No. 3, J. I. Case Co.*

OTHER COMPANIES
* *150 Years of International Harvester.* C. H. Wendel.
* *A Tractor Goes Farming.* Roy Harrington.
* *The Agricultural Tractor: 1855-1950.* R. B. Gray.
* *Allis-Chalmers Farm Equipment, 1914-1985.* Norm Swinford.
* *A Guide to Allis-Chalmers Farm Tractors.* Norm Swinford.
* *Classic Tractor Collectors: Restoring and Preserving Farm Power from the Past.* John Harvey.
* *Farm Tractors: 1950-1975.* Lester Larsen.
* *Farm Tractors: 1975-1995.* Larry Gay.
* *Ford & Fordson Tractor Buyer's Guide.* Robert Pripps.
* *How to Restore Your Farm Tractor.* Robert Pripps.
* *How to Restore Tractor Magnetos.* Neil Yerigan.
* *International Harvester Tractor Buyer's Guide.* Robert Pripps.
* *John Deere Buggies and Wagons.* Ralph Hughes.
* *John Deere Tractors and Equipment, Vol. 1* and *Vol. 2.* Don Macmillan, Russell Jones, and Roy Harrington.
* *John Deere Tractors Worldwide: A Century of Progress, 1893-1993.* Don Macmillan.
* *Oliver Hart-Parr.* C. H. Wendel.

* Books can be ordered from the American Society of Agricultural Engineers (ASAE), 2950 Niles Road, St. Joseph, MI 49085-9659 USA. Voice: (800) 695-2723 or (616) 428-6324; FAX: (616) 429-3852.
  If you wish to be kept current on equipment history publications, just ask for your free copy of the *Looking Back* catalog.